Birds in the Garden

EASTERN BLUEBIRD

FEMALE   MALE

JUVENAL PLUMAGE (NESTLING)

ROBIN

MALE

FEMALE   JUVENAL PLUMAGE

Scale about one-half

BIRDS
IN THE GARDEN
AND HOW TO ATTRACT THEM

By MARGARET McKENNY

*With Thirty-two Pages of Photographs and
Sixteen Plates Showing Forty-eight
Garden Birds in Full Color*

Introduction by
CLYDE FISHER

GROSSET & DUNLAP · *Publishers* · NEW YORK

BY ARRANGEMENT WITH THE UNIVERSITY OF MINNESOTA PRESS

PRINTED IN THE UNITED STATES OF AMERICA

I DEDICATE THIS BOOK TO

W. L. McATEE

WHOSE WORK WAS ITS INSPIRATION

AND FOUNDATION

PUBLISHER'S ACKNOWLEDGMENTS

THE author and publisher herewith render thanks to the following individuals, publishers, or their representatives for permission to reprint:

To the author and the Yale University Press, for "Overtones," by William Alexander Percy.

To Messrs. A. P. Watt and Son, London, for "The Birds," from *The Birds and Other Poems,* by J. C. Squire published by Doubleday, Doran & Co.

To Henry Holt & Co., for "The Mother Bird," from *Poems 1901-1918,* by Walter de la Mare.

To J. B. Pinker & Sons, London, for "Bird Watching and Bird Behavior," by Julian Huxley, from *A Book of Birds,* edited by Mary Priestley, The Macmillan Company, New York.

To Little, Brown & Co., for "To Hear an Oriole Sing," from *Poems of Emily Dickinson.*

AUTHOR'S FOREWORD

THIS book deals with the familiar birds of our gardens and fields and the native plants which will attract them. No mention is made of those plants having poisonous properties, such as poison ivy and sumac, though birds are known to eat of them freely.

I feel keenly that the joy of a garden is more than doubled if we know the birds. And I feel also that an intimate acquaintance with the friendly birds that add so much charm and gayety to our gardens will lead to a greater understanding of wild life in general, and of the vital necessity of conserving our natural resources.

For the benefit of readers of a limited technical knowledge, the plant lists are arranged with common names preceding the scientific, giving the preference to the popular name most widely used in each region.

The inspiration of this book, the firm foundation on which it is based, is the work of W. L. McAtee, Technical Adviser of the United States Bureau of Biological Survey.

For many years Mr. McAtee has studied the food habits of birds. Through field trips in every portion of the country he has built up a profound knowledge of environmental factors suitable for birds; through study under the microscope of their stomach contents, he has been able to assemble unquestionable records of food habits.

All the lists of plants attractive to birds and the birds known to feed on them are based on Mr. McAtee's work in the Biological Survey. The many booklets written by him on attracting birds and building up proper surroundings to encourage their presence have been invaluable to me. But I am especially grateful for the constructive criticism of my manuscript given

AUTHOR'S FOREWORD

by Mr. McAtee, and can express only a small measure of my appreciation by dedicating this book to him.

To Mary Leonard Pritchett I owe much gratitude for her unfailing faith and constant encouragement, and to Kenneth Sultzer for his fine research work and his assistance in writing the first and ninth chapters.

Various parts of the manuscript have been read by Richard Pough and Roger Tory Peterson of the National Association of Audubon Societies, and for their inspiring and understanding help in every stage of my work I give many thanks.

I wish to express sincere gratitude for the always cheerful assistance given by Margaret Brooks, Librarian of the National Association of Audubon Societies; to Elizabeth Hall, Librarian of the New York Botanical Garden; to Dr. W. H. Camp of the same institution for help in checking plant names and sources; and to Frederick Packard for his research work. I also wish to express my appreciation of the work of Mary Kirwin, who so patiently assisted me in preparing the manuscript and lists for the publisher, and to thank Robert Underwood and Frank Gehr.

The color plates in this book are taken by permission from *Bird Portraits in Color* by Thomas S. Roberts, published by the University of Minnesota Press. I am particularly grateful to the Press and to Dr. Roberts for their friendly co-operation in permitting me to reproduce sixteen of the plates in this book.

My thanks go also to Dr. Frank Chapman, Head of the Department of Ornithology, American Museum of Natural History, for his advice in regard to illustrations; to Alice Bird Erikson, who drew the designs for the plantings, bird-boxes, and feeding-devices; to the many photographers who have contributed their pictures; to the authors of the many books I have consulted and quoted; and to the many friends who, with their anecdotes of personal experiences with birds, have helped round out the interest of every chapter.

Margaret McKenny.

>>>>>>>>>>>>>>>>>>>>>>>>>>>>>>>>>><<<<<<<<<<<<<<<<<<<<<<<<<<<<<<<<

PREFACE

A GARDEN without birds would be a semi-desert from the esthetic standpoint alone. The beauty of plumage and the beauty of song among our birds are thoroughly appreciated by those who stop to consider the matter. Just as the sentiment for the flowers of our grandmother's garden is strong in us, so it is with the birds that were familiar to us in childhood. How the evening song of the robin can carry us back to the days of our youth!

Birds are individuals in the economy of nature, and their behavior is of absorbing interest. We see ourselves reflected or interpreted in their courtship, their home-making, and their tragedies—in short, in their struggle for existence.

Then there is the economic point of view. Many birds eat the seeds of noxious weeds which the farmer and gardener are combating. It should be remembered, however, that these same birds eat the seeds of plants that are not objectionable. But who would begrudge the bobwhite a few handfuls of corn, if he could have him for a neighbor? Many birds perform a great service in destroying injurious insects. It is no doubt true that these same birds eat many insects that are not injurious. Many birds feed upon mice and other destructive rodents. Other birds are of distinct value as scavengers.

What can be done to attract birds to our gardens? This question has been answered in a thoroughgoing way by a careful naturalist, and her data on the food of birds has been checked by the best living authority on the subject, one who has for many years had charge of the division of food habits research of the U. S. Biological Survey.

Here is a beautiful book, greatly enhanced in its attractiveness by color

PREFACE

plates from *Bird Portraits in Color,* by Dr. Thomas S. Roberts, and it contains a wealth of practical, dependable information that every gardener will want in his library.

CLYDE FISHER
American Museum of Natural History,
New York City.

September 20, 1939.

Contents

CONTENTS

CONTENTS

CONTENTS

CONTENTS

List of Illustrations

COLOR PLATES

LIST OF ILLUSTRATIONS

PHOTOGRAPHS (between pages 14 and 15)

1. "Chickadee-dee." An instant's pause by the tree swallow.
2. Blue-gray gnatcatchers inspect a masterpiece of camouflage. The cardinal's problem. A rufous hummer on its cup of lichens and cobwebs.
3. The mountain-ash invites the hungry migrants. Winking blackberries. A happy throng strips the dogwood. A multitude of revelers.
4. Life is not all song to the Baltimore oriole. Young phoebes doubt that patience is a virtue. The rule of the black-throated gray warbler. The brown thrasher does a thorough job. Young cedar waxwings argue about a cherry.
5. A feeding station camouflaged with cedar boughs.
6. Purple finches on the feeding shelf. The blue jay pre-empts the center of the stage. Mealtime brings strange companions. An impatient chickadee.
7. Purple finches at Aberdeen, Washington. "The Bird's Paradise," Vancouver, B.C. The cardinal's cheer. The chickadee will police your trees.
8. The age of innocence in "The Bird's Paradise." Who's afraid of the big bad gun?
9. The flicker family. The wood pewee on its traditional nest. Princes-to-be in a kingbird's nursery. A stone wall shelters the phoebe's nest.

LIST OF ILLUSTRATIONS

LIST OF ILLUSTRATIONS

DIAGRAMS

Chapter One

VALUE OF BIRDS, ESTHETIC AND ECONOMIC

BIRDS and flowers—they are closely associated in our thoughts—they are a part of our heritage of beauty. But birds, even more than flowers, are significant of vibrant life; they are never static; they are dynamic, pulsating with energy, surcharged with new charm every hour of the day, every season of the year.

If we were asked just what birds meant to us, many of us would say that they meant the freedom of open spaces—wide skies and untouched forest depths. Others would remember the rapture of the dawn chorus, or the simpler but equally moving beauty of the everyday songs and calls of the birds that they have known from childhood. Still others, even though not particularly poetic in feeling, would say they meant the spring, and quote that memorable description from the Song of Solomon: "For, lo, the winter is past, the rain is over and gone; the flowers appear on the earth; the time of the singing of birds is come, and the voice of the turtle is heard in our land"—even though a few of them might, like the ardent young traveler in *Innocents Abroad,* think that the "turtle" was a tortoise and not a turtle dove.

To nearly everybody birds mean something beyond and outside themselves, a part of the mystery and poetry of nature, and so we need not wonder that from the earliest ages birds have had their place in myths and in religions in various parts of the world. To early man they were often semi-divine or closely associated with his divinities, and later, symbolical of divine attributes. Long before the printed word they were a part of folklore and have been immortalized in art, in that of primitive man and in that of

I

periods of the highest civilization. Even now they still hold something of their mystical symbolism and have become an integral part of man's intellectual existence in song and story, poetry and music. William Alexander Percy in *Overtones* expresses this mystic significance:

> I heard a bird at break of day
> Sing from the autumn trees
> A song so mystical and calm,
> So full of certainties,
> No man, I think, could listen long
> Except, upon his knees.
> Yet this was but a simple bird
> Alone, among dead trees.

To return to the early ages: in Greek Mythology the eagle was the messenger of Zeus. Aphrodite was attended by her doves. Pallas had her owl and Hera her peacock. In Egypt the hawk was the symbol for Horus, and the ibis for Thoth. In Scandinavian mythology Wotan had his ravens, and in the Near East Astharoth her doves. The phœnix of India brought wisdom and energy to Buddha, and protected him.

In the Bible, Noah first sent out a raven from the Ark to see if the floods were abating. When the raven did not come back he sent a dove, which finally returned bearing an olive leaf. That dove has become to us more than just a dove; it is a symbol of hope and promise. It is significant, too, that the dove bearing an olive branch has come to mean peace.

Folklore is full of tales of people—usually princes and princesses—who are transformed into birds; to say nothing of talking birds and friendly birds like the robins which covered the Babes in the Wood. We may look on these tales as just good stories for children or simple-minded folk, but very often we can find a deeper significance. The vultures which fed on Prometheus' vitals as he lay chained eternally to the rocks for defying the gods, the phœnix of Herodotus which is resurrected from its own ashes, the birds of Æsop, are really parables.

2

Ernest Ingersoll has an interesting chapter in *Birds in Legend, Fable and Folklore,* on the use of birds as national emblems. When the Sumerian city of Lagash, in Southern Mesopotamia, was conquered by the Babylonians about 2000 B.C., its emblem was an eagle facing us with wings and legs spread and its head in profile. When the Assyrians in turn conquered Babylon, they, too, took over the emblem. Then, when Rome came to be Mistress of the World, it was the eagle which came to be the symbol of her supreme power; it was officially adopted by the Republic in 87 B.C.

Napoleon, when he set out to create a new world empire, also adopted the eagle as his symbol. Throughout the restoration of the Bourbons, the eagle disappeared, but it came back with Louis Napoleon. Again it gave way, this time to the cock—the cock which heralds the dawn, the proud pugnacious cock which Rostand has so glorified and at the same time treated so ironically in *Chanticler.* Probably this symbol came to be associated with the ancient Gauls in Roman days; at any rate, we find it used as an emblem in France as far back as the thirteenth century, and in 1792 the First Republic put the cock on its escutcheon. Displaced by the Napoleonic eagle, it came back again with Louis Philippe, again to be routed by Louis Napoleon's eagle. In the World War the cock once more showed symptoms of arising phœnixlike to shrill forth France's battle cry.

To return to the eagle: when the Assyrians took it over as an emblem, it gradually evolved into the two-headed eagle which later, probably some time after the tenth century, became the symbol of the Byzantine Empire. Eagles were carved on the standards of the Roman legionaries, while at the end of the Holy Roman Empire, Austria fell heir to the double-headed eagle, and from the middle of the fifteenth century Russia, too, adopted the emblem. Germany later was content with a single-headed eagle, which it took over from Prussia.

In America the bald eagle was adopted as the Great Seal and Coat of Arms for the thirteen original States in 1782. We have all come to know our proud emblem; we have all seen many thousands of carved and sculptured and engraved and painted eagles. Postage-stamp collectors, too, will tell you that on many stamps eagles and other birds have been used, and a student of heraldry can give us multitudinous examples of the use of birds.

As is only to be expected, with this widespread interest in birds and attributing of significance to them, in highly developed as well as primitive civilizations, there has been no other symbol used more often in decoration in all its varied manifestations. It is true that the bird is not always used realistically; it is apt to be conventionalized, simplified, stylized, not only in textiles, ceramics and repeat patterns, to which we are accustomed today, but in various art objects or serviceable objects such as primitive bowls, the bronze incense burners of China, the glass "setting-hen salt-cellars" of New England. Such details as the peacock feather have been used in myriad ways: we need only think of the gorgeous designs from Persia, India and Japan, as well as from European nations. As today we consciously turn to nature for motives for our design, so all through the ages men have turned to her both consciously and unconsciously. Study patterns of today as well as of primitive times, and you will be amazed to see how often you will suddenly recognize a bird *motif*.

It is true that we find surprisingly few memorable realistic renderings of birds in Occidental painting until a century or so ago. In the early Italian Renaissance paintings we find birds—who can forget the rare combination of humor and tenderness of Giotto's "St. Francis Preaching to the Birds," or Pisanello's sensitive and meticulous studies of birds? And in how many paintings of this period we see the Holy Ghost in the form of a dove, and angels' and cherubs' wings sometimes exquisitely adapted from birds' wings, to say nothing of bird flights, or single birds, even peacocks, usually introduced only for accent or symbolism or to round out a composition. Then, in the seventeenth and eighteenth century *genre* and still life painters, especially the Dutch and French, like Cuyp, Franz Hals, the Wouvermans and the Aelsts, we find much dead game and barnyard poultry. Yet in this treatment of birds, numerous as the examples may be, beautiful and

4

accurate as some of them are, it is difficult to see a continuous tradition or development in the handling of the subject. Artists had still to realize, though, that, as Barbellion put it, "The flight of the gull is as wonderful as the Andes."

This was precisely what Chinese and Japanese artists had realized for centuries. The more one studies their paintings, drawings and prints, the more one wonders at the reverence, truth and delicacy with which they render birds. We find bird pictographs more than a millennium, and numerous bird bronzes, many centuries, before Christ. By the tenth century A.D., we are getting skilful bird paintings, and as time goes on we get more and more of them. It is important to remember though, that in Oriental art, skilful and delightful esthetically as a bird or flower painting may be, there is always a suggestion behind the subject; the painting is suffused with a meaning that we Westerners do not get without knowing something about Oriental symbolism. A poetic meaning is given to birds, as in our folklore and poetry, which when we understand, intensifies their beauty and significance for us.

Mr. A. de C. Sowerby, who has made a study of the number of common birds which have been identified in Chinese paintings, also classifies into three groups the birds we find in Chinese and Japanese art: first, the purely fabulous birds; second, the semimythological or semifabulous birds, composites which cannot be identified with any existing species, but which are very numerous in paintings and embroideries; and third, the large numbers of native birds and birds introduced from other countries, sometimes conventionalized but often treated with marvelous realism and feeling. The commoner species appear most often, not only the more ornate birds like the golden pheasant, the peacock and the egret, but also geese, ducks, swans, birds of prey (a favorite subject), and simple homely little birds like the sparrow and swallow. The owl, which means bad luck, is a conspicuous omission.

The gorgeous phœnix, usually depicted as about six feet in height and

5

with a tail about six feet long, stands for wisdom and energy. It is very common not only on screens and in embroidery and textiles, but also in sculptured decorations on palaces, shrines and temples, imperial structures and furniture in Japan. In China it was the symbol of the Empress, as the dragon was of the Emperor, and it was also associated with womanhood and brides. The crane signified longevity and immortality, the falcon heroism, the cock valor, the mandarin duck married love and fidelity, the nightingale (especially in connection with the plum blossom) the coming of spring, the cuckoo unrequited love—the list of these symbols could run on indefinitely, both for its symbolism and for the special qualities of such artists as Huang Ch'uan, Chi'ien Hsuan, Wang Lei-Lieh and Hiroshige.

This naturally leads to a word or two about the famous "Chelsea birds" that are such an item for collectors of porcelain. Just as porcelain came from China, so the designs first used on it came from China. Although "Chelsea birds" can be found on porcelain made by the factories which antedated the Chelsea works, they first became famous on Chelsea ware. At first just copies of Chinese originals (of Chinese birds, of course), adaptations were made by skilful artists and new subjects were attempted. As the Chelsea works were patronized by George II and his court, they had plenty of money. Colorful and striking subjects were at first used exclusively, but by degrees English birds were introduced in native settings (sometimes studied by Chinese artists), and, as various works came under the same management or artists traveled, "Chelsea birds" came to be found on Worcester, Derby, Spode and other porcelain. One does not have to be a collector of ceramics to appreciate the beauty of this work, or of the vivid porcelain bird ornaments of the same works that are such a collector's item today.

There is still another field of study for the bird lover: tapestries, especially the *millefleur* or French tapestry of the fifteenth century—those beautifully colored tapestries whose designs are so interwoven with the "thousand flowers" from which they have taken their name. In among

6

BLACK AND WHITE WARBLER
MALE, BREEDING ADULT
FEMALE, BREEDING ADULT
JUVENAL PLUMAGE (NESTLING)

PROTHONOTARY WARBLER
MALE, BREEDING ADULT
JUVENAL PLUMAGE (NESTLING)

PARULA WARBLER
MALE, BREEDING ADULT
FEMALE, BREEDING ADULT
JUVENAL PLUMAGE

GOLDEN-WINGED WARBLER
MALE, BREEDING ADULT
FEMALE, BREEDING ADULT

BLUE-WINGED WARBLER
MALE, BREEDING ADULT

Scale about one-half

the flowers and trees we find many delightful birds. Then, when Arras fell, to be supplanted by Flemish tapestry works, and designs by the great Renaissance painters of Italy supplanted the Gothic ones, the bird still held its own, as it did when the later French works developed, in tapestry borders, if nowhere else. Later, when William Morris brought new life to tapestry weaving he learned much from these earlier models, and the same birds appear again in his tapestries.

In spite of these achievements in Oriental art and in certain phases of Western art, one of our outstanding ornithological authorities, Dr. Frank M. Chapman, recently pointed out that the well-known drawing of geese from the tomb at Maydoom in Egypt, dating from 3000 B.C., is better than most of the bird drawings which appear in natural histories and works on ornithology up to the close of the eighteenth century. Without discounting Alexander Wilson's work, one can realize why Cuvier called Audubon's *Birds of America* "the most gigantic and most magnificent monument ever erected to nature." One cannot do justice to Audubon in a brief space, but we must remember that, in addition to his minute study of the anatomy and plumage of birds, he considered birds as an artistic end in themselves (which they had never really been in Western art as they had in Oriental art), and was careful to consider them always as living creatures even if he worked from dead models. If he introduced the concept of motion into his study of birds, and if later disciples (like Joseph Wolf in Great Britain) have carried on his meticulous studies, others, notably, Louis Agassiz Fuertes, Allan Brooks, Rex Brasher, Roger Peterson, Francis L. Jaques, Walter Weber and George Miksch Sutton have become what Dr. Chapman calls portrait painters of birds who excel "not merely in accuracy of line and color, but in the subtle intangible qualities approaching spirituality," who get even the facial expression of birds, the queer uncanny intelligence which glints in their eyes. And in the last fifty years or so it is amazing how much the bird has come into its own in art, and it is encouraging to notice how much the artists have learned from the study of the early painters of China and Japan. Nor must we forget what photographers are doing with birds today, especially the magnificent photographs published in Germany in the Blauenbücher series of Langewiesche which gave such an impetus to the movement, while in America we have Dr. A. A. Allen, Henry B. Kane, William Finley, Allan Cruickshank, Hugo Schroder, and others.

Not only do we find innumerable carvings and statues of birds among primitive peoples, we find them among peoples of high civilization—as in Egypt, where the hawk was the sacred emblem of Horus and placed over entrances to temples, where the ibis was sacred to Thoth, or in China and Japan, where the phœnix brought energy and wisdom to Buddha and protected him with its mighty wings, thereby becoming both a sacred and imperial emblem. In the Middle Ages, birds, like animals, acquired symbolical meanings, largely through the influence of Christianity. The pelican, for instance, came to stand for Christ's self-sacrifice to redeem the world. The eagle for a while was the symbol of the Ascension, and later became that of the Evangelist St. John—which is why we find it today on so many church pulpits. The cock found its way onto church towers because of its association with the story of Peter's repentance. The dove, of course, had many meanings, chiefly representing the Holy Ghost. It is not surprising, therefore, that in Gothic carving we find numberless birds. The capitals of columns frequently harbor birds as well as animals and leaves. And the strange monsters of the Middle Ages that we find as gargoyles include birds or fantastic composite figures with bird elements; among the most famous of these are those high up on the roof of Notre Dame in Paris.

In realistic sculpture we are not so apt to find birds except in a position of rest. We do find such representations, though, in Pompeii, and in such famous works as Michelangelo's "Leda and the Swan." In modern sculpture we find many fountains and garden ornaments in the form of birds. And in weathervanes, wrought iron, and, above all, in figures of the

8

American eagle, proudly defiant, fiercely challenging, superbly aloof, we have countless representations. Many of the most beautiful of these bird figures date from a century or more ago, and some of the most memorable are simple and naïve yet strangely forceful eagles and cocks from old weathervanes and signs. And recently Brancusi, in two much discussed figures, has pointed the way to new treatments of the bird in sculpture—his famous "Golden Bird" and "Bird in Flight," impressionistic figures calling attention to the essential qualities of birds rather than attempts to portray them realistically. When we consider all of these treatments of the bird in sculpture and carving, as well as the innumerable pottery and bronze objects such as those found in China, we can see what myriad possibilities there are for treating birds realistically, impressionistically, symbolically and abstractly.

Turn to another of the arts: music. Critics and musical theorists have fought bitterly as to whether it is legitimate just to reproduce literally bird songs and calls in music—whether art is really art unless it has improved upon or refined nature (as if one could "improve upon" some of the bird songs we hear!). Yet even the most captious critics will accept such pieces as the eighteenth-century Rameau's rendering of the hen, or his "Roll Call of the Birds." And one of the most wonderful moments in all music is at the end of the slow movement in Beethoven's Pastoral Symphony, where we have just been beside the brook listening to its rhythm and, quietly happy, are meditating upon nature in thoughts too deep for words. The rhythmical murmur of the brook dies away, and in a strange silence we hear on the flute the brief trill of the nightingale and, just before it ends, even more briefly the notes of the quail on the oboe and of the cuckoo on the clarinet. For a moment the brook resumes, we hear the same notes of the birds again in the strange quiet and the brook fades away into complete silence. What a magic there is in these soft calls after all the richness of the full orchestra! Few people can help catching

9

their breath or feeling a shiver run down their spines at this perfectly simple rendering of three little bird calls.

We have another somewhat similar moment in the second act of Wagner's "Siegfried," when Siegfried forgets he is dragon-hunting and lies down in the forest to dream. We hear the murmur of the leaves in the wind, and the orchestra builds up a superb picture of the depths of the forest and the thought it evokes for the young hero. Then it all culminates in the magic song of the Forest Bird—no such simple songster as Beethoven's birds, but a virtuoso, strangely enough making use of some of our own hermit thrush's unmistakable idioms, which Wagner never heard. It is a perfect evocation of the magic of the out-of-doors.

Another later famous use of a similar device is in Respighi's "Pines of Rome," where, in the midst of the full orchestra, a victrola record of an actual nightingale's song is introduced; effective as the device is, the mood is never quite captured as in Beethoven and Wagner. In Stravinsky's richly colored "Firebird" we meet a Russian cousin of the phœnix of the East— perhaps that very phœnix—glowing in all its magnificent iridescence. We meet an only slightly less colorful nightingale in his opera "Le Rossignol." Other Russians, like Rimsky-Korsakoff, have given us exotic birds, and the American Griffes an Oriental white peacock.

Of course we have innumerable songs about birds, from simple folk songs and ballads like the American "Listen to the Mocking Bird," the French-Canadian "L'Alouette," the German "Vöglein in Tannenwald" and "Kommt a Vogerl geflogen," to such art-songs as Schubert's "Hark, Hark the Lark" and "Carrier Pigeon," Brahms' "Nightingale," Grieg's "Swan" (which reminds us of the legend that a swan sings, when dying, a song that surpasses all earthly music), Sinding's "I Heard the Gull" and Ravel's charming and highly sophisticated bird songs. And such orchestral tone-poems as Delius' "On Hearing the First Cuckoo in Spring," and Sibelius' "Swan of Tuonela" never weary us. Whether you want birds realistically treated in music (in spite of the ban), whether you want them treated sentimentally and romantically, or whether you want them treated with the deepest and most poetic feeling, you will easily find them.

Birds add immeasurably to the poetry and interest of every-day life. Especially if we have a garden, the birds can be our constant companions and helpers. In our garden we have an opportunity to study intimately their habits, as they ceaselessly weave an intricate web of song and flight as they go about their many concerns. They are a constant delight to both eyes and ears. The welcome sight of the wild geese winging northward in the spring, gives us courage to look for the first snowdrop; and to hear the dawn chorus of the birds in May and June, that ecstatic expression of pure happiness, is an experience never to be forgotten, an eternal renewal of faith in life.

No bird student is ever bored, for the study of birds is a never-failing source of interest. The mystery of their periodic arrival and departure, the wonder of that migratory urge which leads many of them to travel thousands of miles each year, some of them nearly from pole to pole, casts a glamour over them, while the study of their lives from day to day, their courtship, their care lavished on their offspring, is a well-spring of perpetual pleasure.

Fortunate is the child who has been from early days conscious of this busy world, so unceasingly astir about us. He has a wealth of memories to carry with him through life.

Julian Huxley in *Bird Watching and Bird Behavior* tells of his first vivid appreciation of bird life:

"I had been fond of birds since a child; but it was when I was about fourteen that I became a real bird watcher. The incident, which precipitated the change was this. One morning of late winter, crossing the laundry yard of my aunt's country house, I saw a green woodpecker on the grass only a few yards from me: I had just time to take in the sight of it before the bird was off to the wood beyond the hedge. The green woodpecker is a common bird enough; but I had never seen one close. Here

I saw every striking detail: the rich green of the wings, the flash of bright yellow on the back when he flew, the pale glittering eye, the scarlet nape, the strange moustache of black and red; and the effect was as if I had seen a bird of paradise, even a phœnix. I was thrilled with the sudden realization that here, under my nose, in the familiar woods and fields, lived strange and beautiful creatures of whose strangeness and beauty I had been lamentably unaware."

As our knowledge of birds grows more intimate we have a feeling of oneness with nature which no other branch of study of our world supplies so richly. Every day will add to the delight of companionship with new friends. What you see may not be new to the veteran bird student, but to you it is a virgin nugget of knowledge, and new and endearing traits will be disclosed every day in the year that you watch these never-tiring inhabitants of our trees and shrubs. Thomas S. Roberts in his *Birds of Minnesota,* says: "The beginning of bird study has many wonderful disclosures and many thrilling experiences, never to be duplicated and never to be forgotten. . . . Such strangers are we at home until our senses are awakened to the things about us."

Each season will have a new meaning to the bird watcher. Spring will not only reveal opening buds, but also a brave migrant from the South, daring the chilly winds of March and often in dire need of and gloriously appreciative of the hospitality we have prepared in sheltering evergreens and well-stocked feeding shelves. Day by day all spring the interest will increase as the male birds arrive and pick out their stations, singing lustily to let other birds know their territorial boundaries; then the arrival of the females, the courtship and the summer of domesticity, will be followed by the delight of greeting fall migrants and the pleasure of extending hospitality to winter guests. Thus to those aware of birds the year is full of glad surprises—always the chance of a visitor unseen before, a new guest lured to the feeding shelf—observation after observation, adding to the richness of one's store of memories until the bluebird "shifting its light load of song," the robin, singing at the cottage gate, are not only harbingers of spring, but symbols of youth eternal, of a flood of life welling up from an eternal source.

> To hear an oriole sing
> May be a common thing
> Or only a divine.
>
> It is not of the bird
> Who sings the same, unheard,
> As unto crowd.
>
> The fashion of the ear
> Attireth that it hear
> In dun or fair.
>
> So whether it be rune,
> Or whether it be none,
> Is of within;
>
> The "tune is in the tree,"
> The sceptic showeth me;
> "No, sir! in thee!"
> —*Emily Dickinson.*

If there were no other gain than the esthetic pleasure of knowing birds and having their companionship, it would be sufficient, but added to this joy is the positive knowledge of their great economic value.

We often see it stated that, if some catastrophe should wipe out entirely the bird life of the continent, we would starve to death before man could combat through sprays and mechanical means the insect hosts which, having no enemies, would destroy all crops. Ornithologists say that is too sweeping a statement, and entomologists say also that "parasitic insects would develop and prevent any major catastrophe," but, nevertheless, it is almost impossible for us to realize how much birds do to keep down the ravages of insects and rodents.

Birds are intensely active; their hearts beat very rapidly and in order to keep up their store of energy they have to eat often and plentifully. A good share of their waking hours is spent in the pursuit of food, and this constant feasting benefits the fruit and foliage of our trees and gardens. The United States Biological Survey by the examination of stomach contents, has proved beyond question of a doubt the vast good that birds do. Many birds, like swallows and swifts, course through the air and eat a multitude of insects, such as gnats and mosquitoes, often destroying them while they are mating and thus preventing a vast increase. The nighthawk patrols the air all night and part of the day, and eats mosquitoes, winged ants, June bugs, potato and cucumber beetles, boll weevils, squash beetles and many others; while other familiar birds like the chickadees, the woodpeckers, the warblers and the tiny kinglets, all war on egg masses and larvae as well as on the adult forms of the insects infesting forest and garden. Think of the reward given us for putting out a lump of suet for the happy chickadee when we know that his presence helps to free our trees from the egg masses of tent caterpillars and cankerworms, also from bark lice or scale insects, plant lice, leaf hoppers, and the larvae of codling moths and many bugs, flies and moths. E. H. Forbush, in his *Birds of Massachusetts,* says that it has been estimated that one chickadee would destroy 138,750 eggs of the cankerworm moth, during the twenty-five days in which the female moth lays her eggs. Professor E. D. Sanderson has estimated that the chickadees in the State of Michigan destroy eight thousand million insects annually.

Spring brings myriads of warblers ready to rid our trees and shrubbery of the multitude of insects feeding on the tender foliage. It has been calculated that one warbler can destroy 3,500 aphids in an hour, and as aphids produce from ten to thirteen generations in one summer, one can realize how sincerely we should welcome their arrival. Dr. Elliot Coues, the great authority on birds, gives the following tribute to the value of these little-known workers:

"With tireless industry do the warblers befriend the human race; their

A, A. Allen

"Chickadee-dee"—his spirits rise as the mercury falls

An instant's pause in the tree swallow's aerial search for harmful insects

William L. and Irene Finley

The blue-gray gnatcatchers inspect a masterpiece of camouflage

Whose turn comes next—seems to be
the cardinal's problem

An arrested flame—a rufous hummer
on its cup of lichens and cobwebs

The mountain-ash invites the hungry migrants

Winking blackberries lure a host of feasters

A happy throng soon strips the dogwood

A multitude of revelers seek the ripening mulberries

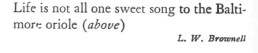

Life is not all one sweet song to the Baltimore oriole (*above*)

L. W. Brownell

Young phoebes doubt that patience is a virtue (*top, left*)

L. W. Brownell

Turn about is fair play, is the rule of the black-throated gray warbler (*upper center*)

William L. and Irene Finley

The brown thrasher does a thorough job (*lower center*)

L. W. Brownell

"Cherry, cherry, who'll get the cherry?" Cedar waxwings and young (*bottom*)

A. A. Allen

A feeding station, protected from the prevailing winds by glassed-in sides and back, and so camouflaged with cedar boughs that it seems a part of the woodland

Blown in by a "norther" purple finches cluster on the feeding shelf (*above*)

A. A. Allen

The impudent blue jay pre-empts the center of the stage (*top, left*)

A. A. Allen

Mealtime brings strange companions at "The Bird's Paradise" (*center*)

Charles E. Jones

An impatient chickadee awaits his turn at the cafeteria (*bottom*)

A. A. Allen

Sara Durno Wilson

Charles E. Jones

The thrill of feeding a wild bird! Purple finches at Aberdeen, Washington

Where is his sling shot or BB gun? "The Bird's Paradise," Vancouver, B. C.

One of the most delightful experiences that can come to the owner of a garden is the pleasure of winning the confidence of the birds that seek it as a haven

A fair exchange—the cardinal's cheer for a few sunflower seeds

For a bite of suet the chickadee will police your trees

A. A. Allen

A. A. Allen

The age of innocence in "The Bird's Paradise," Vancouver, B. C.

Who's afraid of the big bad gun?

The flicker family has accepted modern architecture

The conventional wood pewee broods on its traditional nest

Princes-to-be in a kingbird's nursery in an orchard

A stone wall shelters the untidy, bulky nest of the phoebe

The carefully woven cradle of the white-eyed vireo hangs firm and safe

The blue jay with native cunning often secretes its nest in an evergreen

Young robins hesitate before making the leap into the unknown

Confident of a welcome, the robin usually builds near our homes

A house finch weaves a nest of everlasting flowers on David Burpee's California Seed Farm

A wood thrush builds as its ancestors did

A bluebird's nest on old-fashioned lines

The purple martin welcomes a g[ourd]
for a home just as it did in the day[s of]
the Red Man

S. A. G

A skilfully woven structure of lichen
shelters the Acadian flycatcher's nestlings
Courtesy of U. S. Bureau of Biological Survey

Suet is fuel to stoke the furnace of
the brown creeper

With appetites insatiable, young
Seattle wrens demand more worms

A yellow warbler appreciates a gift
of cotton for her hope-chest

Red-shafted flicker ready to pump
ants into its nestlings

Poised in air, the hummingbird considers the nectar value of a balsam

Jacob Staub

The house wren's babies are cradled in a gourd

Esther Heacock

U. S. Bureau of Biological Survey

All God's chillun get worms, when it's dinner-time with the catbird family

This saw whet owl is out on a limb, but only far enough to see the camera

H. H. Pittman—Courtesy National Association of Audubon Societies

D. W. Dumser

The snow flies, but many birds remain—if they are given shelter and food

No sign of shopper's fatigue after the house wren's trip to market

*Robert G. Elliot—Courtesy National
Association of Audubon Societies*

H. D. Kimball

Even a kingbird must condescend to bathe

Young robins argue a nice question of precedence

Esther Heacock—Courtesy National
Association of Audubon Societies

An ever-welcome guest at any season, a song sparrow enjoys a doughnut at the city cafeteria

The white-throated sparrow often stops at the haven of the city garden on his way north or south

The parula warbler is one of our forest guardians

The black-chinned hummingbird seems a part of its cup of felted plant down

Three of a kind—young Cassin's vireos in an alder tree (*above*)

William L. and Irene Finley

The "upside down" bird, or white-breasted nuthatch, inspects every crevice in your trees (*left*)

Allan D. Cruickshank—Courtesy National
Association of Audubon Societies

A worm a minute keeps the young scarlet tanager in the "pink" (*below*)

A. A. Allen

Tree swallows awaiting the mystic signal for the southward flight

A brown thrasher
held for banding.
He is quiet and
not frightened

"Bobby" has received his band and is now "warming up" for the flight

A. T. Beals

A cardinal is quite calm about receiving his identification mark

Hugo Schroder

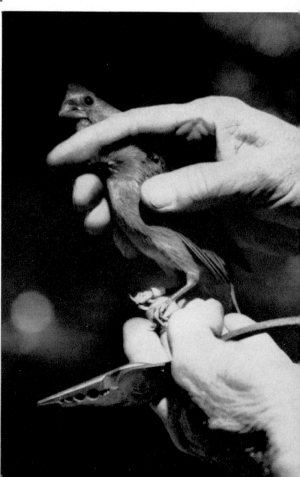

*H. H. Pittman—Courtesy National
Association of Audubon Societies*

Rain or shine, rings out the silver lay of the optimistic song sparrow

"A rapture of Western meadowlarks"—a song of the billowing prairies

*H. H. Pittman—Courtesy National
Association of Audubon Societies*

Too young to leave their mother—baby birds thrown out of a nest by a storm

Parental love overcomes the shy redstart's usual fear of man

A baby killdeer in its first neatly belted uniform stands at attention

Within sight of his mountain home, the bald eagle broods as if lost in thought

Courtesy of U. S. Bureau of Biological Survey

A young red-tailed hawk ready to pounce on an unwary meadow mouse

H. H. Pittman Courtesy National Association of Audubon Societies

All night, on silent wing, the screech owl
hunts food for its young

The dainty sparrow hawk wages unremitting warfare on grasshoppers

The heart-shape
face and black eye
of the barn owl ar
seldom seen by da

"Oh, woe, oh woe, woe," moans the mourning dove contentedly (*above*)

The Canada goose defends her jewels (*top, right*)

Young bobwhites just out of the egg and ready to scratch (*bottom, right*)

Amidst the bird's foot violets, the upland plover broods her eggs (*below*)

C. J. Henry—Courtesy of U. S.
Bureau of Biological Survey

Advance and rear guard for baby Canada geese, Lower Souris
Government Refuge, North Dakota

No nest for the killdeer's eggs, but the parents are ever on
guard to protect their spotted treasure

Allan D. Cruickshank—Courtesy National
Association of Audubon Societies

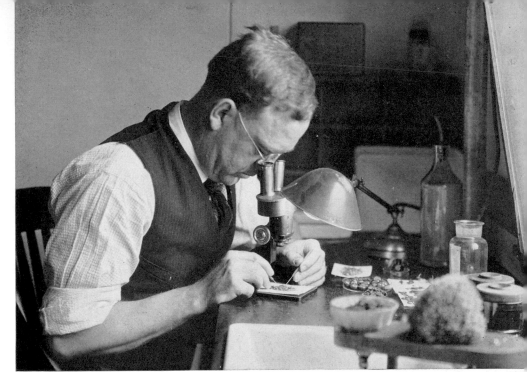

Courtesy of U. S. Bureau
of Biological Survey

"How many seeds did this bird eat?" W. L. McAtee at his microscope

he pokeberry is a prime favorite with the birds
W. L. Brownell

Birds prefer wild cherries to cultivated fruit
W. L. Brownell

The bayberry's "gray pearls" are precious booty to many a hungry wayfarer (*above*)

Drooping clusters of elderberries are food and drink for the birds of field and garden (*right*)

One of the few remaining trumpeter swans at a Government Refuge in Montana

Black ducks still breed in the low swamplands in the Northeastern States

Courtesy "More Game Birds in Amer

Where wild ducks find rest and food—a State Game Refuge at Seattle, Washington

Safe from hunters' guns, the mallard floats contentedly on the home sanctuary

Paul J. Fair—Courtesy National Association of Audubon Societ

unconscious zeal plays due part in the nice adjustment of Nature's forces, helping to bring about the balance of vegetable and insect life, without which agriculture would be vain. They visit the orchard when the apple and pear, the peach, plum and cherry, are in bloom, seeming to revel carelessly amid the sweet-scented and delicately-tinted blossoms, but never faltering in their good work. They peer into the crevices of the bark, scrutinize each leaf, and explore the very heart of the buds, to detect, drag forth, and destroy those tiny creatures, singly insignificant, collectively a scourge, which prey upon the hopes of the fruit grower, and which, if undisturbed, would bring his hopes to naught. Some warblers flit incessantly in the terminal foliage of the tallest trees; others hug close to the scored trunks and gnarled boughs of the forest kings; some peep from the thicket, the coppice, the impenetrable mantle of shrubbery that decks tiny watercourses, playing at hide and seek with all comers; others more humble still descend to the ground, where they glide with pretty mincing steps and affected turning of the head this way and that, their delicate flesh-tinted feet just stirring the layer of withered leaves with which a past season carpeted the grounds." *

Aiding the warblers are the soberly clad vireos, that, giving forth as if in soliloquy their sweet, disjointed songs, more deliberately examine the foliage for insects. A song, a pause—and down goes a cankerworm! Besides there are the flocks of kinglets which because of their minute size (hardly four inches in length) can penetrate every crack and cranny, and find obscure egg masses which have been overlooked by the other birds and which no spray can reach.

Among other insect-eating birds which are likely to help us are the nuthatches, orioles, hummingbirds, tanagers, wrens, waxwings, thrushes, titmice, cuckoos, shrikes, thrashers, bluebirds, robins, mockingbirds, catbirds and rose-breasted grosbeaks. A number of these birds live almost

---

* *Birds of the Colorado Valley;* Elliot Coues.

entirely on insects while others vary their diets with plant food. The following list of unwelcome visitors to the garden with the number of birds feeding on them is very illuminating.

The army worm has 43 bird enemies; billbugs, 110; the browntail moth, 31; chestnut weevils, 85; chinchbugs, 29; clover root borers, 94; the clover weevil, 48; the codling moth, 36; cutworms, 98; the forest tent caterpillar, 32; the gypsy moth, 46; horseflies, 49; leaf hoppers, 175; the orchard tent caterpillar, 43; the potato beetle, 34; white grubs, 95, and wireworms, 205.

Among seed-eating birds, the members of the sparrow or finch family are pre-eminent. It is almost impossible to estimate the amount of harmful weed seed that they destroy annually. Think how much back-breaking labor with the hoe is saved the home gardener if weeds are not allowed to seed in the garden; and in addition, think how much soil fertility is conserved, for the weeds, if allowed to grow, would have stolen much nourishment with their greedy roots from the legitimate crop. It is estimated that in the state of Iowa alone tree sparrows eat over 800 tons of weed seeds annually. It has also been calculated that the value of birds in Pennsylvania in keeping down weed seeds and noxious insects is $7,000,-000 per year. We need their help immeasurably more year by year. The country is flooded by the progeny of imported weeds, which would spread overwhelmingly, not only in the farmer's field but into our gardens if the seed-eating birds were not ceaselessly destroying them without even asking a "thank you."

Now in addition to insect pests and weeds, the gardener may expect that the moles will undermine his lawn and that the field mice will follow in the moles' burrows and feast on the choice tulips and also girdle his trees! Again birds come to his rescue. The much persecuted hawks and owls slip, or rather fly, into the breach and rid him of many of these rodents and also of hordes of grasshoppers and beetles. Only lately has the true value of these birds been appreciated. Although of different families,

16

their food habits are similar; they really supplement each other. The hawks with their swift, daring flight hunt during the day, and the owls, on silent wings, dispatch the enemy at night. Only through disastrous experience (disastrous to the hawks and owls as well as to ourselves) has the value of these birds been proved.

We know now that to offer a bounty on these so-called birds of prey is to bring upon ourselves a great financial loss, as well as an esthetic one, by the destruction of some of our most interesting and beautiful birds. In mistaken zeal, some years ago, Pennsylvania offered a bounty on hawks and owls. This resulted in the killing of over 100,000, and an estimated loss over one and one-half years time of nearly $4,000,000!

It has always been noticed that in times of a scourge of grasshoppers or mice or some similar pest there will be a concentration of birds that prey upon the pest in that vicinity.

The traditional example of birds concentrating and saving a crop is that which occurred in Utah in 1848, when Salt Lake City was less than a year old. That spring the hopeful settlers, about 1800 in number, had tilled the ground and planted potatoes, corn, wheat, beans, peas and oats, all in happy anticipation of not only a bounteous harvest for themselves, but also food for 2,400 immigrants who were about to arrive. The fields were covered with a green veil, when suddenly the sun was hidden by a dark cloud and from the air a million grasshoppers fell on the tender green. The people stood appalled—utterly helpless before the descending horde. Suddenly there was a rush of wings and from the islands on Great Salt Lake came gulls by the thousands and fell upon the insects, gorging themselves on the scourge until not one was left and the greater part of the crop was saved. For this act, which the Mormons considered a direct intervention of Providence, a monument was erected to the gulls, said to be the only one in the world dedicated in gratitude to birds.

These few examples show how valuable birds can be in our garden or in one State. Think what their value must be all over the country! It is truly tremendous.

The Department of Agriculture estimates that every year insect pests do $1,590,040,500 worth of damage, while the value of birds in destroying these pests is over $350,000,000. Those figures should awaken us to the value of birds. Can we afford to ignore and not encourage the presence of these untiring workers? Surely we shall receive back payment tenfold in pleasure and assistance for the time expended if we give some thought to the planting around our homes, endeavoring to design our grounds so that there will be proper cover and shelter for the birds, and also planting trees and shrubs which bear plentiful fruit. We should also provide for a supply of water for bathing and drinking; for supplementary food during heavy storms when ice coats the trees or deep snows cover the ground; and for suitable nesting sites and boxes. Very little effort will result in the garden becoming a Mecca for the birds and a source of undying interest for yourself, where at any time you may see "some modest songster whose delicate beauty surpasses that of the richest fabrics and whose graceful movements charm the fortunate observer who can find and see our birds at home."

Chapter Two

PLANTING IN THE SMALL GARDEN
TO PROVIDE FOOD AND COVER

G RANTED that the birds bring to the garden the joy of life and movement, and to it also, through their destruction of insect pests, a greater beauty of flower, fruit and foliage, it then follows that we must want to do all we can to insure their presence. This can be done more easily than the gardener usually realizes, for birds, whether they are insect or seed eaters, are dependent on vegetation for their existence; all that we have to do is to plant trees and shrubs which are not only ornamental in the garden, but which will be of three-fold value to the birds. That is, they must furnish flowers and fruit for the primary allure of food, and foliage, both for protection from storms, to afford cover for concealment and also for nesting, and pasturage for insects the birds need for food.

If only the real estate dealer would realize the value of trees and shrubs on lots which they so glowingly describe to prospective buyers! Not only trees planted by the development company, but enough of the native growth left to form the keynote of intelligent planting: for instance, an elm where an oriole may hang its remarkable cradle, or a group of dogwoods for the beginning of our bird sanctuary.

But generally the home-builder has to start from "scratch" and that usually a blackberry tangle, which, fortunately, the birds won't object to. Let us take an imaginary bare lot in the suburbs of any city of the eastern United States and plant it with a thought for the birds. The formal area should be kept to the front of the house and need not now concern us.

19

In the rear should be a terrace—an observation gallery for the joyous activities of the birds who are to be the guests or permanent inhabitants of the garden.

By all means have a catproof fence if possible, for birds can survive their *natural* checks, but are powerless against the depredations of the cat, a foe which man has brought from the Old World and has let loose to deplete ruthlessly their ranks. If a catproof fence is considered impracticable, we should in every way try to protect the birds while eating, bathing, drinking and nesting, by planting thickets of prickly, densely-twigged shrubs interlaced with a tangle of profusely growing or thorny vines.

To start with the vines. Along the fence or wall plant Japanese honeysuckle, *Lonicera japonica*, variety *halliana*. It will soon make a thick tangle. This honeysuckle is an exceedingly rapid-growing vine, spreading so fast that where it has become established in the wild it has become a pest, absolutely wiping out by its aggressive growth more attractive native plants. But where it can be kept in bounds, it makes a very valuable tangle for birds, its fragrant blossoms attracting insects, its berries giving food, while its almost evergreen foliage provides good cover.

With the honeysuckle can be planted the ever-charming American bittersweet or waxwork, *Celastrus scandens*, the fruit of which is so often used for indoor decorations. This vine, though not evergreen, has good glossy green foliage throughout the summer, a profuse twining growth, and an abundant crop of brilliant scarlet and orange fruit which lasts well into the winter. Be sure to secure from the nurseryman both the pistillate and staminate (that is the female and male) forms, for only the pistillate vines bear fruit. Both of these vines do well in any ordinary garden soil and endure partial shade.

For more protection add the catbriar, *Smilax glauca*, and the woodbine or Virginia creeper. The catbriar is a vine with spiny underground growth and stems armed with stout, hooked, viciously sharp spines. It makes an impassable barrier for cats when allowed to grow at its own

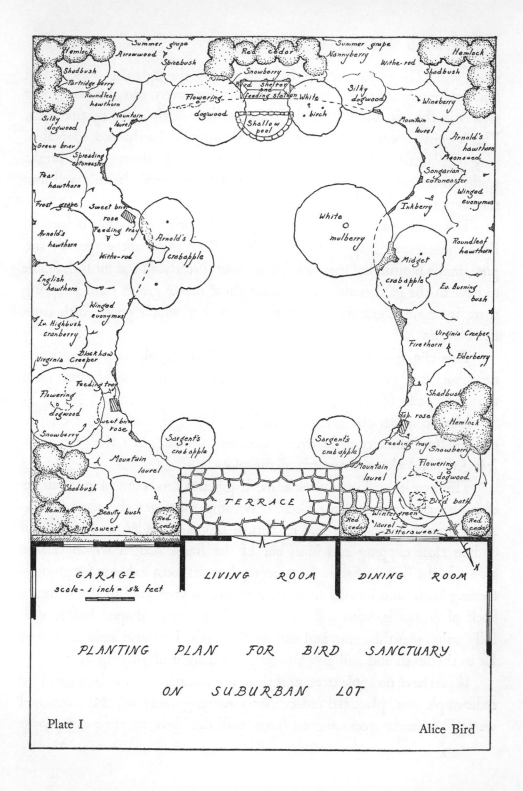

Hemlock · Summer grape · Red cedar · Summer grape · Hemlock
Arrowwood · Nannyberry · Withe-rod · Shadbush
Shadbush · Spicebush · Snowberry
Partridge berry · Bird Shelter and Feeding station · Silky dogwood
Roundleaf hawthorn · Flowering dogwood · White birch · Wineberry
Mountain laurel · Shallow pool · Mountain laurel
Silky dogwood · Arnold's hawthorn
Green brier · Peonseed
Spreading cotoneaster · Songarian cotoneaster
Pear hawthorn · White mulberry · Winged euonymus
Frost grape · Sweet brier rose · Inkberry
Feeding tray · Arnold's crabapple · Midget crabapple · Roundleaf hawthorn
Arnold's hawthorn · Withe-rod · Eu. Burning bush
English hawthorn · Firethorn · Virginia Creeper
Winged euonymus · Elderberry
Eu. Highbush cranberry
Virginia Creeper · Blackhaw · Shadbush
Flowering dogwood · Feeding tray · Jap. rose · Hemlock
Snowberry · Sweet brier rose · Sargent's crabapple · Sargent's crab apple · Feeding tray · Snowberry
Mountain laurel · Mountain laurel · Flowering dogwood
Shadbush · Bird bath
Hemlock · Beauty bush · Red cedar · TERRACE · Red cedar · Wintergreen laurel · Red cedar
Bittersweet · Bittersweet

N

GARAGE · LIVING ROOM · DINING ROOM
scale - 1 inch = 5½ feet

PLANTING PLAN FOR BIRD SANCTUARY

ON SUBURBAN LOT

Plate I · Alice Bird

sweet will. The birds, though, can slip sleekly through the prickles and find secure sanctuary. Its leaves are partially evergreen, often coloring very vividly in the fall, and it bears dark blue berries eagerly eaten by the birds. The Virginia creeper, *Parthenocissus quinquefolia,* hardy and adaptable, may be planted to lace in and out of this tangle. It always turns bright scarlet in the fall and produces quantities of black berries lasting well into the winter.

The wild grapes too, may add to the luxuriance of this hideaway. Both the summer grape, *Vitis aestivalis* and the riverbank grape, V. *vulpina,* make profuse leafage, valuable as cover. Nearly all the birds desirable to have in the garden are known to eat these native grapes, and in spring there is no more entrancing perfume than that which pours forth from the blossoms.

This choice of vines, not being quite conventional, may astonish the neighbors, but you will find that there is nothing more satisfactory from the birds' point of view.

Next consider the evergreen background. If the suburban lot is far enough from the city to be free of dust and smoke, plant the graciously-foliaged hemlock on the north of the plot.

The hemlock, *Tsuga canadensis,* if given a modicum of pure air, is of a very adaptable nature. There is nothing more graceful than its un-shorn growth of branches and its slender drooping leader, and yet it will endure close clipping and form one of the finest hedges which can be grown in the Eastern States. Its sweeping boughs form a shelter for ground-feeding birds, and its tiny cones may attract to your yard in the winter a flock of crossbills, who will, with their little scissor-shaped beaks, skil-fully snip open the cones and extract the seeds. Unfortunately they nest far to the north and will give you only the delight of a flying visit.

If you have no apple trees, or if there is no orchard near to be injured by cedar-apple rust, place red cedars, *Juniperus virginiana,* on the south and west. These cedar trees are great favorites of the birds, for their dense ever-

SCARLET TANAGER

ABNORMAL PLUMAGE (XANTHOCHROISM)		MALE, FULLY ADULT (BLACK WINGS)

MALE, WINTER   FEMALE

JUVENAL PLUMAGE (NESTLING)

MALE, FIRST BREEDING PLUMAGE (BROWN WINGS)

MOLTING MALE

Scale about one-half

green foliage forms a snug shelter for them in the stormiest weather. The blue fruit is eaten by at least half a hundred kinds of birds, among those most desirable in the garden—the robin, bluebird and mockingbird, cedar waxwing and flicker—while its lasting supply of berries may bring a casual myrtle warbler in the winter, or a flock of purple finches or the longed-for visit of that rare northerner, the pine grosbeak, with rose-red feathers warm against the drifting snow.

In front of the hemlocks plant groups of the native flowering dogwood, *Cornus florida,* mixing with them the Japanese dogwood, *Cornus kousa.* The native dogwood is one of the loveliest of small flowering trees. Before the leaves appear in May it is wreathed with a perfect snowdrift of blossoms which are followed by brilliant red fruits, lasting late in the fall, and greatly loved by the birds. Besides the beauty of its flowering, the dogwood is very graceful in its tiered growth, and its foliage turns exquisite shades of rose-red, crimson and deep orange in the autumn. The Japanese dogwood is less well-known; its time of flowering immediately follows that of *Cornus florida,* and its starry blooms are set amidst the glossy, dark-green leaves. The flowers are about the same size as those of our own tree, but the white bracts which surround the central cluster of small greenish flowers are pointed instead of rounded and notched, thus giving the bloom an airier appearance. Its fruit, a bright crimson, is also enjoyed by many, many birds, the fruits of these trees and the shrubby dogwoods being enjoyed by ninety-three kinds. Think of it, ninety-three kinds of birds which we might identify in our gardens! Among these are such delightful ones as the song sparrow, with his simple tune forever uplifted even in the rain, and his great value as a weed seed eradicator; such melodious songsters as the wood, hermit, gray-cheeked and olive-backed thrushes; and such friendly birds, bubbling with song, as the catbird and brown thrasher. Some of these birds may become summer residents through nesting in your shrubbery border.

Near the red cedars should be set a planting of shadbush, *Amelanchier canadensis,* or *A. laevis.* These small trees, in early spring, are garlanded in frail wreaths of snow-white bloom, and later are covered with tiny purple applelike fruits, so loved by the birds that they seldom remain longer than a few days after they are ripe. These fruits are particularly enjoyed by such interesting and attractive birds as the flickers, orioles, cedar waxwings, veeries and robins. Near the shadbush put a mass of the highbush blueberry, *Vaccinium corymbosum,* a shrub too little used in the garden. Its lacy branches are covered with dainty bells in spring, which are followed by blue-bloomed berries, a great treat for young birds, while in the fall the foliage turns rose-pink and deep wine-red. Another shrub for similar use is the chokeberry, either the red, *Aronia arbutifolia,* or the black, *A. melanocarpa.* These shrubs bear fruits which remain on the bushes until next blooming season or even later.

In this portion of the garden the soil should be kept acid, for the welfare of most of the native plants mentioned depends on soil acidity. The cedars, the shadbush, and the high-bush blueberry and chokeberry require an acid soil and the dogwoods do not object to it. This acidity may be maintained by mulches of red-oak leaves or pine needles, or if these are not obtainable, by scattering aluminum sulphate in the proportion of a pound to each square yard.

Now for a ground cover attractive in itself, the fruit of which is also an attraction for birds. Near the red cedars plant a thick carpet of wild strawberry, *Fragaria virginiana.* The glossy three-parted leaves are early in June surmounted by little clusters of the bright red fragrant fruit. Fifty-two kinds of birds eat these and feed them to their nestlings. Whether expressed or not, great will be the relief, if not the gratitude, of a mother robin at finding these easily accessible berries. This planting will mean protection for the patch of strawberries in the kitchen garden, for wild fruits are usually taken in preference to cultivated. Other birds which may be nesting near by and which would enjoy these strawberries are the catbird, the brown thrasher, the wood thrush and the towhee.

FOOD AND COVER IN SMALL GARDEN

Near the hemlocks, where the soil is also acid, plant the wild sarsa-parilla, *Aralia nudicaulis,* in combination with mats of bearberry, *Arcto-staphylos uva-ursi.* The sarsaparilla is a native plant which should be used more frequently, both in the wild garden and in plantings for birds. Often on the edge of a natural growth of hemlocks it will form a uniform bank. It has a pleasing leaf form and its clusters of small black berries are greatly enjoyed by sixteen kinds of birds, among them our dooryard friend, the robin.

The bearberry, as it is evergreen, will supplement the sarsaparilla. Its small pinky-white, urn-shaped flowers appear in spring when last year's fruit is still present, the red berries persisting (if the birds leave them) until the new crop takes their place. The bearberry, a member of the huckle-berry family, requires an acid soil. It is an exceedingly pleasing ground cover, its small oval leaves are a lively green and the new growth is of a beautiful bronze tint. It is a creeping shrub of wide distribution, carpet-ing the sand dunes of Long Island and Cape Cod, the mountain slopes of Montana and Wyoming and the edges of the prairies of Oregon and Washington. Sods of bearberry are occasionally transplanted, but success is insured if pot-grown seedlings are used.

In all localities together, no fewer than thirty-four species of birds are known to feed on the persistent berries, which become a valuable addi-tion to the birds' menu when other more perishable fruits have disappeared. All winter the ruffed grouse eat them greedily and the fox sparrows wel-come them as they stop for a brief visit on their way to the North. Even if the vines are lightly covered with snow, with extraordinary vigor the fox sparrows will dig down to the storehouse. They will leap into the air, then scratch away with both feet at once, scattering the snow behind them, until they reach the buried treasure, which consists of, not only the fruit of the bearberry, but of weed seeds and insects that have accumulated be-neath the leaves. Then pausing a moment, perhaps a young male may give a sample of the song which will ring out in the far North, a sample

25

which does not seem like a bird song, but like the far-off tinkling of silver bells.

Other ground covers which may spread over the bare earth beneath the hemlocks are wintergreen, *Gaultheria procumbens,* and partridge-berry, *Mitchella repens.*

The wintergreen will tolerate a good deal of shade, and like the bear-berry it must have acid soil. It, too, is of the huckleberry family, but is of upright, not spreading growth, reaching a height of four inches. Both the leaves and the scarlet berries have a decided wintergreen flavor. Its foliage is evergreen and very shiny. The partridgeberry resembles the bearberry, but is not of the same family, belonging instead to the madder family; the little paired flowers have bearded petals and a delightful perfume, and each pair is followed by a gleaming twin or two-eyed berry, the two eyelike depressions showing where the bases of the two little blossoms have united. These berries are as persistent as those of the bearberry and the vines are more easily grown, being more tolerant as to soil, and even adapting them-selves to quite an exposed situation in the rock garden. As their name indicates they are beloved of the partridge or ruffed grouse and more than thirty-four other ground-frequenting birds.

In the shrubbery border, which is perhaps an irregular planting flank-ing the vine-covered wall or fence, may be set a combination of the shrubby dogwoods and the viburnums. These shrubs are from the dogwood and the honeysuckle families, which contain enough worth while plants to supply an entire bird sanctuary. Among the most attractive of these native shrubs is the pagoda or alternate-leaved dogwood. It is really a small tree and has an interesting manner of branching in whorls, forming tiers, which has gained it its common name. It has alternate instead of opposite leaves, which makes it easily distinguishable from the other members of this group. The flowers, in flat-topped clusters, are creamy-white, and the fruit is bright blue on red stems. The fruit is presumably held from mid-June to mid-October, but as we are planting for the birds we should be happy to state that the tree is soon stripped. Yes, soon only the bare red stems of the berries remain, but vivid still is the memory of the cardinal's flame, the melodious ripple of the warbling vireo, or the whispered lisp of a flock cf cedar waxwings. No one could begrudge the choicest fruit to any of these birds, especially to the waxwings, so sleek, so trim, so entirely well-groomed are they at every season of the year. And so gentle-voiced and courteous are they too. Their voices are so soft that some persons cannot hear them, and so polite are they that oftentimes, as they sit in groups, when a bird picks a berry it is passed several times up and down the line before one bird will be persuaded actually to swallow it.

The silky dogwood, *Cornus amomum,* is decidedly shrubby in growth. It has creamy-white flowers, similar to those of the pagoda dogwood, but its fruit is not so brilliant a blue, usually cadet-blue or dull white. Its fruiting season is also from June to October, and it does not seem to be quite as attractive to the birds early in the year as later in the fall. But wait until autumn brings a band of migrating bluebirds and you will see a flurry of wings and then a stripped bush.

Another shrub of dense twiggy growth, which makes it valuable as a nesting site, is the panicled dogwood, *Cornus racemosa.* Sometimes in the fields you will see whole hedgerows of this bush. Perhaps long ago there was a wall or fence there and the birds dropped the seeds as they perched upon it. It has flat clusters of small creamy flowers, followed by white fruit which it carries normally until the end of October, thus making it valuable for migrant visitors.

With the dogwoods should be placed the viburnums, which hold their fruit through the winter and well into the spring, and several of them quite through the year. For a shady situation the mapleleaf viburnum, *Viburnum acerifolium,* is excellent, retaining its fruit well. Its flat clusters of flowers are followed by dark blue berries and in the fall the leaves turn to most unusual shades of soft pinkish-lavender and purple. Among the thirty or more birds that feed on the various viburnums is the yellow-billed cuckoo,

27

that eats quantities of the hairy caterpillars which are passed up as distasteful by many birds. It is said that so many of these bristly caterpillars, which are among our worst pests, are eaten by this bird, that the lining of its stomach is set with a thick coating of spiny bristles.

Other viburnums are the nannyberry, *V. lentago,* having cadet-blue long-persistent fruit with a soft bloom, the blackhaw, *V. prunifolium,* and the arrowwood, *V. dentatum,* both of the latter bearing blue-black fruit with a bloom. Among the most beautiful of the birds which eat viburnum berries is the rose-breasted grosbeak, and if only his mate can find a safe place for her rather precariously constructed nest, you will have secured by the lure of this planting one of the treasures of the bird world. How delightful some morning to be greeted by the liquid, mellifluous warble of this grosbeak, similar to that of the robin, but more sustained and much sweeter and smoother. This song will rise from the treetops early and late all through the spring and summer. Yes, the devoted male is seldom silent, for so conscientious is he that he relieves his mate when she is incubating the eggs and sings as he sits on the nest.

The list of garden pests this grosbeak destroys is astonishingly long and includes potato beetles, cucumber beetles, wood borers, moths, curculios, destructive caterpillars and scale insects. W. L. McAtee of the United States Biological Survey says: "Few birds have so good a record." And few birds are more delightful to observe in their family relations. The male not only relieves the female on the nest, but feeds her and is always close at hand, singing his melodious song.

Another viburnum, very brilliant in its fruiting, is the American high-bush cranberry, *Viburnum trilobum.* The bright scarlet, almost translucent, fruit hangs long on the bush. They very seldom tempt the bluebirds or robins, but let the gentle cedar waxwing learn of their presence and every spring a flock will appear on approximately the same date, year after year. With much hissing and whispering they will strip the bush of its bright red fruit, leaving the snow below flecked as if with drops of blood.

Also a member of the honeysuckle family is the common elderberry, *Sambucus canadensis*. In June all through the Eastern States its foamy white clusters top the stone walls and hedgerows, making an unforgettable part of the wayside beauty. Then later it is so loaded with fruit that the bush is actually top-heavy. Although it reaches its greatest luxuriance of growth in moist ground, the elderberry is adaptable and responds readily to cultivation. The only reason that it is not more often planted in the shrubbery border must be because it is so often seen in the wild. But with the generally growing appreciation of our native plants it will be more frequently used in the future, taking the place of the unhealthy-looking golden elder, a variegated form of the European species, which the nurseryman so often urges upon us because he has an oversupply in his fields.

Even in the small bird sanctuary we must have the elderberry, for the United States Biological Survey puts it second only to the raspberries and blackberries in its attractiveness to birds. It is known that over a hundred kinds of birds eat its small black fruits and those of its close relatives, the red elder, *S. pubens*. Here in the East, flickers and other woodpeckers, bluebirds and thrushes and many others feast upon it. And varying his diet of moths and other insects, that interesting member of the flycatcher family, the kingbird, is glad to eat of it. If there is even a small orchard the kingbird might decide to linger, for he often builds in an apple tree and has even been known to put his nest in an eavestrough. If he does nest in the garden woe betide the intruder who would molest his domicile! The kingbird is a fighter from away back. In that sleek slate-gray body with the white breast and white-tipped tail beats an indomitable heart. No crow or hawk escapes his eyes as he sits on guard on some prominent bare twig. Although not as large as a robin and really powerless against a larger bird, he knows no fear and will attack from above, having been known to light on the enemy's back and ride off as his foe flees, punishing him with his short bill. He certainly may have some very human swashbuckling characteristics, but he doesn't boast and not carry out his threats, for never-ceasingly he is on guard for hearth and home and by his unremitting watchfulness, does good sentinel services for less wary species. He is our invaluable ally in the garden, preferring insects to all other food. He is destructive of moths of all kinds, especially the gypsy moth which feeds on our fruit and shade trees. On good authority it is stated that in two and a half hours seven of these birds were seen to take seventy-nine male and twenty-nine female gypsy moths. Besides this they eat June bugs, click beetles, crickets, weevils, grasshoppers and many others.

The kingbird was known by some of the Indians as "the little chief." It is too bad that such a picturesque name could not be retained but it is fortunate that his name of "bee martin" is now seldom heard. The Department of Agriculture has gone out of its way to prove to the farmer that the kingbird is his friend. Many beeraisers have been certain that the kingbird took their bees, but Professor Beal in a Bulletin of the United States Biological Survey says that in his examination of numerous stomachs of these birds, shot to prove their economic status, that only a few bees were found, the majority of which were drones which can always be spared from the hives. In the kingbirds' stomachs, in addition to the remains of the drones, were found the bodies of numerous robber flies which kill many bees.

All the planting spoken of may be considered a prelude to choosing a site for a mulberry tree. This is a tree without which no bird lover's garden is complete. It is attractive to the birds and therefore such a protection for cherries, strawberries and other early fruits, that it is practically indispensable. The native tree, *Morus ruba,* reaches sixty feet. This is somewhat larger than the Chinese white mulberry, *M. alba.* The birds seem to like the two equally well, flocking to both of them continuously during the time of fruiting which is from May to late August. The pistillate and the staminate catkins are on separate trees, so care should be taken to secure the fruiting or pistillate form from the nurseryman, or both, if there are no other mulberry trees in the neighborhood.

FOOD AND COVER IN SMALL GARDEN

The mulberry develops a graceful, rather drooping shape. The leaves are a long oval and coarsely toothed; and the fruit resembles a blackberry in shape, and is rather insipid in taste to us, but a rare dainty to the birds. The fruit of the native tree is dark purple, almost black, while that of the Chinese tree varies from white, through pink to purple. An objection has been made by exceedingly tidy gardeners that the fruit drops badly. This is true, so do not plant it where it overhangs the terrace.

In sections where there is very severe winter weather, the varietal form of the white mulberry should be planted. This is *Morus alba,* var. *tatarica* and the nurseryman will doubtless call it the Russian mulberry. It is a smaller tree and perfectly hardy in the colder States such as Minnesota and North Dakota.

Over half a hundred birds are known to eat the mulberry fruit, and doubtless there are many others. The list includes, not only robins, bluebirds, catbirds, thrashers and various woodpeckers, but also such brilliant visitors (or happily) residents, as the scarlet tanager and the cardinal. And how fortunate we are if we can actually lure a cardinal to stay with us! After he has once discovered the place he will quite likely make it his home if there is a constant supply of food, both natural and what we can supply. All through the winter no cold will disturb him provided there is a bounteous table spread, for contrary to the popular idea, the cardinal does not migrate to the South. Once lure him and his mate to nest on your grounds and you have permanent residents, he and his children after him, that is if that important food question is taken care of and there is a reasonable amount of protection from enemies.

So, even if you were indifferent to the welfare of birds in general, it is worth while to plant a mulberry tree just in the hope of getting such a spectacular visitor as a cardinal. One of the few birds with brilliant plumage who is also a songster, he is a bird few are oblivious to. In various parts of the country he is so well loved that he has received sectional names. In Virginia he is called Virginia redbird, farther west the Kentucky cardinal and sometimes the cardinal grosbeak. As "Kentucky Cardinal" he has been immortalized in literature by James Lane Allen.

The cardinal is of the most vivid vermilion-scarlet color. He has a black mask on his face and throat, but his large stout bill and crest are scarlet. His mate has a crest also, and her plumage is of an olive-grayish tone showing a little vermilion on wings and tail. But she has a gift not generally bestowed on her sex; she can sing and warbles a melodious answer to the male during the time of courtship. The nest is placed from three to thirty feet from the ground in a deciduous or in an evergreen tree, but more often lower in a vine or a thicket. It is a rather carelessly-made structure of twigs, barkstrips, weed stems and grasses, but it is carefully lined with fine grass or hair. Not as devoted as the rose-breasted grosbeak, the male cardinal does not share the incubation of the eggs, but who can blame him? Who wouldn't spy that flame-red, no matter how quietly he sat? But otherwise, he is most attentive to his mate, feeding her, and constantly singing while she is on the nest. And curiously enough, when you think of how much attention his brilliant plumage attracts, for at least three weeks he takes complete charge of the nestlings while his mate lays and broods a second set of eggs.

Although the cardinal is particularly fond of wild fruit, he eats many insect pests, among these cutworms, codling moths, rose beetles, cucumber beetles, plum scale and other plant scales, besides leaf-hoppers and plant lice, to mention only a few of particular interest to the home gardener. Yes, to be envied is the gardener who has a cardinal for an assistant. In every month of the year he may hear his musical whistle, even on the coldest day of January, and against winter's snow, the scarlet plumage stands out in a vivid contrast which never loses its novelty. These birds were once extensively used as cage birds. As far back as 1699 we have a record that they were sold at $10.00 each in Havana, and once in time of public scarcity the Spaniards bought so many that the sum expended amounted to $18,000. They are now protected by laws forbidding the confinement of native birds.

These are merely a few suggestions for a simple planting of shrubs and trees, largely native, on a small lot. There are infinite combinations that can be worked out with native material alone, or this material combined with exotic, or with species native in other parts of the country.

Chapter Three

PLANTING TO PROVIDE FOOD AND COVER
IN THE LARGER GARDEN

O N A place with a slightly larger area than the suburban lot, the trees and shrubs already mentioned and others particularly loved by certain birds should by all means be planted. Unfortunately, if on the larger place you have an orchard the valuable red cedar will have to be omitted because it develops on its branches the fungus called cedar apples. The spores which fly from this fungus cause a destructive rust on the leaves of trees of the apple family, including the native crabapples. But fortunately for us, as well as for the birds, the Asiatic crabapples, so ornamental in flower and fruit, are immune. It is indeed unfortunate in a place designed to attract the birds if the red cedar and the ground cedar have to be eliminated, because they are of great value as shelters and nesting sites, as well as in furnishing food to many birds throughout the year. But if the orchard has to be considered other close-growing evergreens may be substituted. Both the white pine and the hemlock if kept trimmed, make excellent wind-breaks and nesting sites.

A large tree, one of the most characteristic sights of the landscape of the eastern United States, is the American elm, *Ulmus americana*. Graceful in shape, and affording welcome shade and protection, the elm is beloved beyond all other trees by the delightful Baltimore oriole. This bird was named in honor of Lord Baltimore, because its black and gold plumage bears the colors of that family and May sees the flash of gold of this little minion of the peerage in the favorite elm and we hear the warbling whistle of the male. Soon after the female will arrive and after looking the tree over carefully will more than likely choose the very tip of one of the lacy branches for a nesting site. There she will hang one of the most intricately contrived of any of the structures woven or built by birds. It is in the form of a long bag and in making it, the female thrusts a fibre into the side of the nest, then reaching over to the inside pulls it through, weaving, knitting, and felting the whole fabric together so securely, and fastening it to the bough so tightly, that few storms can dislodge the cradle, although a severe wind may crack the eggs. Supplying short bits of string is a great help to the little weaver, saving her much time which would be spent stripping fibre from milkweed and dogbane. Beware though, during the time of nest-building, of hanging any fine linen on the clothesline. Once, an oriole discovered a piece of delicate drawn-work which had been hung out on the line to bleach. Time after time she returned to it, with her sharp bill cutting all the delicate threads and then unraveling them. But just as cleverly will her sharp bill slit every silken cocoon that she can spy on the trees or in the gutter of the roof, and extract from it the dull sleeper, preventing the nefarious activities of the future. And of course when the brood of clamorous nestlings has to be fed, the efforts of the pair are astonishing and an amazing amount of May beetles, grasshoppers, caterpillars, and click beetles, of which the wireworms, such a pest to the gardener, are the larvae, are carried to the youngsters at short intervals all day.

A tree in disrepute with landscape architects and those in charge of street tree planting, is the box elder, *Acer negundo*. Though it grows very quickly and gives abundant shade, its wood is brittle, its shape ungainly, it is comparatively short-lived, and only the pistillate tree bears fruit.

But the bird lover will always cherish a tender feeling for it, for to it will often come when winter snows are deep and storms sweep in from the Northwest, the charming, gentle evening grosbeak. In a livery of black and yellow, with white patches on their wings which make them at rest look as if they had lily petals folded on their backs, these sociable birds may one day descend like a shower of falling leaves on your box elder, and stay until

35

with their sturdy bills, almost like those of little parrots, they have cracked every one of the hanging seeds. These rare, and seemingly exotic birds, whose scientific name means "daughters of the night who dwell on the verge of the world where the sun goes down," come to us in mid-winter. Scientists say their eastern pilgrimages have lengthened since the box elder has been planted. Whether that is true or not, and though they may not disdain the seeds of maple, dogwood, tulip tree, or lilac and even eat some winter fruits, their first love is the box elder, and after it is stripped, off will fly these beautiful "waifs of the Northland," who knows how far, or to what northern waste.

Surely the bird lover can spare a corner for this tree, planting it with the hope that some morning he may be roused by the rather metallic call note of these unusual and beautiful visitors.

Another tree, the hackberry, *Celtis occidentalis,* bears fruit greatly loved by the birds. It is not often planted because it is sometimes attacked by a fungus causing a bunched growth of twigs on the branches called witches' brooms, in the wild, however, it often makes a stately tree. Belonging to the same family as the elm, it resembles that tree in foliage; and, as it is not particular as to soil, will grow in almost any situation. The leaves are a glossy, light green and the tree has an airy cheerful appearance. Of course from the birds' standpoint, the chief value lies in the fruit, which is round, varies in color from orange-red to dark-purple, and hangs on the tree from season to season. Nearly fifty birds have been known to eat this fruit. If the hackberry is planted at the rear of the garden, where the trees and shrubs tend to resemble a wild thicket, perhaps the brown thrasher may discover its persistent fruit and eat of it when he returns from the South in spring.

Although we shall have to be observant to see the thrasher when he first arrives, he is very emphatic in song a little later. At first he will slip silently in and out of the undergrowth, betraying his presence only by a vigorous scratching of the dry leaves. Then, say by May Day, if the sun is

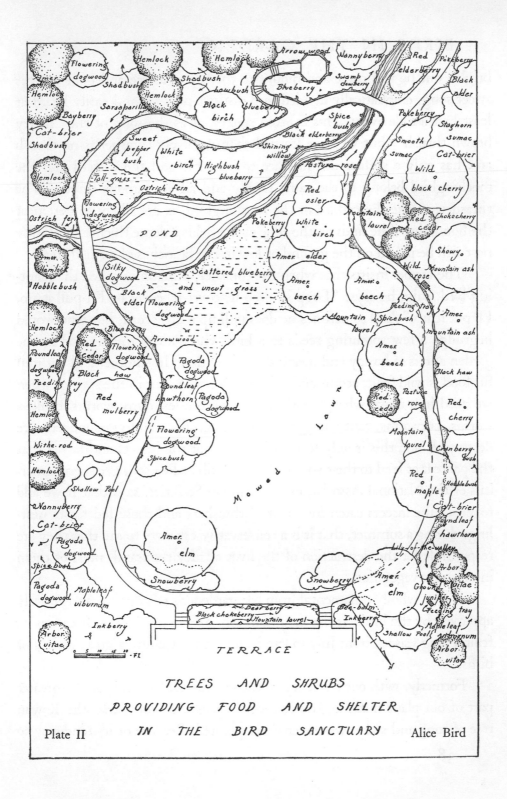

TREES AND SHRUBS
PROVIDING FOOD AND SHELTER
IN THE BIRD SANCTUARY

Plate II   Alice Bird

bright, out he will come and mount to the top of a tree and pour out his sweet song, emphatically divided into distinct phrases, and easily heard at least half a mile away. This is often spoken of as the song of the "merry brown thrush"; but we have learned that our lively thrasher is no thrush and has only a surface resemblance to one. He and the catbird and the mockingbird belong to the same family and all are famous singers. The thrasher, unlike the catbird or the mockingbird, is not likely to nest near the house, but if he finds on the edge of the fields a dense thicket, his bulky nest will be placed on the ground or low in the branches of a small tree.

The farmer insists that when the thrasher, sometimes called the planting bird, sings he says: "Drop it, drop it, cover it, cover it, I'll pull it up, I'll put it up." And sometimes he does pull up a little corn, but who would begrudge a few sprouting seeds to a bird who does so much good in the garden and is so happy and merry about it withal? In summer and autumn his food is wild fruit, acorns and a little waste corn. But in the spring, when we need him most, what quantities of May beetles, army worms, canker-worms, cutworms, tent and gypsy moth caterpillars and grasshoppers, are destroyed; and this is only to mention a few of the insects and larvae that the pair eat or feed to their young. Dr. T. Gilbert Pearson, President Emeritus of the National Association of Audubon Societies, says that if we add together the insects eaten by a pair of thrashers and those fed to six nestlings during a summer, that it is a conservative estimate to say that they are responsible for the destruction of the lives of fifty thousand, most of them injurious to vegetation.

A tree, wholly ornamental from the gardener's standpoint, and entirely approved by the birds, is the mountain ash, *Sorbus americana*. It carries its fruit a long season, from July to late March, thus feeding a great variety of birds.

Formerly, with our tendency to turn to the Old World for the greater part of our plant material, the European species, *S. aucuparia,* the Rowan tree of song and story, was extensively planted. Because of its tendency to

WHITE-WINGED CROSSBILL
JUVENAL PLUMAGE
ADULT FEMALE

RED CROSSBILL
ADULT FEMALE
ADULT MALE
ADULT MALE
JUVENAL PLUMAGE

EVENING GROSBEAK
MALE, JUVENAL PLUMAGE
ADULT MALE
ADULT FEMALE

Scale about one-half

succumb to diseases attacking trees of the apple family, such as rust or scale, it has not been as widely planted as formerly. The American tree is really much handsomer as well as a great deal more resistant to disease. It is also smaller, which makes it more desirable for a lawn specimen. The leaves are feather-form, having from eleven to seventeen leaflets, and the bright red fruits in dense clusters, are very showy. It is not at all particular as to soil and can endure a dry situation.

Another native species of the Eastern States recommended by the Arnold Arboretum is *S. decora*. It is inclined to be shrubby in growth and has even larger and showier fruit which lasts well into the fall.

Among the birds which delight in mountain-ash berries are the gentle cedar waxwing, his larger cousin, the Bohemian waxwing, the Baltimore oriole, evening and pine grosbeaks, the robin, the thrasher and his relative, the catbird.

And how ready the catbird is to nest in our dooryard! Originally a bird of the rather swampy lowlands, he has accepted with true philosophy the changed conditions produced by the coming of the white man, and takes all possible advantage of man's presence. And yet, though he may place his nest in the bush by your door, he is suspicious of your presence in the garden, paralleling your course as you step out to admire the flowers, by slipping along concealed in the bushes, and almost sneeringly giving his catlike cry. And if you should imitate, by sucking on your hand, the cry of a young bird in distress, immediately he and all the neighboring catbirds will appear in full voice to expose and endeavor to expel the barbarian in their midst.

His neat suit of gray feathers, his black cap and tail lined with chestnut, make no gaudy costume, but one which is always sufficiently handsome to secure him a mate after he arrives in May. Then comes the building of the rather bulky nest, which will be placed in a bush or low tree in a spot well-concealed by dense foliage. During the time of incubation the catbird sings his very heart out. The hours of the day are not long enough to contain all his bubbling songs, and sometimes he starts singing at midnight and continues until morning. Some people think his song almost the equal of that of the mockingbird, but it is likely to be interrupted, if he is startled, by his harsh catlike call, and he delights, too, in interpolating sounds he has heard, perhaps the squeak of a wheelbarrow, the rasp of a saw, or the discordant alarm note of some other bird. He is a marvelous singer, nevertheless, and a great imitator of tuneful birds. He has frequently been known to give the song of a house wren or of a Baltimore oriole, of a bluebird and a song sparrow, all birds habitually nesting near him; and many specially-gifted individuals possess a much greater repertoire.

But when the nestlings are hatched there is less time for music. What a concentrated bundle of suspicion is the male catbird at this period! Let a blue jay appear, the catbird will come to the attack, and ruffling himself to twice his size will drive off the potential foe even though the jay is a larger bird.

The catbird is a true appreciator of the wild fruit in the garden, eating besides the berries of the mountain ash, mulberries, wild cherries, fruit of the dogwood and honeysuckle, those of sour gum, buckthorn, elder, spicebush, black alder, cat brier, holly, shadbush, and many others. As a novelty in vegetal diet one catbird was observed carrying bits of mushrooms to its nestlings. In return he and his mate and usually his two broods will consume potato bugs, locusts, crickets, hairy caterpillars, including those of the gypsy-moth, weevils, plant lice, chinchbugs and many more of the worst pests in the garden.

Dr. Witmer Stone says: "Let us bear in mind the needs of the catbird when we care for our grounds, and leave him a corner where he may find a shady thicket. . . . It would be to me a poor garden indeed that did not have some retreat from which I would hear that harsh complaining cry of the catbird when I chanced to stroll by. Every bird note brings back to us some association, some memory of the past, and with the cry of the catbird there comes before my mind's eyes the old garden with which as a boy I

40

was so familiar. I see the thicket of lilac and mock oranges, and the goose-
berry bushes bordering the path, the spreading boughs of the apple trees
with the sunlight filtering through; the smell of ripening fruit is in the air,
and the stillness of a quiet summer afternoon is broken only by the hum of
insects and the complaining voice of the catbird from his shady retreat." *

Even in a place of an acre in extent, one or more of the wild cherries
should be planted. The choke-cherry, *Prunus virginiana,* has fallen into disrepute, even in native plantings, because it is subject to black knot, a fun-
gous disease which renders it unsightly. This is unfortunate, for this shrub,
so often seen in the eastern hedgerows, has attractive white flowers in
drooping clusters, borne with the leaves early in the spring, and the translucent red or orange fruit is a great favorite of the birds. Its shrubby growth
also makes good nesting sites.

The wild red cherry, *P. pennsylvanica,* is sometimes shrubby, but often
becomes a small tree. It has white flowers in clusters and small red fruits in
early summer. As wild cherries are generally preferred to the cultivated by
the birds, this tree, as it fruits early, is a protection to the cherries in the
orchard.

The largest of our native species, often attaining the size of a forest
tree, is the wild black or rum cherry, *Prunus serotina*. Its fragrant white
flowers are in graceful clusters and its purple-black fruit follows in time of
ripening that of the wild red cherry, thus furnishing a continuous supply of
fruit for nestlings.

It seems almost incredible that seventy-four kinds of birds are known
to eat the fruits of these cherries. What a world of good would this number
of birds do for the farmer if instead of clearing out his fence rows he would
plant groups of wild cherries at short intervals!

Among the birds that may be attracted to our garden by this fruit, and
perhaps then come to nest there, are flickers, woodpeckers, kingbirds, ori-

---

* National Association of Audubon Societies Educational Leaflet No. 70, 1913.

oles, rose-breasted grosbeaks, thrushes, robins, catbirds, brown thrashers, and that far-famed singer, the mockingbird.

The mockingbird is only occasionally found in the Northeastern States; he finds the country farther south more to his taste. But as more and more records are being made of his presence in New England and New York, perhaps some glad day we may see the happy songster in our own garden. If he does nest with you, like the cardinal, he will stay with you through the winter, for he is not a migratory bird and would leave the neighborhood only in search of food.

E. H. Forbush's account of his song is so fine that it is given: "The mockingbird stands unrivaled. He is the king of song . . . He equals and even excels the whole feathered choir. He improves upon most of the notes he reproduces adding also to his varied repertoire the crowing of chanticleer, the cackling of the hen . . . the plaints of young chickens and turkeys and those of other birds . . . He even imitates man's musical inventions." He also quotes the following: "The mocker is more or less a buffoon, but those who look upon him only as an imitator or clown have much to learn of his wonderful originality. His own song is heard at its best at the height of the love season when the singer flutters into the air from some tall treetop and improvises his music, pouring out all the power and energy of his being in such an ecstasy of song that exhausting his strength in the supreme effort, he slowly floats on quivering, beating pinions down through the bloom-covered branches until, his fervor spent, he sinks to the ground below. . . . On moonlight nights at this season the inspired singer launches himself far into the air, filling the silvery spaces of the night with the exquisite swells and trills, liquid and sweet, of his unparalleled melody . . . and so he serenades his mate throughout the livelong night."

Like the catbird the mockingbird builds near man, seeming to prefer the risk of the prowling cat, one of his worst enemies, to the dangers of brushlands. The nest is often found in shrubbery or in a vine near the house, and sometimes in an apple tree, or farther south, in an orange tree.

The gay singer is also a fighter; when the nestlings are to be defended he will even attack an enemy as large as a hawk or a cat. He bristles up to flickers and even to blue jays, often sending them discomfited from the feeding station. The kingbird is his match though, and often makes his feathers fly when the mocker becomes too pugnacious.

The list of the wild fruits which the mockingbird eats includes almost everything that grows in the woods and fields, and cultivated kinds are taken also. But in the spring the lively pair eat as well as feed to their nestlings many caterpillars, beetles, grasshoppers, ants and wasps. In the South, the cotton boll weevil and the moth of the cotton bollworm are often eaten, therefore no Southerner should object too strenuously if a little cultivated fruit is sampled by these birds later in the year.

Food shortage would be the only reason this gallant songster would leave your neighborhood. Dr. Frank Chapman tells of a mockingbird that stayed all winter near the Museum of Natural History in New York City, even though the thermometer fell below zero. He ate the berries of Virginia creeper and later those of the privet, and appeared quite at home in the snow, though it seems as if he must have been haunted by ancestral memories of the perfume of orange groves under the southern moonlight.

Small trees, too little used in the garden, are the various hawthorns. We are rich in them in this country and should use them more freely especially in planting for birds. True, they are subject to some fungus diseases, and are attacked by a number of insects, but we presume that our bird allies will moderate the latter evil.

For a tall hedge, reaching twenty-five feet and practically impenetrable, the cockspur thorn, *Crataegus crus-galli,* is invaluable. All the branches are covered with long and exceedingly sharp spines. The white flowers are followed by dull red fruits which are held on the tree from late August and sometimes to April. The applelike fruits are one-half inch long, big enough to make really a good bite for a bird, and add appreciably to the menu of winter visitors such as pine grosbeaks and purple finches, as well as to that of the hungry robins when they arrive, half starved after their long flight in the spring. The mockingbird also is glad to find a winter feast of these "haws."

With less brilliantly colored red fruit than the cockspur thorn, is the thicket hawthorn, *C. intricata,* formerly known as *C. coccinea.* Its fruit is also attractive to the birds and because of its bushy growth, which reaches about 10 feet, it makes excellent nesting sites.

Another bushy hawthorn is *C. rotundifolia.* It grows to about 15 feet and has good-size fruit, nearly round, with bright red skin and yellow flesh. Trimmed back severely so that it branches profusely, this hawthorn planted closely, make ideal tangles for cover and nesting.

Another large shrub of this family, the Washington thorn, *C. phaeno-pyrum,* reaches 20 feet in height and has very long sharp spines. It has small bright red fruits and grows particularly well toward the southern part of our range, for it is native from Virginia to Alabama.

Growing about the same height as the Washington thorn is the Arnold hawthorn, *C. arnoldiana.* It has shining leaves and fruit nearly an inch long, and is a hardy species, native of Massachusetts and New York, and therefore likely to do well in the Northern States. All these hawthorns grow naturally in an open sunny position, and prefer a rather limey soil, though any good garden loam will suit them. In trimming those to be left in the open, care should be taken to preserve the characteristic angular shape of the branches which makes an interesting design against the snow when the plants are leafless and laden with scarlet fruit.

Related to the hawthorns are the crabapples. Both the native and the Asiatic species are used in the garden, but the Asiatic species are freer from disease than our own shrubs. Their fruit is small but it is often borne in great abundance and is very ornamental in the garden, while numbers of birds are known to eat it. These Oriental crabs bear fruit varying in size and color—the small, waxy yellow and red apples of the Siberian crab, *Pyrus baccata,* have been used for jelly for many years. The flowers are white and the tree will reach 40 feet. It is lovely both in flower and fruit.

Arnold's crab, *Pyrus floribunda,* var. *arnoldiana,* has large, rosy-red flowers and small bright red fruit. Though this crab may eventually reach 25 feet it is inclined to be bushy. One of the most delightful of these crabs, for both flowers and fruit, is *P. toringoides,* the cutleaf crab; the red and yellow miniature apples are very showy, and it never looks more beautiful or seems more worth while, than when a flock of cedar waxwings discovers it, and, after much confabulation and passing of fruit from one to another, do you the honor of harvesting the whole crop.

In a garden of even moderate size there is always room for some of the birches. Perhaps at the end of the lawn, a group of the graceful canoe or paper-white birches, *Betula alba,* var. *papyrifera,* or perhaps amidst the tangle a few of the gray birch, *B. populifolia.* If there is a stream in the woodland on its bank should be placed the yellow birch, *B. lutea,* and the black birch, *B. lenta.* No bird sanctuary of any extent is complete without these trees, for they carry in their cones a supply of tiny seeds which siskins, redpolls, and goldfinches will seek all winter. The siskin is particularly fond of these seeds. These birds are rare visitors, but perhaps some morning you will awake and looking out on your birches will think they have blossomed birds, so thick the little northern visitors will be upon them. Chittering and whistling, they will make the scales of the cones fly in a shower through the air as they nip out the nutlets, then, as if with one will, off they will sweep, giving simultaneously a harsh wheezing note, which sounds like a gigantic sneeze.

A shrub which bears fruit eaten by nearly a hundred kinds of birds is that unassuming plant the bayberry, *Myrica caroliniensis.* We little think, when we see the barrow-loads of the fruiting branches for sale in the city, of how many birds are being robbed in the wild. And it is the part of the good conservationist to prevent such depredations. In this case, not only is the countryside despoiled, but thousands of migrating birds are deprived of food.

The bayberry in nature grows in sandy, acid soil where little else will thrive, so we should not give it too kind treatment in the border. Plant it in the open where you feel that the soil is poor and let it produce its mound of aromatic, glossy, green leaves all summer, and all fall and winter, its waxy fruit, which clings to the stem nearly all year.

The chickadee will eat of it all winter, and so will the flicker and our downy woodpecker, who comes so confidingly to the feeding station. If a myrtle warbler winters in the North, as it occasionally does, to the bayberry it will go, and some December day we may see this little dandy in bluish-gray with a white throat, busily fluttering over the stiff branches laden with "gray pearls." Many myrtle warblers stay part of the winter on Cape Cod feeding on this fruit. But now the hordes of starlings sweep down on the fields where the bayberry grows, and the valiant little warbler has to move on or starve. Perhaps if he finds your planting he may linger, eking out his food with the fruits of red cedar, juniper, and other plants. If he stays all winter, in the spring he will come out in his nuptial plumage, showing a yellow spot on his head, one on his rump and one on each side. He and his mate will destroy literally thousands of caterpillars, various types of flies, scale insects, weevils, woodborers, woolly appletree aphis, plant lice and their eggs, and many other evil "beasties" seemingly born to give the gardener sorrow and to the warblers a grand feast.

Three of the hollies, the American holly, *Ilex opaca,* the black alder, *I. verticillata,* and the inkberry, *I. glabra,* bear abundant crops of berries that are particularly appreciated by the birds in the late spring.

South of New York, the American holly reaches the proportions of a tree, but farther north it is shrubby. It is the evergreen that has been so ruthlessly gathered for Christmas greens, pickers often cutting down a tree, rather than taking the trouble to clip the branches carefully. Thus is destroyed, not only a beautiful tree in the woodland, but a supply of food for

RUBY-THROATED HUMMINGBIRD

MALE

FEMALE

YOUNG MALE

Scale about one-half

some of our most valuable birds, such as the kingbird, catbird, bluebird, orchard oriole and hermit thrush.

Therefore if we can plant a thicket of holly it serves a double purpose, for we have in the garden the cheering sight of evergreen leaves against the snow, while the bright red berries stand out in glowing contrast to the green and will tempt many a hungry bird to linger longer at our feeding station in the time of dearth in a cold spring. Like the mulberry and the bayberry, only the pistillate or female shrub of holly produces berries. Care should be taken to plant three to six pistillate plants to one staminate or male form.

Although the black alder or winterberry, *Ilex verticillata,* grows naturally in swampy land, it will thrive in ordinary garden soil that is not allowed to dry out. It has excellent foliage during the summer, but in the autumn the leaves fall, showing the clustered brilliant red berries on the naked stems. As the fruit is so bright and conspicuous, groups of the black alder are most effective planted in front of the American holly. Both pistillate and staminate forms of this shrub should be planted. Both these species of holly require a well-drained soil and will endure some shade.

The inkberry, *I. glabra,* abundant in the pine and oak barrens, where the soil is very acid, nevertheless, adapts itself to garden conditions very readily. It is evergreen and will grow in shade, producing a crop of black berries. Often during the winter the chickadee and tufted titmouse will discover the fruit, their beady black eyes as shiny as the glossy inkberries.

The shrubs and trees, vines and perennials which we have spoken of are some of the most outstanding ones that the United States Biological Survey recommends for birds. We may add to our main planting of trees and shrubs a number of commonly cultivated annuals, using perhaps some of the same families as the weeds which the seed eaters used to enjoy before every fence corner was tidied up. We can plant extra sunflowers, zinnias, coreopsis, bachelors-buttons, and cosmos in the cutting garden and let the plants stand to furnish food for goldfinches and others of the sparrow family.

Other annuals recommended by the United States Biological Survey, of which we may make extensive plantings without fearing they will become garden pests, include the two amaranths, love-lies-bleeding and the prince's-feather. These are tall many-branched plants which will hold their panicles laden with seed high above the snow and furnish food for tree sparrows, juncos and others. The China aster, also has a full head of seeds; other profuse seeders include California poppies, forget-me-nots, blessed thistle, (*Carduus benedictus*) tarweed, (*Madia elegans*) and portulaca.

If we wish for

> The hummingbird's arrested spark
> Half-flame, half-flower, blossoming where
> Emerald and ruby burn in the air,

as Louis Untermeyer has it in his poem, *The Hummingbird,* we must see that we have many red, orange, and pink flowers. Among the blossoms favored by the frequent visits of the hummingbird are those of the trumpet creeper, bee balm, tiger lily, scarlet salvia, hollyhocks, cardinal flower, scarlet runner bean, fuchsia, geranium, pea tree, or *Caragana arborescens,* phlox, bachelor's-buttons, delphinium, (both annual and perennial,) columbine, sultana, gladiolus, canna, azalea, weigela and nasturtium. The pea tree flowers have great attraction for hummers, although they are yellow instead of the prime favorite in colors, red. The horse chestnut is a favorite among the trees, and among wild flowers, the hummingbird is particularly fond of the jewelweed, and often hovers over the inconspicuous catnip, an escape from the herb garden.

If you can spare a corner of your vegetable garden for the birds, sow there some of the millets, so greatly relished by all seed-eating birds. Common millet or barnyard grass, *Echinochloa crus-galli,* and German millet or Hungarian grass, *Setaria italica* are excellent. Plant Japanese millet where it can grow up through a screen or lattice-work, placed in a horizontal position, that will support it through the winter. It holds its seeds and makes a valuable food for graminivorous birds. The seeds of canary grass may be scattered in corners and should be allowed to grow and mature undisturbed for winter feed. Buckwheat planted in an unproductive patch of ground makes excellent cover and food during the winter. A planting of red clover will not only produce food, but will enrich the ground for growing vegetables in the future. If unused salsify, turnip and lettuce are allowed to go to seed and stand in the garden, the goldfinch will delight in them as well as in the sunflowers.

Study the following lists and plan a garden that will carry the birds through the year. And remember also that the warblers, both the migrants and those that nest with us, such as the redstart and the yellow warbler, are insect eaters and that the shrubs with conspicuous flowers will by their perfume and nectar attract a host of insects and thus many winged visitors. E. H. Forbush, who proved so conclusively the value of birds in the garden says: "It is evident that a diversity of plants, which encourages diversified insect life and assures an abundance of fruits and seeds as an attraction to birds, will insure their presence."

Give careful thought to the time of flowering and fruiting. Plant the shrubs in drifts as they are so often found in nature, and let a drift of early-fruiting kinds intermingle with another that holds its fruit through the winter. For instance, the berries of sumacs and hollies are not popular in fall or winter, but in early spring they are eagerly stripped by such hardy migrants as bluebirds and robins. Plant them with summer fruiting shrubs and birds will find hospitality all the year.

49

Chapter Four

FEEDING DEVICES

The Snow Lies Light

The snow lies light upon the pine
The winds are still, the day is fine;
My guests come trooping in to dine.
There are so many to be fed
I have a generous table spread
With corn and nuts and fat and seed
To suit each vagrant taste and need.
From far and near the jays convene,
And redpolls leave the evergreen,
The finch that wears a splendid crown,
Is also of the company.
Goldfinches with their gold turned brown,
Juncos with peeping petticoats,
Tree sparrows lisping whispered notes
With downy, nuthatch, chickadee
I welcome to my almonry.
—*W. W. Christman.*

THERE are people who say that we merely pauperize the birds by feeding them and that it is pure sentimentality on our part to want to see the birds near us.

It is true that all summer the birds have a bountiful larder, but it is also true that whatever food we offer them winter or summer is only a supplement to their natural diet. Who hasn't seen a chickadee leave a lump of suet after a bite or two and start busily inspecting a twig, attacking it from every angle, even hanging upside down in order to peer into an obscure crevice?

It has been stated that, considering their numbers, the winter birds do more good in the garden than those of the summer. The woodpeckers are busy drilling out grubs, thus stopping their damage, while the chickadees, creepers, nuthatches, and kinglets destroy millions of eggs of plant lice, moths and other insects.

E. H. Forbush, so long the State Ornithologist of Massachusetts, believed thoroughly in feeding birds. An account of his own experience is most convincing. He writes:

". . . my small orchard became very seriously infested with cankerworms, tent caterpillars, codling moths and gypsy moths. No attempt was made to protect the trees from their enemies, until the fall, when, by feeding, numbers of birds were attracted to the orchard. Immense numbers of the eggs of the fall cankerworm and the tent caterpillar moth were already deposited upon the trees, and toward spring large numbers of spring cankerworm moths began to ascend the trees and lay their eggs. So many chickadees and nuthatches were attracted to the orchard during the winter that they destroyed nearly all the insects and their eggs, and the next season, which proved to be one of great insect multiplication, my orchard was the only one in the neighborhood which produced good crops of fruit, while most of those in town produced little or no fruit. That part of the orchard of my neighbor across the way . . . retained most of its foliage and set a fair crop of fruit, showing how his orchard had been benefited by its nearness to my own. My assistant, Mr. C. E. Bailey, who watched the feeding of the birds, estimated that one chickadee would destroy 138,750 eggs of the cankerworm in the twenty-five days in which the female moth lays her eggs."

And as for sentimentality—birds often perish by the thousand during a heavy snowstorm that covers all natural food, or when there is an icestorm and all twigs and branches are sealed with a glittering armor. The bluebirds were almost wiped out a number of years ago in an unseasonable storm. If it is sentimentality to assist the birds through such a time of stress, then sentimentality is a good thing. How much better to feed the birds through the year, getting them accustomed to a secure source of supply, than it would be to go out some subzero morning and find a chickadee frozen in a knothole, or the stiff form of a downy woodpecker or a brown creeper at the foot of a tree.

Many birds can endure great cold if only there is a sufficient food supply. Their hearts beat very rapidly and their feathers are very warm. The chickadee seems to enjoy the ice and snow and so do the snow buntings. But look out on the feeding shelf some cold morning and you can see the song sparrow shivering even in his warm coat, and sometimes the little juncos will stand first on one foot and then on the other, warming their toes in their feathers. Birds do feel the cold, but can defy the frost if only the little furnaces hidden beneath their feathers are kept continuously stoked.

Yes, it is perfectly all right to feed the birds all winter, for many of them, because of the confidence developed over the months of stress, may be much more likely to stay with us when we need them in the summer. But always remember to keep a continuous supply at the feeding places. Don't let the birds become accustomed to finding food in a certain locality and then go away and leave them unfed. If you have to leave, hire some reliable person to keep a constant supply of the proper food on the shelves until your return. Place food at night, for birds breakfast early.

The permanent resident birds of the Northeastern States which will be most likely to visit your winter cafeteria are: song sparrows, white-breasted nuthatches, chickadees, downy and hairy woodpeckers, goldfinches, blue jays, crows and sometimes cedar waxwings, flickers, and purple finches. Birds that nest farther north but which may winter with us are tree sparrows, juncos, white-throated sparrows, red-breasted nuthatches, brown creepers, golden and ruby-crowned kinglets and that little

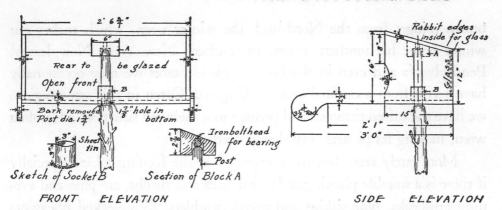

FRONT ELEVATION — **SIDE ELEVATION**

WEATHER-COCK FOOD HOUSE

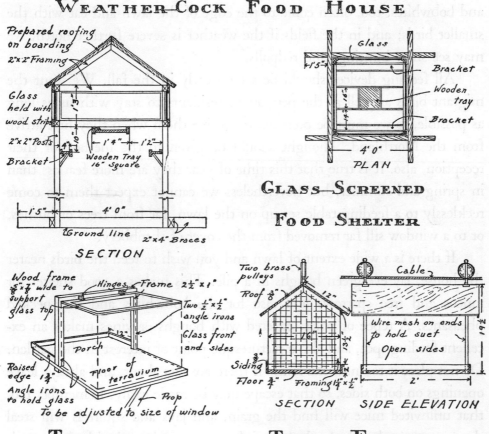

GLASS-SCREENED FOOD SHELTER

TERRAVIUM

TROLLEY FEEDER

Plate III

brown midget from the Northland, the winter wren, which makes our winter home his southern resort. In southern New York, New Jersey, Pennsylvania and even in the New England States we may occasionally have a visit from a cardinal or a mockingbird. Often in this same region, we have the tufted titmouse and perhaps in a sheltered situation, a Carolina wren, making its pioneer way slowly north.

More rarely seen, but to be expected at the feeding table, especially if there is a suitable planting of berried trees and shrubs, are pine and evening grosbeaks, pine siskins and myrtle warblers. Ring-necked pheasants and bobwhites, too, often come to the edge of the lawn and eat with the smaller birds; and in the fields if the weather is severe further north, we may see snow buntings and redpolls.

All feeding devices should be set up early in the fall. We want the migrant birds as well as the permanent residents to stay with us as long as possible, so we must be prepared to receive them when they first arrive from the Northland. Thought should be given to the method of their reception, also. It is true that this time of year they are more fearless than in spring and summer, but nevertheless we cannot expect them to come recklessly to a feeding table set up on the lawn, far from trees or bushes, or to a window sill far removed from the cover of shrubbery.

If there is a wide extent of lawn and you wish to feed the birds nearer the house, lay evergreen boughs in a pile. This makes a good shelter for juncos and tree sparrows and also for the bobwhites and ring-necked pheasants. A tepee of poles, covered with boughs or vines makes an excellent feeding spot, and also a picturesque point of interest in the garden. Do not place it too near the house if there are cats about, and always leave openings on both sides, so that escape may be made easily. Remember too, that uninvited mice will find the grain, and jays and squirrels will steal the suet, so see that the food supply is kept constantly replenished. If weeds are cut early in the autumn, the seeds will ripen but not fall, and the sprays

TUFTED TITMOUSE   RED-BREASTED NUTHATCH
MALE

BLACK-CAPPED CHICKADEE   FEMALE

BOREAL CHICKADEE

WHITE-BREASTED NUTHATCH
MALE

FEMALE   BROWN CREEPER

Scale about one-half

can be woven in among the boughs or the poles. The goldfinches would be delighted to work at mullein, evening primrose, and hollyhock.

In addition to the weeds we may let turnip, salsify and lettuce go to seed in the vegetable garden and use them in the same way. Sheaves of grain with heads hanging can be woven in also. Red cedar boughs, plentifully supplied with berries, are the very best type of cover to use, but if evergreens are hard to obtain, cut a supply of deciduous bushes while the leaves are still green and store them until time to make the shelter. The leaves will cling to the twigs and provide an excellent protection. If fruiting boughs of wild cherry, mountain ash, chokeberry, black haw, and sumac are gathered and dried they may be brought out during the late winter and early spring and will be hungrily stripped by cedar waxwings, or by robins or bluebirds returning from the South.

Under these shelters, whenever it is mild enough, in addition to the food there should be a dish of water. Grit should be supplied in the form of sand or very fine gravel, for when the ground is heavily covered with snow it is exceedingly hard for birds to find this material so necessary for their digestive processes. A hollow spot filled with soft loam for a dust bath will also be greatly appreciated.

Near the shelter may be set a covered feeding shelf. This part of the winter cafeteria, may be hung from a tree or placed on posts. If on posts, a funnel-shaped piece of tin with the opening downward fastened on each post, or inverted tin pans just below the tray will prevent visits of cats or mice. The feeding shelf should be roofed, not only for protection from the snow, but in order that the grain may not sour from frequent wettings. A moulding on the edge will prevent the food from slipping off. A large feeding station of this type may be used to supply both shelter and food. Evergreen boughs may be placed beneath the main feeding shelf to form a windbreak and sheaves of wheat interwoven for the quails and pheasants. While in the tray above, glassed in on three sides, may be placed the suet and seed for smaller birds. It is well, too, to bore holes in each of the corners

55

of the shelf for drainage in case the rain blows in. A piece of wire netting over each hole will prevent loss of loose grain.

If the tray is small, instead of a conventional roof, one can fasten four supple twigs, one at each corner and tie them together at the top, then place burlap or evergreen boughs on three sides. Similar to this tray, is one made from the top of a barrel. A few of the hoops are fastened over half of it, canvas or burlap tacked over them and evergreen boughs laid over its top.

Dr. Frank Chapman describes an attractive rustic feeding shelf that fits unobtrusively into the garden picture. He recommends, instead of the usual flat tray, hollowed-out limbs with the bark left on them. Two such hollow troughs are nailed at about four and five feet upon a post, while a large hollowed-out slab is fastened over the top for the roof. The base of the post may be protected from cats by the funnel-shaped tin, or less conspicuously by being bound with barbed wire. Holes may be bored in the upper part of the post and suet forced in the apertures or pieces of suet may be bound to it with many layers of string between and above the two hollow shelves.

Various forms of these feeding stations may be obtained on the market. The National Association of Audubon Societies has a number which it recommends, and will send a list if so requested. Or they may be made at home, ordered from the manual training shops of the public schools, or from the Boy Scouts or other boys' clubs in the vicinity. Their making is an excellent project for any of these organizations. An interesting variation is the weather-vane food house which has but one side open and, because of the vanes (Plate III) swings with the wind, so that the walled sides, which may have glass in them, thus letting us see our customers, are always toward the cold blast.

If birds are very shy and it is desired to bring them near the house, a trolley feeder may be used. This is a roofed shelter run on a wire attached to the house at one end and to a tree or post in the shrubbery at the other.

This tray may run on one wire but if it is arranged from a second-story window, two wires are more satisfactory. If the tray is 20 inches square, the wires should be slung 20 inches apart and stretched taut at the same height between the house and a wooden bar nailed to a tree or post at least 100 feet from the window. Place a pulley wheel on each corner of the tray, if the farther end is on a level with the window. But if the wires slant down, the two wheels on the corners nearer the house should be screwed to short wooden uprights fastened to the corner of the tray. Thus, even though the wire runway slants, the tray retains its horizontal position.

This easily-moved tray may be brought a little nearer the house each day. Move it after the birds are through feeding in the evening; the morning's hunger will cause them to overlook the few feet difference in the situation. Foot by foot the distance may be lessened until at last we can see the beady sparkling eyes and exquisite plumage at arm's length. Another obvious advantage is that in extremely cold and stormy weather the food may be replenished from the house, thus obviating the necessity of the cafeteria proprietor tramping through the snowdrifts.

When there is sufficient near-by cover, a shelf outside the window may be made a point of attraction for both birds and the family. Even if there are no shrubs near the window a few stout branches may be set up near the tray or branches can be nailed below the window sill. A small evergreen in a pot can be set on the tray or a cut one can be nailed to it.

These shelves may be open or roofed. If covered, glass is the preferable material to use, for then we may see our guests' appreciation, for the birds, once they have gained confidence will congregate early and late, and especially *early*. Dire will be the epithets poured on your head and bitter the reproaches if you as host or hostess of the cafeteria are slow in supplying the "daily bread," and also the butter in the form of suet. Many delightful experiences may occur when birds have once overcome their initial fear. An incident is recounted that in the State of Washington, California purple finches that had been used to their daily allowance of hemp seed, not obtaining it one morning, flew into the open dining-room window and lighted on the shoulders of their friends as they ate their own breakfast.

The most elaborate form of dining table is that devised by Mr. and Mrs. Spencer Marsh of Madison, New Jersey. It is an adaptation of the original "Dutcher feeding shelf," so-called from Mr. William Dutcher, a former President of the Audubon Society. Through permission given by Mrs. Marsh, the following is copied directly from her leaflet called *The Terravium for Birds:*

As the terrarium owes its heritage to the Wardian case, a miniature glass-enclosed garden, so the terravium may claim kinship to the terrarium. The name terravium (*terra,* for earth, and *avis,* bird) which we have coined, implies its use for birds.

This diminutive wild garden or rocky glen, built within a glass case, rests on the sill of our dining-room window, having a southeast exposure, and is open to the outside to admit the birds. It contains many a treasure from woods and field; these are all evergreen as the terravium is essentially a winter garden retreat. But even after the little birds have deserted it, we enjoy the spring awakening of the little glen with its opening leaf buds and unfurling fern croziers—with sometimes an added clump of violets for color.

The illustration on the first page shows the terravium as viewed from inside the room. The three-sided glass case, having a glass lid, is closely fitted into the window opening so that the wild birds can wing freely to shelter and refreshment within, during the cold season when food and drink are often scarce.

An entrance porch extending beyond the window, encourages the birds to hop further into this woodsy retreat. Two cedar trees about a foot high, stand rooted in soil among the rocks at each side of the entrance. Other interesting rocks of various shapes and sizes provide a natural setting for the little glen, while mosses, lichens, creeping vines, colorful bits of fungi, small ferns and wild plants, tucked into crevices with leaf mold, or banked irregularly against the glass sides, lend charm and reality to the picture; frequent spraying of these is necessary. The planting is kept mostly low, so as not to obstruct the view of our swiftly moving visitors.

In the right center, anchored by rocks, stands an old, gnarled laurel root, whose numerous branches provide perching accommodations from which our guests may easily reach the suet fastened to the branch tips by means of rubber bands. A few red-berried twigs at Christmas time bring added cheer to both guests and hosts; but of the many varieties of food offered, none has proved as popular as the suet and sun-flower seeds.

On a flat rock under an overhanging laurel branch, is a little pottery water basin with tiny pebbles in the bottom. On many a cold day one may see a thirsty chicka-dee perched on the rim with its little toes in the warm water frequently sprayed into it, and several times injured birds have sought hospice here and have received first aid at the little font.

Our most constant visitors are the tufted titmouse, chickadee, and nuthatch, while the woodpeckers, both hairy and downy, and other more shy birds frequently dart in for refreshment, when they believe themselves unseen. Although apparently indifferent to noise within the room, sudden motion alarms them.

A step preliminary to inserting the finished terravium into the window open-ing, is the making and fitting of a wooden frame into the aperture left by the raised lower sash. This frame, as shown, is formed of a top, bottom and two uprights, bolted together. The raised window sash rests firmly upon the top of the frame, into which the completed terravium is locked by means of Fitch window catches to afford quick removal when desired; otherwise ordinary screws or bolts may be substituted.

Illustration Number Three shows the completed terravium before fitting into the window.

A wooden shelf 36 inches long, 12 inches of which extends outside for the entrance porch, is designed to rest on the bottom of the framed-in window open-ing; it is covered with copper sheeting. Pairs of narrow brass angleirons screwed to the frame and to the shelf form the slots between which the glass sides of the terravium are inserted and held in place. All glass edges inserted between the angle-irons are bound with adhesive tape. Between the two corner-joining glass edges, narrow strips of felt are substituted for angle irons to afford a more artistic and less obstructed view. Glass cement welds these edges together.

Various means of insulation are all important in protecting the room from cold, as the lower window sash must necessarily remain open. Strips of felt insulate all the contacting edges of the two frames described above. Best materials, such as copper sheeting, heavy plate glass—with polished edges where exposed—are used, not only to enhance the appearance of the terravium, but also for better protection and endurance; the passing years prove the advisability of this.

The glass lid of the terravium rests on a narrow felt-covered wooden frame fitted to the top of the glass case; this slides open easily, or may be removed en-tirely in the care of plants and bird feeding.

It will be noted that the top of the case slopes slightly to a lower height at the inner or room edge, to give a better proportion; therefore, to prevent the glass lid from sliding off, two small upright brackets are screwed to the felt-covered frame to hold it in place.

A diagonal prop from the baseboard of the room to the edge of the terrarium shelf prevents it from sagging.

As each terravium must necessarily conform to the size of the individual window, exact dimensions must be worked out by the terravium builder. He may allow his imagination and ingenuity wide scope if he will keep in mind, a few important points:—good proportions, thorough insulation from cold, use of durable materials, placing of terravium where most attractive to birds, suitable choice of plants, naturalness of arrangement, and unobstructed and pleasing view from both indoors and out.

Note—Mosses may be collected in the fall and stored in a cool place for replenishing the terravium.

This terravium makes possible a delightfully intimate type of bird study. Seemingly because of the way the glass reflects the light the birds appear quite oblivious of spectators, but are plainly visible to their entertainers, and every morning you feel as if you and the birds were breakfasting at the same table.

Where English sparrows are common, until they can be trapped and gently disposed of, the tilting food table is often desirable. With it can be combined the food-hopper, so convenient when one has to go away for a few days. The spring allows the board to sag with a bird's weight. The English sparrow, made wary by many years adventuring where he is not wanted, fears a trap and will not venture on the tilting shelf. The other birds do not seem to mind at all.

Chapter Five

SUPPLEMENTARY FOOD

SO MUCH for the various types of cafeterias, now for the "fixin's." For the insect-eating birds, like the woodpeckers nothing is better than suet. Among other birds attracted by it are the chickadee, brown creeper, golden-crowned kinglet, and the white-breasted nuthatch. The blue jay, too, is exceedingly fond of it. He should have some of course in payment for the beautiful picture he makes against the snow, but not the whole piece which he will surely take if the lump is merely nailed to a tree. Various devices for feeding suet have been manufactured. There is the regular suet box (see p. 3 Audubon Society's Leaflet—Bird Study for Schools, part III Winter Feeding by Roger Peterson). This is a three-sided box with projecting hinged roof and the front covered with chicken-mesh. The wire prevents the jays and squirrels from taking the whole lump but allows the smaller birds to get their share. An ordinary wire soap-dish or broiler is often used, or wire-netting fastened down over the front of the shelf. It may be noted here that the wire is sometimes considered dangerous for birds. In their eagerness they might injure their beaks against it, and in very severe weather they could possibly freeze their tongues against it or lose an eye.

One of the simplest ways to feed suet is to bind a large piece on to a limb with many strands of cotton cord. Chickadees and downy wood-peckers will peck at this. Kinglets, though, are more likely to eat it if it is in very small pieces fastened to the twigs of evergreens. It may also be put in coarsely crocheted bags made of white cotton cord which can be hung from limbs of trees or fastened on bars nailed to posts. Another method is

to bore holes in a cut section of a limb, two or three feet long, always point-
ing these holes upwards and inwards. Melted suet can then be poured into
the holes. A little log of this type can be set up on the food tray, fastened
above or below it, or nailed on a tree or post. Similar in principal is the
foodboard, which is made by boring holes part way through a heavy plank,
then running the melted suet into the holes and fastening it up in a horizontal position. The chickadees will cling to it and find shelter and food
at the same time. A hollowed-out cocoanut may be filled with melted suet
and will be eagerly sought by the birds. Another attractive method of feeding suet is to dip fir or spruce cones into melted fat then suspend them
from a growing tree. The chickadees are always delighted with these and
play many acrobatic feats on them. Nut meats may be inserted under the
scales while the fat is still soft.

Peanut butter is almost as attractive as suet to chickadees, blue jays
and tree sparrows. Pack it in half cocoanut shells and hang the shells from
limbs, or put it in flat dishes on the tray. It also may be spread thick on
low branches. The jays, juncos and tree sparrows as well as the chickadees
will find it there. If it is plastered in cracks of rough-barked trees the nuthatches, woodpeckers and brown creepers will greet it as a glad surprise.

To add to the calories of the above menus and suit a number of birds
the following two recipes are given for tasty puddings. They have been used
by very successful bird cafeteria-keepers and have drawn and kept many
enthusiastic customers.

No. 1. Chop suet and heat it. While warm, add canary seed, chopped
peanuts and raisins, oatmeal, sunflower seeds, cooked and uncooked rice,
scratch food and honey or sugar. Large pine cones may be dipped in this
mixture and then hung in trees, or it may be run into a groove bored in
a stick, or into earthern dishes.

No. 2. Take one pound of suet, and try it out, add one pound coarse
cornmeal, one pound sunflower seeds, one half cupful chopped raw pea-

nuts, one cupful oatmeal, one half cupful coarse bran and one cupful of dried currants. This will fill several hollowed-out cocoanuts.

A bird's Christmas tree will attract many customers. A small cut evergreen may be obtained and fastened securely near the house. Over its branches may be poured a mixture of fat and other bird food. The following proportions are given in one of the leaflets of the Audubon Society, and the recipe is an adaptation of the famous Von Berlepsch Bird Food Mixture. Its ingredients are as follows:

Bread, dried and ground	5 oz.
Meat, ground and dried	3 oz.
Hemp seed	5 oz.
Millet	3 oz.
Ants' "eggs"	2 oz.
Sunflower seed	3 oz.
Dried berries	1½ oz.

Add to this one and one-half times as much suet or fat melted, and stir the mixture thoroughly, pouring it while hot over the branches of the tree. Of course, a live tree should never be so treated. This formula may be varied to suit circumstances and supplies available. Chopped nuts, preferably raw peanuts may be added and where available dried elderberries, pumpkin seeds, and ground bones. A small quantity of sand or coal-ashes is sometimes mixed in for "grit."

Pour this mixture with a ladle when very hot on every branch of the tree. Stir constantly when ladling and have some one with you to catch the drip in a frying pan or other receptacle. What remains may be poured into cake-tins and used on the trays or poured over a smaller tree or branch fastened to the shelf near the window.

Another Christmas tree is a favorite with the children and the birds. It may be growing this time if it is properly situated. It can be a gay surprise for the children or better still they may prepare all the gifts. On it can be hung net bags filled with berries which the children have collected and dried during the summer. Elderberries, dogwood fruit, mountain ash berries, wild cherries, blueberries—all will be acceptable. Other bags may contain crumbled doughnuts, suet, or the pieces of the bird food left after covering the dead evergreen. Several small cocoanuts stuffed with either one of the two Christmas puddings, or with what Dr. A. K. Fisher says is a favorite combination for his bird customers, that is, fresh pork fat and black walnut kernels. They may be filled also with coarsely ground raw peanuts, rolled oats and popped corn.

A great variety of food may be spread on the feeding trays. Of course, the chickadees, titmice and woodpeckers are happy with a plentiful supply of suet, but we have to think also of juncos, song sparrows and other birds of the sparrow family. They will want seeds and instead of buying a number of kinds and mixing them you will find it easier to obtain from the Audubon Society or pet store what is called "wild bird seed mixture." This should consist of a combination of hemp, canary seed, cracked corn, Kafir corn and millet. A good addition to this is pounded up dog biscuit and a little grit. Juncos will feed indefinitely on ordinary chick feed, especially if greasy crumbs are combined with it. The song sparrows enjoy the crumbs and often take a nip at the suet. Crumbled up corn bread seems to be another popular item. Hemp is a favorite because of its nourishing oily content. Millet is a close second. Goldfinches are particularly fond of both hemp and millet as well as of sunflower seeds. A sunflower head with the seeds in it fastened to the shelf is greatly enjoyed by them; there is something about picking the seeds out, themselves, that particularly appeals to the birds. Above all they prefer to have the sunflower head left in the garden, but that of course keeps them far away from your interested companionship, and it is pleasant to see the little fellows doing their own "shelling" right at the window. The seeds may also be glued to a feeding post.

Other "titbits" that birds enjoy include lettuce and cabbage leaves, celery tops, hard boiled eggs, milk curd and boiled rice, though these soft foods are not advisable in freezing weather. It is especially interesting to see how all-embracing in their tastes birds can become, especially those that usually go farther south, but have lingered with us through the winter because of an assurance of food.

The catbird, which, on rare occasions, winters in the North has been reported to partake of the following varied menu: boiled potato, cold mush, fried fish, beefsteak, chopped peanuts, moist bread, bits of beef scraps, suet, raisins, currants, cut apples and hemp seed. Surely variety enough to give him his vitamins even though he gets no cod-liver oil.

Another rare winter customer in the North, although it is not migratory, is the mockingbird. As all during the fall he lives on the wild fruit in the shrubbery; if it runs short, he is glad to eat the following at the feeding shelf: cut apples, chopped figs and raisins, various chopped nutmeats, dried prunes and apricots, and dried raspberries, currants, elderberries and blueberries and also bread and doughnut crumbs and suet. For his protein he will eagerly eat any dead insects offered to him. All together this is also a pretty well balanced winter menu even for a Southerner used to taking his share of the exasperated planter's crop of cultivated fruit.

From the experience of various people who have maintained feeding stations the following preferences of birds for food are listed:

Suet	Chickadee, downy woodpecker, hairy woodpecker, flicker, white-breasted nuthatch, tufted titmouse, brown creeper, golden-crowned kinglet, blue jay and occasionally the song sparrow.
Sunflower seeds	Chickadee, white-breasted nuthatch, cardinal (also likes squash and melon seeds), goldfinch, evening grosbeak, pine grosbeak, purple finch.
Mixed small seeds, hemp, millet, etc., and chick feed	Junco, tree sparrow, song sparrow, goldfinch, fox sparrow, catbird, purple finch, pine siskin.

Peanut butter	Chickadee, tree sparrow, song sparrow, blue jay.
Crumbs of bread, doughnuts and cheese	Chickadee, cardinal, white-breasted nuthatch, tufted titmouse, blue jay, junco, fox sparrow, catbird, purple finch, song sparrow, tree sparrow, goldfinch.
Coarsely ground raw peanuts, cracked butternuts, black walnuts, etc.	White-breasted nuthatch, red-breasted nuthatch, chickadee, cardinal, tufted titmouse, blue jay, pine siskin, catbird.

Ears of corn impaled on nails which have been run through a board provide excellent food for bobwhites and ring-necked pheasants, and an ear hung in a tree is enjoyed by both blue jays and cardinals, their plumage making a pretty color combination whenever they consent to feed together.

Now we come to the most pleasant experience which can fall to the host or hostess of the winter refuge, and that is to have the birds become friendly enough to take the food from your hands. Walter Pritchard Eaton in one of his essays on the New England countryside gives a delightful account of how his wife, holding a bit of suet in her hand, whistled the chickadees' love notes, until the birds, answering flutelike, circled and, lighting on her fingers, confidently pecked at the coveted morsel.

It is most amusing to watch the chickadees overcoming their initial fears. If you whistle their two "phoebe" love notes, they will first gather in curiosity in the surrounding trees or bushes. Hold out the suet and at length one will venture to fly toward you, only to stop in mid-air within a few inches, whirring his wings just as if he were "back-pedaling." Back he will turn to the branch, then venture out again and perhaps this time really land on your finger. He will clasp your hand, holding tight with those tiny, thread-like claws. You will never forget the first time this occurs, and always whenever you receive this mark of confidence, it is the greatest thrill that can come to a nature lover. Dr. Frank Chapman says:

"On several occasions chickadees have flown down and perched upon my hand. During the few seconds they remained there I became rigid with the emotion of this novel experience. It was a mark of confidence which seemed to initiate me into the ranks of woodland dwellers."

Many delightful stories are told of the chickadees. Often they will attain the utmost confidence, settling on your head and shoulders and even eating a morsel held between the lips. Mr. Ernest Harold Baynes tells how a band of the little rascals would actually hold up any one who came out of his house in Meriden, New Hampshire, demanding food even though there was a plentiful supply on the shelves. And often they would flutter to him and eat of his sandwich if he took his lunch to the woods.

A number of other birds will also learn to eat from your hand. Both the red- and white-breasted nuthatch after patience and gentle treatment often become tame. Miss Mabel Tilton of Vineyard Haven tamed a red-breasted nuthatch so completely that it would come to her hand as confidently as a chickadee. It took all kinds of liberties with her finger nails and seemed to enjoy warming its cold feet on her hands. It would drive a nut meat down between her fingers and eat it with many a tiny contented squeak.

A story told by Mr. Forbush in *Birds of Massachusetts* illustrates graphically how confiding birds may become and how much pleasure and entertainment may be derived from feeding them. He writes that a flock of 150 pine siskins, little striped brown birds, closely related to the goldfinches, had been fed all winter by Mr. Davis, and had grown very tame and confiding. The birds one morning were ready for breakfast long before he was awake, but there was no food in the trays. For awhile the birds sat around in forlorn groups in the trees, then they began to fly into the open windows of Mr. Davis' bedroom. By this time he was awake but pretended to be still sleeping, so several of the siskins hopped on the bed and then came to his face and pulled at his hair. He still pretended sleep, and they braced themselves and pulled still harder, and even began to tweak his nose and ears. One morning he covered his face with a cloth, leaving only a peephole, but one bird discovered the hole and tapped through it on his forehead. He then turned to the dish in which he kept the seed and one little fellow lit on his hand and rode over on it so as to beat the others to the feast.

Song sparrows, especially in the Far West, become very tame and confiding. In Olympia, Washington, a song sparrow which had fed all winter at the food tray, became so trusting that it would flutter into the dining room and pick up the crumbs under the table. Miss Mabel Tilton tells of one in her yard at Vineyard Haven, Martha's Vineyard, which retained in the summer the confidence gained in the winter, taking a nut meat from her hand as she held it on the ground under a rose bush.

Thoreau in *Walden* speaks of his experience with a sparrow: "I once had a sparrow alight upon my shoulder for a moment while I was hoeing in a village garden, and I felt that I was more distinguished by that circumstance than I should have been by any epaulet that I could have worn."

Bluebirds, robins, pine and evening grosbeaks, redpolls, pine siskins, blue jays, crossbills and purple finches have all been known to feed from the fingers, not to mention the impudent gray jays or "whiskey jacks" of the West and North, who calmly demand that attention.

When one thinks of the prevalent human attitude of hostility toward wild life, it seems amazing with what gentleness and kindness nearly every one responds when one of our smaller birds shows confidence in approaching. E. H. Forbush quotes the story of a farmer sitting on a snow drift surrounded by about a hundred redpolls, some of them feeding on scattered hayseed, some of them perched on his head and shoulders, and one on his knee. The farmer, one in his emotion with poet and philosopher, said that he had enjoyed himself more than at any other time he could remember, and that any man who would kill one of those little birds should go to the "pen."

Usually the most thrilling experiences in feeding birds take place in the winter when natural food is scarce, but Miss Tilton has also won the confidence of the catbird in summer. This bird, that so often seems suspicious of our intentions, will eat raisins out of her hand as readily as the chickadee eats suet from her fingers in the winter. She says a pair of catbirds often brought their young ones with them when they came for food, and one day both father and mother and two little ones tried to land on her hand at the same time. Another catbird in Miss Tilton's garden was so fond of butter that when he came for his breakfast of raisins would help himself to butter from her breakfast tray.

In the West and North the gray jays or "whiskey jacks" seem to be born without fear. Often in the fir forests on the foothills of Mount Rainier, a clear ringing whistle will bring a flock circling around you, literally demanding a share of your lunch. Sometimes in the morning they will light on the blankets of the sleepers in a camp, wakening them so they may get busy over the camp fire. They know they will have a share of the flapjacks to be cooked for breakfast. In the high meadows on Mount Rainier, when you are eating they will often alight on your toe, leap to your plate and make a dive for a mouthful, then flutter off triumphantly "taking home the bacon."

Mr. A. W. Anthony says: "While dressing deer in the thick timber I have been almost covered with jays flying down from the neighboring trees. They would settle on my back, head, or shoulders, tugging and pulling at each loosed shred of my coat until one would think that their only object was to help me in all ways possible."

Chapter Six

PROTECTION

THE most effective protection that can be given our birds is properly selected planting, which means a growth of plants which as nearly as possible duplicates their natural habitat. In the close-set belt of sheltering evergreens they will find protection from cold rainy winds and from snow and ice, and in the tangle of thorny shrubs and vines they can get the cover necessary for nesting.

When we think of the life in our gardens we are inclined to consider only the plants and the song birds. We not only enjoy the birds but appreciate the benefit they do us by keeping in check the insects that despoil our shrubs and flowers. But if our planting approximates natural growth we will find in it many forms of life, all depending on one another for existence and maintaining a balance of which we are often quite unaware.

In the first place are the plants themselves. They are the only forms of life that can manufacture food. Through the chlorophyll, or green coloring matter in their leaves, they make food from sunlight, soil and water. The tender green leaves are pasturage for myriads of insects, which in turn become food for song birds and their clamoring young. This is as far as we usually go in our analysis. We bend all our efforts toward the preservation of these song birds, but we should realize that the same planting which so admirably serves the birds will also attract squirrels, rabbits, skunks and snakes, not to mention hawks and owls. Some of these animals are frequently classed as "enemies" of song birds and also of man because at times they live upon birds or plant material that we wish to preserve. But all these animals have developed through the ages side by side with the birds

MAGNOLIA WARBLER
MALE, BREEDING ADULT
IMMATURE, FALL

YELLOW WARBLER
MALE, BREEDING ADULT
FEMALE, BREEDING ADULT

BLACK-THROATED BLUE WARBLER
MALE, BREEDING ADULT
FEMALE, BREEDING ADULT

KIRTLAND'S WARBLER
MALE, BREEDING ADULT

MYRTLE WARBLER
IMMATURE, FALL

MALE, BREEDING ADULT

Scale about one-half

and even the sentimentalist must learn it is right for a certain percentage of birds to succumb to natural causes other than old age, for otherwise the country would be overrun with the progeny of the more prolific species which can reach only a certain level without there being a lack of food and nesting sites.

So, though the sharp-shinned hawk may feed upon small birds, it is no more cruel than a bluebird or a wren devouring a grub. It is only following its instinctive behavior pattern or natural bent, and as it is a native bird, for thousands of years it has existed under the same conditions with song birds and has caused no extinction of species or even undue losses in their ranks. And, though the screech owl may take a few birds during the time it is feeding its young, it is also a check on meadow mice and other rodents. Hawks also do much good by picking up birds weakened or made unwary by disease. In Scotland, on some of the big game preserves, hawks and owls are shot most conscientiously by gamekeepers, and here it is found that disease spreads very rapidly, the weakened birds not being picked out by the alert hawks, which are in reality guardians of the grouses' health. Plant life suffers, too, when the hawks and owls are destroyed. In a game farm in Connecticut where all predators have been shot, the meadow mice attracted by grain scattered for food, built up a large population, and in the spring it was found that they had girdled a plantation of 1,500 five-year-old pine trees.

But we can use protective measures against "unnatural enemies" which have been introduced unknowingly and carelessly by man himself. These take a toll beyond the natural loss which is not always compensated for by the annual increase. There are three outstanding menaces to our bird life in and about suburban districts and they are: the house cat, the English sparrow and the European starling. These are all species not native to this country, and experience has taught us in many cases that introduced species often become menaces by upsetting the balance of life. Examples of this

71

are the rabbit in Australia, the muskrat in Austria and the so-called Norway or brown rat that has traveled all over the world.

Few people realize what a menace the cat is to our bird population. It has been estimated that fifty millions is a low estimate for the number of small birds that cats consume in the state of Pennsylvania in one year. This is fifty millions beyond the total loss which would take place naturally. This estimate is for one State. Is it not appalling to think of the sum total in all our States? Can the gardener afford this loss of bird life? Not if he realizes what the birds can do for him as well as for agriculture all over the country.

Birds will not linger where they see a prowling cat. A cat's presence in or near a garden terrifies them. Almost every bird has a distinctive alarm note when it sees a cat. Even a well-fed, well-cared-for cat, that may not be an habitual hunter cannot resist the temptation to kill a young and helpless robin or bluebird as it flutters helplessly on the ground. The cat has never become a domesticated animal. It is almost impossible to train it. Ever it walks—and most commendably so in its own eyes—by its "wild, wild lone." If this is true of the petted house cat, think of the slaughter caused by the thousands of unowned cats that have gone entirely wild and live by foraging in the woods and fields.

A nice sleek cat is a pleasurable companion to many people. But the best place for it is in the city. There are thousands of cat lovers in the world, but if you want birds, you cannot have cats. They just don't mix, or rather they mix too well. It is just as natural for cats to catch birds as it is for them to lap milk, much more natural in fact, and cats can't be blamed for this perfectly normal impulse which has come to them through the generations as a behavior pattern which shows when the tiny kitten leaps on a ball or on any moving object. We merely have to choose between the voluptuous sinuous beauty of the cat and the presence of a yardful of glancing wings and glad carefree songs.

The United States Biological Survey advises placing a catproof fence around the bird sanctuary. Such a fence is made of strongly woven wire of not more than one and a half inch mesh. It should be six feet high with an outward over-hang of two feet. Sometimes this over-hang consists of horizontal rows of barbed wire or is arched and the wire left loose.

A very inexpensive catproof fence is made of tarred fishnet or seine six feet high, attached at the top to flexible poles; at the bottom it is threaded by rods pinned to the ground by tent pegs. If a cat jumps against this fence, the poles bend toward her so that she falls backward and is unable to recover herself quickly enough to make the spring over.

If these fences do not seem suitable to the neighborhood, a high, closely-built lattice on which thorny roses and vines are planted forms a small measure of protection. This protection though is only partial and therefore the humane cat trap should be used. The United States Biological Survey says "stray cats become skilled hunters and severely menace song, insectivorous and game-bird life, and as an act of mercy to the cats themselves, all unowned cats should be destroyed." They can be readily caught in a well constructed baited trap, which is described in Leaflet No. 50, *How to Make a Cat Trap,* sent out by the Biological Survey, and here quoted:

The trap consists of a box with a drop door, held up by a projecting wire, one end of which is attached to a false floor, or treadle. The weight of the cat on the treadle beyond the fulcrum pulls back the wire and releases the door.

Any one who can use a square, a saw and a hammer can make the trap from the following instructions, using well-seasoned, dressed, pine lumber three-fourths of an inch thick:

The following materials are necessary for building the trap:

1 12-inch board 14 feet long
1 1½-inch strip 7 feet long
1 ¾-inch strip 2 feet long
20 inches of No. 3 gauge wire

2 small screw eyes
1 piece of 2- or 3-mesh wire netting
6 inches square

Cut the 12-inch board to make the following pieces:

1 bottom board 30 inches long	1 treadle board 27 inches long
1 top board 28½ inches long	1 drop door 13½ inches long
2 side boards 29¼ inches long	1 end board 10½ inches long

Cut the 1½-inch strip to make the following pieces:

2 drop-door guides 24 inches long	1 fulcrum piece for treadle 10½
2 drop-door guides 11¼ inches long	inches long

Cut the ¾-inch strip to make 2 center guide strips 1 foot long.

Cut or plane a quarter of an inch from the edge of the treadle board so that it will move inside of the trap without binding. Cut a V-shaped groove about a quarter of an inch deep across the treadle board at right angles, and 13½ inches from the front end to fit over top of fulcrum. Cut or plane the fulcrum piece to a ridge, 1 inch high, to fit into the groove in the treadle. Cut or plane edges of drop door so that it will slide freely in guides. Cut an opening 4 by 5 inches in center of the rear end board and tack a piece of 2-mesh or 3-mesh wire netting over it to provide ventilation. The cut-out section may be used as a door to make the trap airtight for fumigation.

Nail the bottom, sides, top, and end in position to form the box. Fasten the fulcrum at right angles across the bottom board, 15 inches from the front end. Nail the drop-door guides to front of trap to form grooves for the drop door, as illustrated in Figure 1, A. Screw one screw eye into the top side of the treadle half an inch from the right side and 17½ inches from the front end. Screw the second screw eye into the under side of the top board one-half inch from the right side and 1 inch from the front end. Fasten one end of the trigger wire to the screw eye on the treadle by bending to form a loop through the eye. Set the treadle in place so that its groove fits over the fulcrum. Pass the loose end of the trigger wire through the upper screw eye and bend the end back sharply at a length that will allow it to project just enough to hold up the door when the trap is set and to release it when the rear end of the treadle is pushed down. (Fig. 1, B.) The trap should be given two coats of good paint inside and out, to prevent warping when used outdoors.

Fresh fish is undoubtedly the most attractive food bait for cats. A fish or fish head, should be hung on a nail or hook provided for the purpose at the back end of the interior of the trap. When fish is not available, fresh meat of any kind, cooked or raw, may be used. A half ounce of dried catnip tied up in a cloth or preferably catnip oil, if available, also makes excellent bait and sometimes attracts a well-fed cat into a trap when food bait has failed.

The trap should be set in or near places that stray cats might be expected to visit in search of food. Open garbage cans at the rear of dwellings, as well as those that occasionally over-flow, are visited regularly and furnish good trapping prospects.

The trapped animal should be inspected by looking through the screened opening in the rear end of the trap. If a neighbor's pet cat or other valuable animal has entered the trap, it can be taken out, unharmed, and returned to its owners with a warning.

In almost all cities there is a Humane Society which cares for stray animals. Such animal rescue leagues can be notified when cats are caught and will be glad to take charge of trapped cats which have no owners.

If it is impossible to eliminate the cat, great care should be taken to protect all nesting boxes and feeding shelves where a cat might climb and catch unwary birds. Posts should be of metal, or if of wood, can be protected in several ways. A tin pan upside down may be placed just below the box or shelf, or a metal guard shaped like a funnel can be placed high enough, (six feet or more) to prevent the marauder from springing and catching hold above. The posts may also be wrapped with barbed wire or sheathed with metal tacked closely to the support.

Now to consider the English sparrow, really a weaver bird, not a true sparrow, which was brought from its European habitat to this country in 1852. Here it found things quite to its liking and very little in the environment to check its increase. The original number has increased prodigiously; they have spread from the cities to the country and, by riding on grain cars, have reached from coast to coast and from the Arctic to the Tropics. William Leon Dawson considers that bringing the English sparrow into this country was one of the most regrettable events in the history of American ornithology, and he deplores the sentimentality of people who build birdhouses and throw out crumbs, not bothering themselves to know whether our valuable native birds benefit or only the usurping English sparrow.

When it was definitely decided that this bird was a nuisance and a pest by no lower authority than the Department of Agriculture, much effort and many thousands of dollars were spent to prevent its spread and increase. But it was soon found that the species had come to stay. Finding no opposition in the cities the sparrows overflowed into the farmyards and then mobbed together and drove away many of our valuable birds which nest in boxes or in hollow trees. House wrens, swallows, martins, all fell victims to the newcomers' pugnacity, and even as large birds as flickers and robins were dispossessed.

But fortunately for our native birds the motorcar was invented; the sparrow could no longer find horse-droppings full of undigested grain, and in some places it was starved out. In suburban sections the house wren again made its appearance, but even to this day where these "hoodlums" collect in farmyards the lovely martins and barn swallows still remain aloof.

Aside from their detrimental effect on beautiful and valuable birds such as bluebirds and martins which we desire to have near us, English sparrows are directly destructive in our gardens, for they pull up young corn, peas, lettuce and other vegetables.

Local control of the English sparrow can be accomplished if a persistent campaign is set up. Aside from all material considerations, why should we have the delight of the morning chorus ruined by the monotonous cheeping of these intruders? Trap two or three of them and you will find they give your yard a wide berth. Of course, this is only driving them to your neighbors'; the only lasting solution is an united campaign against them, especially during the winter, in order that there may be no breeding stock left for increase in the spring.

Methods for combating these birds by trapping are to be found in Leaflet 61, *English Sparrow Control,* sent out by the Department of Agriculture.

The other introduced enemy of our native birds is the European starling which was, after many previous attempts, first successfully introduced into this country in 1890 and 1891. Since then it has spread over the greater part of the Eastern States and even toward the South and as far West as Salt Lake City.

There is a great difference of opinion with regard to the value of the starling. The Biological Survey, after an examination of over 2,000 stomach contents, says that the animal food—that is, insects, etc.—is 57 per cent of the whole, thus showing that the bird's food habits are to some extent beneficial to man. It undoubtedly destroys many injurious insects, but also whole flocks will often sweep down and devastate a cherry orchard or a vineyard. And as for what it does in small vegetable gardens! A flock of the handsome rascals will descend and up will come all the prize young tomato plants, all the cucumbers, peas, beans and the cherished muskmelons! If we have many more such visitors from abroad we shall have to "net" our gardens just as they do in England.

When there is a choice between our native birds and the starling there is no doubt that the swallows, the martins and the bluebirds should be given the preference. After the attacks of the English sparrow had somewhat lessened, the gentle, sociable martins were just beginning to return to their many-roomed homes and now they have to contend with this larger, stronger newcomer, a fighter who, with the greatest persistency, will endeavor to secure a nesting site. As the starling nests early, the martin's house can be protected by corking the entrances until the first martin arrives. Bluebirds, swallows, and wrens can be protected by narrowing the entrance holes, but this cannot be done on flicker or martin houses, and in the garden for birds the presence of these "outlanders" should be discouraged.

Chapter Seven

BIRD HOMES

The Mother Bird

Through the green twilight of a hedge
I peered, with cheek on the cool leaves pressed,
And spied a bird upon a nest:
Two eyes she had beseeching me
Meekly and brave, and her brown breast
Throbbed hot and quick above her heart;
And then she opened her dagger bill:—
'Twas not a chirp, as sparrows pipe
At break of day: 'twas not a trill,
As falters through the quiet even;
But one sharp solitary note,
One desperate, fierce and vivid cry
Of valiant tears, and hopeless joy,
One passionate note of victory.
Off, like a fool afraid, I sneaked,
Smiling the smile the fool smiles best,
At the mother bird in the secret hedge
Patient upon her lonely nest.
                              —*Walter De LaMare.*

A GARDEN with a planting that provides food and cover, and where there is water and a constant supply of supplementary food, will attract birds all winter. But when spring comes and the urge to mate and nest is upon the birds, will the majority of the guests leave? They frequently do, and to keep the birds with us at this time is most desirable, for not only is this mating season the season of greatest beauty of plumage

GOLDEN-CROWNED KINGLET
ADULT MALE
ADULT FEMALE   **RUBY-CROWNED KINGLET**
ADULT MALE
ADULT FEMALE

BLUE-GRAY GNATCATCHER
ADULT MALE

Scale about one-half

and song, but a most desirable time from the utilitarian standpoint to have the birds in the garden. After the eggs are hatched, nearly all birds, whether seed eaters or not, feed their young soft-bodied grubs and insects, and thus the gardener benefits enormously by the added mouths that have to be fed. Think of the tireless activity of the chickadees that feed a family of nestlings, every few minutes from dawn to dark! We should do everything we can to keep as many as possible of our winter guests with us as permanent tenants.

Many birds will find protected nesting sites in the luxuriant shrubbery. We can add to the attractiveness of this tangle by doing as Baron Von Berlepsch did on his remarkable bird sanctuary in Germany, that is by drawing together a cluster of twigs or boughs with a wire or cord, thus making a sheltered nook which catbirds or birds of similar nesting habits will find much to their taste, and also by trimming some of the shrubs and small trees severely so that they will make a twiggy growth with many crotches.

In the scrupulously tidied garden birds often have difficulty in finding materials with which to build their nests, so as nesting time approaches a few bits of tempting furnishings may be distributed about the yard. Surely, though, Johnny Wren's twigs are always contemptuously thrown out when Jenny arrives, a collection of choice sizes near the box might lead him to start to build in your yard. One observer found in a wren's nest 702 twigs, three shingle nails, and a safety pin, and not even a feather for a mattress for the babies. Think of having to look up such a pile of wood!

Robins will appreciate string, in short lengths, and a pile of dried grass, also a spot of damp earth for the mud cup so essential a part of every proper robin's nest. Orioles delight in raveling out gunny sacks. Cut them in small pieces and attach them to a tree or board by a tack in one corner. They also like short lengths of string and knitting yarn, and both orioles and vireos appreciate foot lengths of shoemaker's flax. In a bag

79

made of string, or a basket of straw or wire, may be placed bits of hair, non-absorbent cotton, kapok, worsted threads, raveled rope, lamb's wool, small pieces of cloth, especially woolen cloth with a long nap, and also feathers. Both tree and barn swallows adore feathers. Throw them out of the window so they will flutter through the air at first. The birds will soon watch for them and even fly to the window sill and learn to take them from your fingers.

Many birds, among them the chipping and song sparrows, used to line their nests with horsehairs. But now owing to the shortage of horses, they have to be contented with hair gleaned from combings or perhaps stolen from the family watchdog. Occasionally a bird becomes desperate for nesting material when the supply runs short. Maurice Broun, in charge of Hawk Mountain Sanctuary, tells of seeing a nuthatch fly down to the ground and tear off a piece of fur as large as its head from a dead squirrel. Another observer saw a goldfinch strip the wool from an angora sweater on a sleeping baby. Occasionally vireos make use of paper which, when water soaked, gives way with disastrous results.

The most picturesque nesting material was that used by a house finch in California. Mr. David Burpee has a vast acreage in California given over to raising flowers for seed. Naturally the land is in a high state of cultivation and birds are "hard put" to find nesting material. A year or two ago Mr. Burpee had next to his house a large planting of a new yellow everlasting flower, and what was his surprise one morning when he went out on his porch to see a nest made of these flowers! A nest as beautifully designed as any lady's flower turban, for the stems were skilfully woven in and out, leaving the flower heads all on the outside. Mr. Burpee promptly named the new plant "Birds' Nest Flower."

But in addition to those birds which can find a home thus easily, there are others needing either a hollow in a tree, or a suitable place in which to excavate one. In the modern, well-cared-for garden, every decayed branch has been removed, every cavity has been filled and all dead trees are immediately cut down. So what are the poor hole nesters as the wood-peckers and chickadees who have been with us all winter to do then, not to mention spring's gift of bluebirds and wrens and swallows? We want these birds to stay with us. But we must realize that a garden will accommodate only a certain number of pairs. If there are too many houses set too near one another there will be a series of squabbles. Each bird has a certain area which he patrols as his own and he is exceedingly jealous at least toward his own kind, of his territorial rights. He patrols his chosen premises constantly, even before his mate arrives and sings lustily from various singing posts, not only to attract the female but let all and sundry know that a certain bit of the garden is his very own.

The territorial rights of birds vary in extent. Usually the only community nesters you should provide for are the martins. The attractive houses made for several pairs of wrens will only be a source of continual warfare. As a rule three single-apartment wren boxes per acre are sufficient, but there are records of many more to such an area being occupied. Robins occasionally nest within twenty-five feet of each other, but the gentle blue-bird, the poet's symbol of happiness, will tolerate no other pair within a hundred yards!

Therefore, as there now remain so few natural nesting sites in our well-groomed gardens and orchards for the birds formerly nesting in cavities, we must set up suitable nesting boxes. The time to put them up is in the early fall. Many of the birds who winter with us would be exceedingly glad to have a box for a roosting site at night during the cold weather. Birds which would gladly occupy these shelters are woodpeckers, titmice, nuthatches, chickadees and owls. If these boxes are put up early in the fall they will become weathered and thus a familiar part of the surroundings. When nesting time comes, no new and jarring element will have to be introduced into the landscape by putting up a new box, and many a pair of birds which usually retires to the secluded woods, for the summer, will remain to nest near us. Frank Chapman Pellet tells of how he saw thirty-one tiny winter wrens crowd for shelter into a box used by a violet-green swallow in summer, and in another garden in Washington, a chickadee used to retire every night at sunset into a bluebird box, singing himself to sleep,—chickadee-dee-chickadee-dee, fainter and fainter, until all was silence.

East or West, the brave little chickadee, such a tireless bundle of gray with black cap and throat, whose cheery call rings out even in subzero weather, makes a jolly summer companion if he consents to nest with us. All winter, although he has enjoyed his supplementary food of suet and sunflower seeds, he has searched every crack and crevice for insect eggs and larvae. It has been estimated that one chickadee may destroy one hundred thousand eggs of the cankerworm within twenty-five days. He is the most easily tamed of all our winter birds and after having been fed all through the cold weather, has been known to nest in a rustic house within plain view of the terrace. Then all summer he and his mate, and later the energetic nestlings, will continue their indefatigable warfare on spiders, beetles, wasps, bugs, ants, grasshoppers, caterpillars and moths, the latter two forming about one-third of their food. The proper proportions for his home are a floor four by four inches, walls eight to ten inches high, an opening one and an eighth inches in diameter, set eight inches high in the front. This box should be placed six to fifteen feet high in a tree, in not too heavy shade, or against an outbuilding. (See page 108, plate IV, figure 6.)

Even those master carpenters, the woodpeckers, including the flicker, will frequently deign to accept a man-made substitute for their own craftsmanship. And that brings up the thought, will the woodpecker, if he constantly has his work done for him, forget how to excavate? Why not occasionally fasten up a decayed limb and let him do his own work? But that is beside the question now. If we can keep these cheery "tappers" near or in our orchard we are very lucky.

The little downy woodpecker is likely to have been our constant guest all winter. How assiduously he sounds out the death knell of every hidden larva that he unerringly detects beneath the bark. He is larger than the chickadee, six inches in length, and may be known by his distinct black and white coloration, the male having a dab of red on the back of his head. His box, too, should be of the woodland type, even more rustic than that of the chickadee. The proportions of this box should be the same as that of the chickadee with a slightly larger opening, one and one-quarter or one and one-half inches in diameter. Be sure to put in the bottom of the box sawdust or chips, mixing them with a little moist earth, for woodpeckers carry in no nesting material and sometimes a box suitable in every other way has been refused merely because of the lack of a carpet! But if "downy" is suited he will continue all the year to hunt wood-boring grubs and scale insects, tent caterpillars, moth larvae, ants and sawflies, which, with other insects, constitute at least three-quarters of his menu.

Also a valuable destroyer of tree-infesting larvae is the downy's slightly larger relative, the hairy woodpecker. He is shyer than his little cousin, and usually seeks the deep woods during the nesting season, but if he has been fed consistently, he will sometimes accept a box proportioned as follows: a floor six by six inches; walls twelve to fifteen inches; entrance hole one and one-half inches in diameter, set twelve inches high, and the box placed twelve to twenty feet above the ground. (See page 108, plate IV, figure 7.)

Of the three most familiar woodpeckers, the flicker mourns most sadly the work of the tree surgeon in dappering-up the orchard and home grounds. He does very much less work on trees than his two cousins, obtaining a greater part of his food from ants on the ground. The downy and hairy woodpeckers' bills are straight, like little chisels while his is slightly curved, so he prefers to work on rotten wood, though in desperation he sometimes makes a hole in a telegraph pole! But, alas, let winter or the pestiferous tree surgeon take toll of a favorite dead tree where generations of flickers have been born and reared, great will be the lamentations on the arrival of the nesting season. "What, no tree?" You can fairly read the question like a smoke advertisement across the sky as the pair loop back and forth showing the yellow lining of their wings, their white rumps and their black neck crescents, while the air fairly resounds with their frenzied "wick, wicks." And unless you wish them to retire to a less progressive neighborhood, a large box meeting flicker specifications should be set up on a pole twenty feet high where it is not too shaded. A bark-covered box is considered the most satisfactory and the floor should be at least seven by seven inches, the depth of the cavity from sixteen to eighteen inches, the entrance hole two and one-quarter inches in diameter, placed sixteen inches above the floor. After much debating, if you haven't forgotten the chips or sawdust mixed with moist earth on the bottom of the box, this modern departure from old-time flicker ways will be accepted and peace will descend on the flicker tribe. Soon the glossy, pure white eggs will be laid, and when you see both male and female making countless trips back and forth, you will know that the eggs are hatched and that the pair are pumping the young nestlings full of ants. They feed the young entirely by regurgitation, with their sticky tongue pulling as many as 5,000 ants out of the ground for a single meal, and then relaying them to the youngsters.

Found in some districts and never seen in others, that striking bird, the red-headed woodpecker, has occasionally been known to nest in a box. The one which it is most likely to take is the Berlepsch type of chiselled-out log. Although he prefers decayed stubs, in some localities he has been known to work his chisel in the perfectly sound wood of a telegraph pole, thus showing how much in need of help he is. So, set up a box in the woods in an oak tree where it isn't too shaded and the red-headed wanderer may adopt your neighborhood for his home. The floor space of the box should measure six by six inches, and it should have a depth of twelve to fifteen inches, with a hole two inches in diameter, set nine to twelve inches above the floor; it should be placed twelve to twenty feet high in a high-branching tree.

The redhead combines fly-catching in the air with the usual woodpecker drilling for grubs in the bark of trees. He eats much more fruit than the other woodpeckers, and has been accused of destroying cherries, apples and other cultivated fruits, but, doubtless, as is the case with almost all fruit-eating birds, he would prefer to eat mulberries or wild cherries if these were available, as they would be in a planting for birds.

Even if "redhead" does a little damage it is compensated for by the amount of woodborers, grasshoppers, May beetles and weevils that he destroys, and besides that he is such a bright-colored, conspicuous rascal in his coat of red, white and black, that it is a great pleasure to have him near us. It is said that when Alexander Wilson saw his bright plumage that he made up his mind then and there to become an ornithologist.

And then out of the sky comes the bluebird, melodiously warbling, as he flies along, but not from "fencepost to fencepost," for he can find no soft, decayed fenceposts in the modern garden. Long before nesting time has come he will have canvassed every nook and hollow in the orchard. And usually in vain. Again the tree surgeon has preceded him. Not long ago there was an article in the newspaper telling of the desperation of a bluebird, which insisted upon nesting in a mailbox. Several times the pair were turned out, but at length the box was given to the determined nesters and another box set up near by to receive the mail. The mail man had to stop and get out, but he said he didn't mind.

Roger Peterson in the Audubon Leaflet on Birdhouses makes a special plea for help for the bluebird. He says everybody puts up houses for the wren, but it is really the duty of the conservationist to encourage the bluebird as due to the persecutions of the English sparrow and the starling it is a diminishing species. He gives as an example of what can be done the experiment of Mr. T. E. Musselman of Quincy, Illinois. Mr. Musselman set up 102 bluebird boxes along 43 miles of country road and later found 88 of these houses were occupied. Besides this practical bit of housing Mr. Musselman has distributed nearly 3,000 mimeographed plans for a bluebird house project. If such projects were carried out systematically in the schools throughout the country, the bluebird would no longer be considered "a diminishing species."

BIRDS IN THE GARDEN

Bluebirds are not hard to please and if a rustic bungalow has the dimensions according to the best bluebird conventions, that is, a floor five by six inches, a ceiling height of eight inches, and a hole one and one-half inches in diameter set six inches above the floor, it is very likely to be accepted. There may be a few days gentle consultation between the two, but at last the matter will be settled and you will have with you a bit of "the sky above and the earth beneath," as Thoreau describes the colors of the eastern bluebird, and all through the spring and summer it will be a joy to watch them. They are charming in their family life, the male always attentive and often feeding his mate choice bits most gallantly. But they are very jealous of their territorial rights, so remember not to put another bluebird house within a hundred yards. In Forbush's *Birds of Massachusetts* he tells of bluebirds attacking downy woodpeckers and pulling feathers out of their backs and using the feathers for their nests. He tells of another instance where two dogs chased a cat to the top of the bird house when the male bluebird attacked the cat so fiercely that it scrambled down, preferring to face the two dogs rather than the cerulean fury. Ornithologists tell us that song has been developed in birds so that they may let others know their territorial limits, so perhaps the bluebirds' soft "truly, truly," has to be supplemented by more warlike actions. Much of the bluebird's food is of animal nature and the list of pests eaten shows how greatly its presence benefits the gardener. Among those it feeds on are May beetles, cutworms, army worms, wood-boring beetles, tent caterpillars, gypsy-moth caterpillars, cankerworms, plant lice, white-pine weevil, leaf hoppers, cicadas and tree hoppers. It delights in eating wild fruits and only occasionally takes a cherry or a currant from the garden. It is useful as well as beautiful and a most desirable guest or rather householder to have in the garden.

And the wrens—it would be hard to suppress them! How easily satisfied they are! So determined are they to nest and to nest near man that almost any usable place will be pre-empted by the busy midgets, and the day is never long enough for their bubbling songs and ceaseless activities.

86

RED-HEADED WOODPECKER
ADULT   JUVENAL PLUMAGE

RED-BELLIED WOODPECKER
MALE
          FEMALE

YELLOW-SHAFTED FLICKER
FEMALE
MALE

Scale about one-third

Mr. Forbush says: "The house wren is a modestly colored, cunning little elf but true modesty isn't in him. . . . He is a bold and happy warrior."

The male usually arrives first from the South. Immediately, if there is a suitable box he takes up his stand upon it and from then on until the female arrives he spends his time casting his bubbles of song toward the sky to let all and sundry know about his territory. Between intervals of song he carries into the box the most impossible looking twigs, so that things will be well started when the laggard mate turns up. And when she does arrive! Such ecstasy! Showering a very cascade of notes he will throw himself skyward, only to arch downward toward the beloved one who, ignoring him, as soon as she arrives, begins to throw out every stick which her mate has so laboriously dragged in. And the strange places they will nest in! In old satchels, in the door pocket of a motor car, the pocket of a coat, the skull of a cow or horse set up in a pole or tree, and an old hunting bag. Even penetrating the house, one pair set up housekeeping in the human skull in a doctor's office and another pair in a clock in the living-room, where, ignoring the whirr of the machinery and the striking of the hours, as well as the activities of a busy household, they went back and forth through the window left open for their convenience.

The conventional measurements for a wren box given by none less than the United States Department of Agriculture (and constantly and contemptuously ignored by the wrens themselves) are a floor four by four inches; depth of cavity six to eight inches; entrance above the floor six inches; size of hole seven-eighths of an inch; the box placed six to ten feet above the ground. They love to nest in a gourd, and as it would not be convenient to clean out a gourd through a seven-eighth inch hole, the big end of the gourd should be sawed off and then wired to a board. Whether the bottom of the nest is a board or not, a few small holes should be provided for drainage.

It is important to have the opening only seven-eighths of an inch in diameter, to keep out larger birds. For a number of years the wrens failed to hold their own against the rowdy aggressive sparrows and they became quite rare in the dooryard. Then since the decrease of the sparrow the wrens have come back, now to be met with a new siege from the starlings. Keeping the hole too small for the starlings will protect the wren boxes, but as the wrens often have difficulty in dragging in their beloved twigs through this opening, it is a good idea to keep it seven-eighths of an inch high but make it three inches wide. (See page 108, plate IV, figure 1.)

It is claimed that where there are many birds nesting near by that wrens occasionally pierce the eggs in other birds' nests, and even throw out the young. But this is quite local, not a general habit, and the wren ranks high among our useful birds. Its food is almost entirely animal and with their immense energy they search every crevice, hunting out bugs, spiders, caterpillars, grasshoppers, beetles, and taking delight in cutworms, weevils, ticks, and plant lice. One has but to watch a pair for an hour in order to appreciate the almost incredible amount of soft-bodied moths and flies which are fed to a clamoring boxful of six or eight nestlings.

Both the beautiful blue and white tree swallow and the violet-green swallow of the West will nest not only in hollow trees but also in boxes of the same dimensions as those suitable for the bluebird. The box, however, should be set five to fifteen feet up on a telephone pole, dead tree or post standing in the open. (See page 108, plate IV, figure 3.)

Both of these swallows love to line their nests with feathers and take great pleasure in capturing them if they are thrown in the air. In the West so eager are the swallows for these choice bits of upholstery that they will sit in rows on the apartment house windowsills waiting for feathers even after the nesting season is over.

The tree swallows are charming birds to have in the garden, and seem to be constantly looking for new nesting sites. Roger Peterson says that when at the Jones Beach Sanctuary on Long Island a number of boxes were set up, six pairs moved in immediately. Similarly at the Austin Ornithological Research Station at Cape Cod, the tree swallow population was built up to over 100 pairs where previously none had nested.

Tree swallows are the first of their tribe to arrive in the spring and the last to leave in the fall. Their continuous chirping leads the morning chorus and from before dawn until after dusk they course through the air destroying myriads of insect pests. They eat quantities of flies, weevils and other injurious beetles, ants and moths. Unlike other swallows they vary their diet with wild fruit and berries, particularly those of the wax myrtle, and this explains their ability to stay with us longer in the fall. They are as valuable as the barn swallow and quite as ready to nest near man, doing incalculable good near cranberry bogs and mosquito-infested marshes.

With its long, forked tail, its steely black back and reddish underparts, no bird should be better known to young and old than the barn swallow, and few birds are more useful near our homes. Even more adaptable to changing conditions than the tree swallow, the beautiful barn swallow with its superlatively graceful flight and extreme usefulness in destroying insect pests, has learned to shelter itself most companionably about man's abode. Except in the Far West, they have abandoned their dwellings in the wild, on cliffs or in hollow trees, and now make use of man-built structures for their nesting sites, liking especially well barns or unused out-buildings. When they arrive from the South, it may be that they will find their usual nesting places closed to them. They seem to realize the need of human aid and if a person appears they flutter about and twitter beseechingly until a door or window is opened. Then, seemingly overjoyed, they fly into their old haunts. Oftentimes farmers, who appreciate their value, cut holes in their barn gables so that the birds may have easy ingress.

The number of insects that barn swallows destroy seems almost incredible. On cloudy days they fly low, sweeping near the earth for gnats and other small insects. When it is fine, up they circle to reach the small insects flying high, and because of this in many sections they are called the "farmer's barometer." Sometimes when they build in too prominent positions in the barn, farmers object to the litter which falls from their nests, but the wise ones supply them with little shelves placed in more convenient situations. By putting up similar shelves in a garden house or building we may have the pleasure of these graceful birds near our homes.

The barn swallow's platform should be six by six inches, and should have one or more walls six inches high, while the remaining sides should be left open. These platforms may be placed in groups, for these birds are very sociable.

If the platforms are accepted, nest building becomes an absorbing interest, to us as well as to the swallows. You may help operations, if you will, when the weather is dry, by mixing a little earth and water for the plaster for their homes. Perhaps they will swoop back and forth over your head, keeping mosquitoes away from you as you work, and as soon as you leave will immediately accept your offering. And if you will supply some feathers—how they adore them! Mr. E. H. Forbush paints a delightful word picture of a little boy standing shoulder-high in a field of buttercups and daisies, and holding up a fluffy white feather. As he stood looking laughingly aloft, in a long graceful arc, a barn swallow descended and took the feather from his fingers.

When the nestlings are to be fed, the swallows fly constantly, even before dawn and after dark, literally packing their gullets with insects, which they regurgitate into the mouths of the hungry, twittering nestlings.

With the exception of the tree and barn swallows, which occasionally nest in colonies, all the birds we have spoken of insist upon owning their homes as individual pairs, and are quite jealous of their territorial rights. But if you can induce a colony of the predominantly social purple martins to adopt your garden as a homesite, you have brought personified "good luck" to the whole neighborhood.

The martins are true swallows and are birds of the open, never nesting in the forest, though, strange to say, in these modern times, so hard put are they to find hollow trees in the open, or boxes that suit them, that they nest in crevices of cornices in buildings in busy cities!

The Indians appreciated the martins' usefulness in destroying mosquitoes and flies and used to hang gourds on the limbs of dead trees or on trimmed-up saplings. The negroes of the South have followed their example and hang gourds on trees, or on poles with crossbars. And we might follow their example, for these rows of hanging gourds would make a picturesque addition to our own garden.

Before the coming of the English sparrow, martin colonies were quite common, but when spring after spring, the martins, that become greatly attached to their homesite, returned from the South only to find their homes full of rubbish, and were in addition beset by a crowd of ruffians in feathers, they were discouraged. At first they defended their homes and threw out nests and eggs, but the pressure became too great and they retired—who knows where?

Now, the few remaining brave ones, which have lately returned since the English sparrows have decreased in numbers, have to contend with an enemy of still larger size, the starling. It is certainly a sad commentary on man's short-sightedness in introducing foreign species when a native bird, so useful, so beautiful and so well adapted to its environment, is so persecuted by these usurpers that in localities where they were once abundant they are now seldom seen.

But it is well to be ready with hospitality, for one never knows when a wandering pair may be the "avant couriers" of a flock of these cheerful aerial coursers, whose family life is so interesting and who with true social spirit, band together so valiantly to defend their homes from an enemy. From long before daylight until after dusk they wheel through the air, destroying thousands of ants, flies, bugs and beetles, as well as numerous other insects. They feed quantities of these insects to their young, arriving at the nest with crammed crops and mouths.

Sometimes martin houses are made on an elaborate scale, but the type of architecture doesn't seem of much concern to the birds. Perhaps half a dozen pairs will be the first to take the house, and gradually, year after year, the number will be built up until dozens of pairs may be happily housed in the original and supplemental houses, if these happily are provided.

The accompanying diagram shows a simple form of martin house that has been worked out by the Department of Agriculture and accepted by the birds in many localities. (See page 108, plate IV, figure 5.)

Each story is made a unit and supplementary ones may be added. A colony may be started in one story of eight rooms. Three stories, providing twenty-four rooms, will accommodate about as many martins as would ordinarily be desired in one colony. The roof, has over-hanging eaves which are desirable as a protection from heavy storms. The porches, attached by angle irons, also provide protection from the weather for the story below them and provide a place for these sociable birds to congregate or to walk along and seemingly pry into their neighbors' housekeeping. The rooms in this house, have separate entrances and by leaving out the floor of what would have been the central compartment, circulation of air is obtained. A hole at each end of the table also provides ventilation. The young martins often suffer greatly from heat in poorly-planned houses and to escape it, and the persecution of vermin, may come out of the nest too soon and fall to the ground and die. The parents do not even attempt to feed them when they suffer this catastrophe.

This box is held together entirely by hooks and screw eyes and may be cleaned easily by taking the house apart and dumping out the rubbish. The entire house with its support may be hinged for lowering, or, if the pole is set firmly in the ground, a ladder leaned against it will permit taking down the house, section by section. Such a house of two stories built of soft pine will weigh about 65 pounds. The materials for the walls and floors should be three-quarters of an inch thick, and that for the roof and interior partitions should be one-half inch. A light-weight roofing paper cut into shingles makes an efficient and neat roof covering. This will prevent dampness, and as martins were evidently originally birds of the tropics, they are extremely susceptible to dampness and cold, both young and old often perishing in a protracted period of unseasonably cold rain which we have occasionally in June and July.

Mr. P. A. Taverner writing in the *Canadian Field Naturalist* gives an amusing account of his attempts to get martins to come to his house. The third season a lonely female arrived first. The place seemed to appeal to her and she tried to induce friends to come with her. She would sit on the gable end and call vainly to them. Then, somehow, she succeeded in bringing a committee of investigation back with her. They swarmed all over the house, into all the rooms, talking and criticising and making comparisons. Mr. Taverner gathered that one did not like the plumbing, some objected to the decorations, and others to the view, in fact none seemed satisfied enough to move in and after emphatic expressions of opinion all left; the single would-be tenant loudly protesting and vociferously calling them back. When she saw that they were actually deserting her off she flew after them and eventually brought them back for a reconsideration, also fruitless. Later she was joined by a mate—a juvenile or last year's male similar to herself in plumage—and they settled down to home-making by themselves. Through the brooding season friends from other colonies came and visited, and it was no uncommon sight to see ten or a dozen martins taking an active and personal interest in the growing family, and when the young came out sometimes as many as twenty circled about the house. The next spring five or six pairs were in possession; and the colony's welfare was established and has increased until about twelve compartments are occupied.

Some advise putting up the boxes early, but keeping the holes corked until the martins arrive from the South. Sometimes the arrivals will greet a newly-constructed box with great delight, circling about it when it is being erected and even lighting on it, and arising with it as it is being placed. It is said that placing the droppings from an old box in a new one will sometimes bring tenants. It is a matter of uncertainty whether your box will be taken.

But if your garden is large enough so that the house may be set up in the open, well away from trees, it is well worth your efforts to try to secure these neighbors "without a single bad habit."

Although fifty species of American birds have been known to nest in boxes, those already described are the most likely to accept our hospitality. Occasional occupants include certain other kinds, about which information is given in the following paragraphs.

That close relative of the chickadee, the tufted titmouse, more frequently seen in the States south of New York, comes regularly to the feeding shelf, calling briskly "peto-peto." Like the chickadee, it is tame and confiding and full of curiosity and energy. It is a small, gray bird considerably larger than its black-capped relative, and may be known by its crest and black forehead. In former years it nested in cavities in trees but now will frequently accept a house of the same dimensions as the chickadee's except that the entrance hole should be one and one-quarter inches in diameter.

Both female and male titmice work at the nest building and they are particularly fond of a hair lining, evidently considering it indispensable. They have been known to light on a man's or woman's head and, bracing their feet, pull out a beakful of hair. Sometimes their choice falls on a squirrel, and in spite of chattering protestations, a tuft comes out of the bushy tail and goes into the nest lining. Another persistent titmouse secured its quota from the back of a very lively dog.

Fifty per cent of the titmouse's food consists of caterpillars and wasps and includes sawfly larvae, tree hoppers, scales, bugs and insect eggs. The members of this family are considered by scientists to be among the "most efficient conservators of the forest."

All winter long the rollicking troups of chickadees, titmice and white-breasted nuthatches have enlivened our woods and orchards. The nuthatch, as well as its companions, will often become tame enough to eat from our hands. Then as spring comes we hear the rather melancholy "yank, yank," more often; and presume that a nesting site is being sought. The nuthatch is in the same plight as the other birds—"nary" a hollow in a decayed limb is to be found to work on, and as for an abandoned downy woodpecker's nest, a favorite apartment—good-bye, a reproachful "yank, yank" and white-breast will retire to the forest to look there for it. But this little nuthatch, so called because it takes acorns or seeds and wedges them in a crack in the bark and then proceeds to hack them open, is too valuable a garden ally to part with without some effort put forth to keep him. This busy "devil down-head" or "upside-down bird," as the country people call him, because he not only runs up the trees peering into the bark for insects, their larvae and eggs, but also runs down again head foremost still searching diligently, perhaps may stay with us if he finds a hollowed out type of house like figure 7. It looks very much like an abandoned downy woodpecker's hole and perhaps the little acrobats in sleek gray and white may stay to nest in it and continue to help rid the orchard of scale insects, nut weevils, leaf beetles, plant lice and their eggs, and many other pests notably the eggs of the fall cankerworm, moths, and pear-tree psylla. He may occasionally nest in a box of the same size as that used by the titmouse.

According to the United States Biological Survey, the stomach contents of one white-breasted nuthatch, examined in Massachusetts, contained 1,629 eggs of the fall cankerworm moth. Its prowess in the orchard may be gauged by the following report. "A pear grower near Rochester, New York, lost his entire pear crop by the pear-tree psylla, an exceedingly destructive pest. In the autumn the eggs of the pest were so numerous that there was little prospect of a crop the following year, but . . . the white-breasted nuthatch came in numbers to the orchard and in spring hardly an insect could be found on those trees. Thus these birds saved the grower thousands of dollars."

Many close observers have noticed the interesting fact that the white-breasted nuthatch is something of a weather prophet, betraying great un-

95

easiness and activity just before a storm, flying from the nest straight up in the air and diving down again. They also call their nasal "yank, yank" more frequently.

More strictly a bird of the woodland than the orchard, the great crested flycatcher may occasionally be tempted to nest in a box. About the body size of a sparrow, but appearing much larger because of its longer tail, he first lets us know of his presence by a series of rather harsh whistles and we see him sometimes passing from limb to limb among the trees, then posing on the end of a branch as most flycatchers do, before he darts out to capture some hapless insect with a snap of his bill. Often he will choose a favorite perch where he may be seen at certain hours every day. As he darts out among the dark branches his olive-brown back is hardly perceptible. He is noisy, active and very valuable in the orchard as he eats many flies, the strawberry weevil and crickets, locusts and many caterpillars, moths and beetles. In lieu of an abandoned woodpecker hole, which is increasingly difficult to find, he will use a box with a floor space six by six, the walls eight by ten inches in height, the door opening two and one-half inches in diameter, set eight to ten inches above the floor. It should be placed eight to twenty feet up on the edge of a groove in a situation as nearly as possible like this flycatcher's natural habitat.

The male crested flycatcher usually arrives in late April or early May. Then if there are two males and one female, what a battle royal ensues, for the great crested flycatcher is almost as pugnacious as the kingbird, that the scientists called "tyrant of tyrants."

After the feathers have stopped flying, the successful cockbird and the female start nest building. If the house you have put up is of the proper proportions, all they will have to do will be to fill in the cavity with trash, moss, hair, twigs and feathers which seem to them the proper materials. They have been known, when they could only find a cavity much too large for them, to build up in it a big collection of rubbish and then put their nest on that. This flycatcher desires above all things one bit of furnishing,

96

the reason for which scientists to this day have not figured out—that is, a cast-off snake skin! If it is possible to obtain it, no respectable great crested flycatcher will be without this valuable household accessory! William Dawson found in one nest a harsh, rustling piece of tissue paper and thought that the explanation of the presence of skin or paper was that its rustling warned the birds of enemies. But no one has decided. Perhaps if you have a friend at the zoo or museum a few snakeskins scattered about the yard might tempt our belligerent friend more strongly than anything else, to stay with you.

A guest frequently visiting the garden, but more often heard than seen, is the little screech owl. Its name, if intended to represent its call, is certainly misleading, for its quavering whistle coming softly and plain- tively through the dusk is far from a screech. Perhaps it freezes the blood of field mice, but to our ears it is certainly musical.

This little owl, if he is sad at all, which is doubtful, mourns the loss of hollow trees and as he eats quantities of mice, so destructive in the garden, should be encouraged to nest near us. True, when his nestlings become too clamorously hungry, a few small birds may be brought to fill their empty maws. But so valuable is he in exterminating field mice, house mice, cut- worms, moths and beetles, and so amusing a tenant is he as he sits at dusk staring out of his home with his great yellow eyes or flying to its defense with snapping bill and a weird "who-who," that the pleasure of his pres- ence is worth the loss of a few less interesting birds, which often increase too rapidly. A house to attract him should have a floor eight by eight inches and walls twelve to fifteen inches high. The entrance hole should be twelve inches above the floor and at least three inches in diameter. Nail the box firmly, no lower than ten feet above the ground. A greater height, even up to thirty feet, is better but prevents you as landlord or landlady, having as good an insight into this little nocturnal hunter's domestic life. Although seldom seen in the daytime this little owl (a little larger than a robin) works constantly while the other birds sleep.

BIRDS IN THE GARDEN

E. H. Forbush, author of *Birds of Massachusetts,* tells of his observation of a pair of screech owls near his cottage. Their nesting box was near an orchard and that year the field mice did no damage to the trees. The next year the box fell to the ground and the birds disappeared; that winter the field mice girdled nearly every tree. Immediately a number of boxes were erected; they were occupied and there was no more trouble from the mice.

Sometimes, in winter, your little screech owls will disappear, but they have not migrated. Unless they have had the sad fate of becoming the food of some larger owl, March will find them again, looking for the old box. They have only been widening their hunting territory, as many birds do that are not truly migratory; they are only driven beyond their usual range by lack of food.

The little saw-whet owl, often known as the Acadian owl, is the tiniest owl to be seen in the East. Much more than the screech owl is it a bird of the woods, where we may perhaps hear its "saw filing," but seldom see it, for all day it stays hidden, dull and sleepy. It is not much larger than a towhee, but is a mighty hunter of the everpresent field mouse and also of insects.

This "little elf of the forest" usually nests in an abandoned flicker hole, or in a natural cavity in a dead tree or stump, but has been known to accept a nesting box. The floor should be six by six inches, the depth of the cavity ten to twelve inches, the entrance hole should be two and one-half inches in diameter and placed eight to ten inches above the floor. The box should be set twelve to twenty feet above the ground in the woods, preferably near swampy ground.

The barn owl, true to his name, will nest in homes of man's handicraft. He has been known to nest in towers, cupolas and steeples and even in banks as well as in deserted buildings or barns. That is, he has been known to nest in such places, but he is seldom allowed to linger long near man's habitation because of the web of lies and superstition with which both hawks and owls are enveloped.

98

Merely because they fly on noiseless wing at night and their cry (to them doubtless most tuneful and beguiling) seems to us uncanny and melancholy, for ages owls have been associated with warnings of death and disaster. But trace the records as we may we can find nothing but good to be said of the barn owl. His food consists almost entirely of mice and rats and what a quantity of these he requires. An English observer tells of seeing a half-grown barn owl swallow nine mice, one after the other, the tail of the last one hanging out of the glutton's mouth. From this meal he estimates that a family of seven young owls would require in twenty-four hours at least one hundred and fifty rats, mice and other small animals to give them the proper amount of calories.

The barn owl is about the size of a crow. It has light colored feathers and a curious, almost heart-shaped face. For a nesting site it will sometimes accept a box of the simplest construction. The box should have at least ten by eighteen inches of floor space, have a height of from fifteen to eighteen inches, an entrance six inches in diameter, set four inches above the floor. This box should be nailed twelve to eighteen feet high in some secluded spot or on some unused out-building.

For many years a pair of barn owls nested in one of the towers of the Smithsonian Institution at Washington, D. C. This was certainly far from their usual woodland habitat, in fact, in the center of an extensive park system. Roger Peterson says that at the Rainey Wild Life Sanctuary, in Louisiana, the barn owl had never nested in that vicinity, until the Audubon Society warden in charge put up several boxes. Then as many as three pairs of barn owls raised their young there in one season.

And then a house for the sparrow hawk! What a triumph it would be over those who, "because their father shot them," kill any and every hawk on sight, to have these beautiful little falcons nesting peacefully in your yard, never disturbing the other bird residents. This is quite possible, for unless pressed by hunger the sparrow hawk's chief food is grasshoppers, mice and small reptiles.

BIRDS IN THE GARDEN

Although James Fisher in *Birds as Animals* says birds are not very intelligent, this little sparrow hawk seems to evince by its adaptability no small measure of intelligence, and also to show its cleverness in taking advantage of unusual circumstances.

Naturally birds of the open woodland, sparrow hawks have accepted the limitations brought about by man and will now nest in the orchard, the village street or even in the city. They have followed the flickers' trail along the telegraph poles clear out on the prairie and nest in the abandoned hole of that indefatigable anteater.

E. H. Forbush tells of a pair nesting most appropriately near the Boston Society of Natural History, and another near the State House on Beacon Hill, while other records of urban homes are becoming quite common. That much for adaptability—now for intelligence.

In the West, when a forest fire is raging, sparrow hawks repeatedly take advantage of the flight of small mammals before the fire, and dash down, almost into the line of advancing flames, to secure their prey. Mr. Forbush tells that a female sparrow hawk, when its young fell to the ground, flew down and caught the helpless nestling in her talons and carried it to the roof, some fifty feet in the air.

The house for this, the smallest and most brightly colored of our hawks, should have a floor measuring eight by eight inches, walls twelve to fifteen inches high, an entrance hole three inches in diameter set nine to twelve inches above the floor. The box should be placed ten to thirty feet above the ground in some rather sheltered, but not too shady, situation.

Then when in spring you hear the gay "killy-killy-killy-killy," you may have, as a friend of mine did, the pleasure of entertaining these lovely little birds, closely allied to the falcons of Europe, which, because of their bravery and skill, were trained by the nobility of the Old World, to attack and kill birds much larger than they are and then return to their masters' wrists.

Is the song sparrow everyone's favorite bird? Almost every ornithologist confesses a preference for this incurable little optimist, who will sing at all times of year and even in the pouring rain. "A little brown bird," inconspicuous, if he weren't so curious that he is always present with his ready questioning chirp. He is striped on back and head and underneath dull gray, shading to white with a black splotch on his breast. In the East and West, North and South, we find the song sparrow, the first to welcome, or often foretell, spring, and one of the first to welcome the day in the morning chorus.

Usually the song sparrow nests on the ground, or in a low bush, but after he has become tame from a winter's acquaintance, he has occasionally been known to nest on a shelf set at a suitable height. This shelf should be open on all sides and should measure six by six inches and be nailed in an inconspicuous place, one to three feet above the ground. A nesting site near the birdbath will be most acceptable, for song sparrows are inveterate bathers. Before the coming of man they probably nested chiefly near streams and swamps, and now where there is a stream or shallow water they splash in it blithely, sometimes adding a hapless minnow to their menu. The song sparrow's food consists mainly of weed seeds. But of course while he and his mate are feeding their young they carry to them quantities of cutworms, canker and army worms, gypsy-moth caterpillars, many cabbage worms, and also weevils, locusts, grasshoppers and crickets.

Cats are serious enemies of song sparrows, for the young are out of the nest and in the grass and near-by bushes for several days before they can fly. Often you may hear the alarm notes which, to ears attuned to the birds, is absolutely unmistakable, and on rushing out to the rescue see a cat disappearing through the shrubbery; whether with or without a baby song sparrow, rests upon whether you heeded the call for help promptly or not.

This best loved of our sparrows often becomes quite friendly, even coming into the house to pick up crumbs under the table. Although he doesn't seek a quarrel, he has quite a sense of property rights, will linger long in the birdbath, drive English sparrows away from the food tray and defend his nest from catbirds or other busybodies.

His optimism is unbounded. W. L. Dawson tells how a song sparrow cheered him one time on a photographic trip in Washington by perching in the pouring rain on a twig just outside his tent and singing with great emphasis on the last word, a phrase which to Dawson's ears sounded: "Cheer, cheer, cheer, count your mercies *now!*"

"Phoebe, phoebe"—"a wee, sad-colored thing," slips up from the South, long before there seems to be enough insects to make it worth while. For the phoebe, calling and listening as he sits on the telephone wire wagging his tail is a true flycatcher, and must be hard put many a spring for insect fare, for March is a cold and treacherous month, with few days warm enough to set the gnats a-jigging in their endless dance.

Phoebe loves water so we often find rows of nests which have been used one year after another on the stringers of an old bridge. Here the little gray bird snaps up the midges that fly over the water and the mosquitoes which breed in the stagnant pools. It is handy to have a larder so near and also "a bathing place to dash through with wings wide spread."

But phoebe has learned too, that there are many insects near our houses, so the barn, the porch, the garage, or any place where there are projecting eaves and a platform may receive the bulky, and unfortunately, untidy-looking nest. And unfortunately, too, the phoebes are not the good housekeepers that the wrens are. The nests and the nestlings are often literally alive with mites. But these mites will not live on the human skin; our bodily heat is not great enough to keep them alive, and so, instead of knocking down the nest, as so many do, sift some insect powder in it, and keep with you these indefatigable workers.

Here, so near you, the phoebe will become a part of the home picture, a little gray flitting shadow to be looked for at the same nesting site year after year. We can encourage them to nest where their activities may be

BARN SWALLOW   CLIFF SWALLOW

MALE   ADULT

FEMALE   JUVENAL PLUMAGE

PURPLE MARTIN

FEMALE   MALE

Scale about one-half

observed, but not cause inconvenience because of the litter, by putting a little nesting-box under the front or back porch eaves. The platform should be six by six inches, the height of the back and sides six inches, there should be a sloping roof with a slight overlap beyond the platform, while the front should be left entirely open. (See page 108, plate IV, figure 8.)

The phoebe's voice is not melodious but has the feeling of home in it. Witter Bynner says of it:

> And when you bring your brood its fill
> Of iridescent wings
> And green legs dewy in your bill
> Your silence is what sings.

And during that busy, silent time when those wide-mouthed nestlings continually demand food we can know that the garden is being diligently searched for houseflies, codling-, gypsy- and brown-tail moths, elm-leaf and cucumber beetles, besides ants, grasshoppers and many other pests feeding on our trees and shrubbery.

As a rule the phoebe, unlike its cousin, the kingbird, lives peacefully with other small birds. It has been known to kill house wrens, but doubtless this was because it felt its territorial rights were invaded. The wrens' box was probably put up too near to where the phoebes had been accustomed to nesting year after year. The remedy would be, when phoebes seem inclined to resent the presence of wrens to move the wrens' box promptly to another convenient place beyond the territory claimed by the phoebes for their own. If they no longer attack the wren after the box is in the new place you will know it is well beyond their invisible but important territorial limits. Dr. Frank Chapman tells a most amusing story of how he was able to define the territorial limits of a cardinal. He set up a mirror where the cardinal habitually came to feed, and the bird fought his image. Day by day Dr. Chapman moved the mirror 25 feet at a time, and at 109 feet beyond his song perch the cardinal no longer attacked his supposed rival.

Slightly larger than the house wren, the Carolina wren may be known by its curved bill, its reddish-brown coloration and the white stripe over the eye. Like the mockingbird, the Carolina wren is not migratory and unless the winter is bitterly cold and no food is set out for this little pioneer, you will have him with you all winter if he has nested in one of your birdboxes in the spring. This box should be of the same dimensions as that of the house wren, except that the entrance hole should be one and one-eighth inches instead of seven-eighths of an inch in diameter.

Originally a bird of the woods and thickets, he has after much trepidation accepted man's presence and has made known his willingness to share his home. E. H. Forbush tells of one pair that put their nest in a basket containing sticks of dynamite! As restless and energetic as the house wren, he sings every month of the year, a loud, clear, ringing song, often mounting on a bush in the middle of winter and reminding his mate, who remains with him all year, that eventually spring will be here, by singing in his emphatic way, "Sweetheart, sweetheart, sweetheart, *sweet*."

The Carolina wren is a valuable and vivacious guest to have in the garden. His food, according to the Biological Survey, is nearly all insects, but he has been known to eat lizards, tree frogs and small snakes. In the South he destroys the cotton-boll weevil, and helps rid our gardens of caterpillars, moths, cucumber, bean leaf and flea beetles, and also of grasshoppers, crickets, cockroaches and their eggs, flies, spiders and millipeds.

The Carolina wren, though often hiding deep in the shrubbery, can be lured by his curiosity to come quite close to an observer. By making a sucking or kissing sound with your lips on your hand his attention will be attracted. In *Birds of Ohio*, W. L. Dawson says: "Bustling and tittering and talking excitedly to himself he hurries up. At first sight of the stranger he jumps as if shot, but he has the presence of mind to dodge behind a log and take chattering counsel of his fears. Then, more cautiously, he emerges—now scampering along a log with tail in air like a chipmunk, now squatting in sudden alarm, and craning and bubbling apprehensively, the little feathered ferret turns up first on this side of you, then on that, until his curiosity is thoroughly satisfied."

Occasionally nesting in central Pennsylvania as well as in southern Michigan and northern Illinois, is Bewick's wren. Smaller than the house wren, but having a long white-tipped tail, it may be known from the house wren by its white eyebrow line. It will accept a nesting box or really demand one, or often take a curious substitute, if the box is not forthcoming. The box should be of exactly the some dimensions as that of the house wren. (See p. 109.) The Western form of this bird is called the Seattle wren, because the type form was first found near Seattle. In Washington it is much commoner than the house wren and takes the place of that midget, omnipresent in the gardens of the East. Sometimes, he preempts the mailbox for his nest; again, he has been known to nest in the pocket of an old hunting coat or in a corner of a toolbox. In hope that this sprite, this always tuneful garden companion, may appear, put up a suitable box early, for like the other members of his family, the Bewick's wren in the East or the Seattle wren in the West, is of great value in the garden, an untiring foe of all those myriads of insects that unchecked would despoil our flowers and shrubbery of their beauty.

The following principles of nest-box construction are quoted from Farmers' Bulletin No. 1456, *Homes for Birds* by E. R. Kalmbach and W. L. McAtee, of the Bureau of Biological Survey:

Materials

For the person wishing to construct his own bird houses, wood is by all means the best building material. Metal should be avoided because it is a great conductor of heat. Pottery nest boxes have some points in their favor, but there are no facilities for their manufacture in the average home workshop. Nest boxes constructed of tar paper or similar products have no particular advantage over the wooden ones, and the use of these materials is impracticable for some of the larger houses. In the choice of wood, an easily workable kind, as cypress, pine or yellow poplar, is preferable; the first-named is the most durable. Sawmill waste (rough slabs with bark on) furnishes cheap and satisfactory material for rustic houses.

Paint

Where a rustic finish is not sought, paint is unobjectionable and greatly enhances the weathering qualities of bird houses. Modest tones, as brown, gray or dull green, are generally to be preferred. Martin houses and others that are placed in exposed situations, however, may be painted white to reflect heat.

Protection from Rain

Roofs should be made with a sufficient pitch to shed water readily; or, if level, or nearly so, they should have a groove cut across the under face of the overhanging part (Fig. 1, A) to prevent water from draining back into the interior. This overhang in the average house should be from 2 to 3 inches, so as to protect the entrance hole from driving rain. The opening of the nest cavity itself may be bored at an upward slant to aid in keeping out water. A strip of metal or roofing paper often helps to make the ridge of the nest box thoroughly waterproof; flat roofs should either be wholly covered with some such material or else heavily painted. In latitudes where freezing weather is the rule in winter, bird houses will last longer if the sides are prolonged beyond the bottom of the box, thus draining off water which otherwise might freeze in the crack between bottom and sides and wedge them apart. To provide for the contingency that some water may get inside the box, a few small holes may be made in the bottom.

Protection from Heat

If attention be paid to the principle of cool construction, death of nestlings during periods of excessive heat may be lessened. Wood is in itself a fairly good heat insulator; but it must be remembered that the interior of the average nest box is small, and a single opening near the top permits little ventilation. One or two small auger holes through the walls near the top of the box will give a limited circulation of air without producing drafts. A double roof or a compartment above the nest proper will also serve as an excellent insulator. In the colony houses built for martins this feature can be easily included, and the added comfort and safety afforded the nestlings will more than repay for the extra work. In martin houses, however, owing to the low position of the entrance hole and the possibility of producing objectionable drafts, ventilating holes in the compartments themselves should be confined to a single one of small size near the top or left out entirely.

Accessibility

All bird houses should be placed so as to be readily accessible and built so as to be easily opened and cleaned. To those interested in studying the life history of the nestlings a readily opened box is a great aid. A number of arrangements may be used to permit inspection of the nest, several of which as applied to simple houses are illustrated in Figure 1. A pane of glass sliding in a groove just beneath the removable side will allow observations without subjecting the birds to exposure or causing a disturbance of the nest material. Other reasons that demand accessibility to the interior of bird houses are mentioned in the section on sanitation, pages 18-19. (In Farmers' Bulletin 1456.)

Entrances

Entrance holes for bird houses in most cases are placed near the top of the box, and if the inner side of the lumber used is dressed it should be roughened, grooved, or cleated to assist the young in climbing to the opening. Houses longer than high are comfortable and convenient, and seem to be liked by some species, particularly woodpeckers or birds that are partial to old woodpecker holes. Perches at the entrances seem more of an assistance to enemies than a requirement for the occupants.

Dimensions and Elevation

The simplicity of construction of the single-room bird house does away with the necessity of detailed working drawings in most cases. Table 1 gives the proper dimensions for the various species and the height at which the boxes should be placed above the ground.

Principles of Location of Bird Houses

E. H. Forbush, formerly State ornithologist of Massachusetts, concluded from a statistical study of the subject that failure to attract feathered tenants may be attributed mainly to the following faults: (1) Entrance holes too small for the birds desired; (2) boxes put up in dense woods; (3) boxes placed in trees, and therefore accessible to birds' enemies, instead of on posts or poles; and (4) care not taken to protect birds nesting in boxes from their enemies. Three of these

107

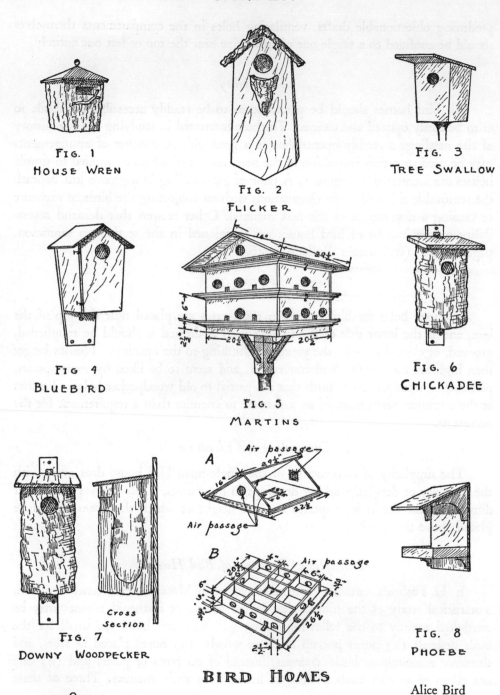

FIG. 1
HOUSE WREN

FIG. 2
FLICKER

FIG. 3
TREE SWALLOW

FIG. 4
BLUEBIRD

FIG. 5
MARTINS

FIG. 6
CHICKADEE

FIG. 7
DOWNY WOODPECKER

Cross
Section

Air passage
Air passage

Air passage

FIG. 8
PHOEBE

BIRD HOMES

Alice Bird

Table 1.—Dimensions of nesting boxes for various species of regular box-inhabiting birds and the height at which they should be placed above the ground

Species	Floor of cavity	Depth of cavity	Entrance above floor	Diameter of entrance	Height above ground
	Inches	*Inches*	*Inches*	*Inches*	*Feet*
Bluebirds	5 × 5	8	6	1 ½	5–10
Robin	6 × 8	8	(¹)	(¹)	6–15
Chickadees	4 × 4	8–10	6– 8	1 ⅛	6–15
Titmice	4 × 4	8–10	6– 8	1 ¼	6–15
Nuthatches	4 × 4	8–10	6– 8	1 ¼	12–20
House wren	4 × 4	6– 8	1– 6	1	6–10
Bewick's wren	4 × 4	6– 8	1– 6	1	6–10
Carolina wren	4 × 4	6– 8	1– 6	1 ⅛	6–10
Violet-green swallow	5 × 5	6	1– 5	1 ½	10–15
Tree swallow	5 × 5	6	1– 5	1 ½	10–15
Barn swallow	6 × 6	6	(¹)	(¹)	8–12
Purple martin	6 × 6	6	1	2 ½	15–20
Song sparrow	6 × 6	6	(²)	(²)	1– 3
House finch	6 × 6	6	4	2	8–12
Starling	6 × 6	16–18	14–16	2	10–25
Phoebe	6 × 6	6	(¹)	(¹)	8–12
Crested flycatcher	6 × 6	8–10	6– 8	2	8–20
Flicker	7 × 7	16–18	14–16	2 ½	6–20
Golden-fronted woodpecker	6 × 6	12–15	9–12	2	12–20
Red-headed woodpecker	6 × 6	12–15	9–12	2	12–20
Downy woodpecker	4 × 4	8–10	6– 8	1 ¼	6–20
Hairy woodpecker	6 × 6	12–15	9–12	1 ½	12–20
Screech owl	8 × 8	12–15	9–12	3	10–30
Saw-whet owl	6 × 6	10–12	8–10	2 ½	12–20
Barn owl	10 × 18	15–18	4	6	12–18
Sparrow hawk	8 × 8	12–15	9–12	3	10–30
Wood duck	10 × 18	10–15	3	6	4–20

¹One or more sides open.   ²All sides open.

faults concern location—the second and third obviously, and the fourth indirectly, for it is manifestly easier to protect a bird house and its occupants if readily reached. "Easily accessible" means not beyond the reach of an available ladder; houses placed higher inevitably will be neglected. Houses on poles seem more acceptable than others to various birds, and this probably is because they impress the birds as being safer. Isolated trees can actually be made safe with tree guards, but perhaps they do not look so to the birds. Premises fenced against vermin probably will give such security that other precautions against enemies can be dispensed with.

To sum up, it would seem that houses should be fairly low, should not be put in dense woods, and seem more acceptable on poles than in trees. If possible, they should be placed with the opening away from prevailing winds.

It is not well to have a large number of boxes on a limited area especially those designed to attract the same species. Birds insist on territorial rights, especially in competition with other individuals of the same species, and if houses are too close together conflicts between prospective tenants may result in none being occupied. The purple martin is our only gregarious nesting species that breeds in bird houses, and houses for colonies of these birds should be on poles well separated from trees or buildings. Tree swallows, however, are sociable and several individual boxes for them may be near together.

BROWN THRASHER   TOWNSEND'S SOLITAIRE

CATBIRD   MOCKINGBIRD

Scale about one-half

Chapter Eight

WATER IN THE GARDEN

THE birds are our guests in the garden. We should see that they have not only food and nesting sites, but also something to drink and somewhere to bathe. These are most essential parts of our hospitality. Fortunately, though we have given great thought to food and have provided an elaborate menu, we need not compile a wine list. We need never serve any drink except Adam's ale, but from a selfish standpoint alone it will pay us to provide water, for birds often pick at and ruin cherries and berries, not so much because they are hungry, but because they need the water which the fruit contains.

Water is the only beverage needed, but in drinking or bathing devices, so great is the diversity of form allowable, from a simple clay saucer to an elaborate pool or fountain, that we may let our imaginations run riot.

Lucky is the bird lover who has a natural stream or a spring on his grounds. Birds seem to love the sound of running or dripping water, or perhaps they know they will find more food in the lower spots where water is usually found. Some of the great migration routes follow the courses of rivers and often migrating birds will congregate along the banks of a shallow lake or follow a little stream for miles. They are cleanly creatures, too, and during hot weather will fly for some distance to refresh themselves in a favorite bathing spot.

The song sparrow, one of the most welcome of our guests, is particularly fond of his bath. Often, in an early morning stroll through the vegetable garden, you will see one taking a dainty dip in the rain collected in the outer leaves of a head of cabbage or flirting onto his feathers the sparkling dew collected on the lettuce. And frequently, at dusk, when all birds excepting nighthawks and owls are safely at roost, you will see a song sparrow crouched in the bird bath, reluctant to leave his shower. The daintiest bath of all, perhaps, is taken by some of the warblers who bathe by shaking onto their plumage the shining drops of dew or rain edging blades of grass or leaves of trees.

An excellent natural bathing place is a boulder with a slight depression in it. Sometimes one may be found in the woods and, if it is in a sheltered but not too shady spot, you will find the birds flocking to it. If you want a boulder bath near the house you may find that one is available in a near-by field. If it is on land beyond your own, the farmer will nearly always be glad to dispose of it, and will help you move it and set it on the edge of the shrubbery. If there is not enough of a depression in it, a stone-cutter can easily deepen it. The hollow should never have a greater depth than two and one-half inches, sloping to that depth from one-half inch at the edge; it should be left rough and small pebbles and sand may be scattered over the bottom in order to give the birds a foothold.

So far as possible a bath of this type should have a natural setting. But always remember the prowling cat if it has not been eliminated from the garden or sanctuary. Birds with water-soaked feathers are almost helpless, so shrubbery in which a cat can hide should not be too near, nor should it be too far away for the bird to reach easily.

In a protected place an earthenware saucer sunk in the ground, and kept constantly filled with water, will often draw many birds. Or hollows may be scooped out of the lawn and lined with cement. A pool of this type without any outlet is exceedingly easy to make. Dig out a hole about four by three feet in size and four to five inches deep in the center. Then place in a box or tub one part of cement to four of sand, adding enough water to make the mixture like mortar. Plaster this mixture with the hand, a trowel or large spoon all over the surface of the hollow in the earth. Put in enough cement so that the depression will be only two and a half inches deep in the middle, and slope it gradually to the sides. Leave the surface rough and while it is still moist set in a few small stones and place a few irregular mossy boulders around the edge. This pool will hold about two pails of water; in order to keep it fresh you should sweep out the water with a broom and renew it daily.

If one is fortunate enough to have a spring, a basin of the type described can be sunk just below it in order to catch the seepage. Roger Peterson in *Song Bird Sanctuaries* says that a birdbath like this at Camp Chewonki, on the Maine coast, attracted not only the birds of the woods but also those of the open country. Red-breasted nuthatches, hermit thrushes, warblers, goldfinches and field sparrows, all came to share the refreshment.

If a more elaborate pool is wanted, the excavation may be made larger and a tub containing water lilies or other aquatic plants set in as a centerpiece. Then the hollow may be cemented from the tub to the edge of the excavation, making depressions in which the birds may bathe. The depressions may be separated from each other by small mossy stones, and the edge finished with similar stones set in an irregular manner.

A cement bath invented by the bird lover, Ernest Harold Baynes, is made on the principle of broad steps, two feet long and seven inches wide. There are five of these steps, each one-half inch lower than the last, and water flows over them from the top, from a spring or from a concealed pipe. By this arrangement the water is half an inch deep on the top step and two and a half inches deep on the bottom one. In a bath of this kind the birds invariably enter the water at the top step, showing their preference for shallow water. As they overcome their first timidity they descend to the second and third steps, the latter, two inches deep, being their favorite. They seldom use the one with the fearsome depth of two and one-half inches. In all these baths the birds seem to enjoy a layer of sand and pebbles at the bottom because of the footing it affords.

If cats are prevalent, or if a more formal type of bird bath is wanted, a shallow basin on a pedestal may be used. And here the diversity of forms and shapes to be obtained, either by your own ingenuity or by purchase, is very intriguing. If you desire to make a bath of this kind at home, it is really a very simple thing to do. Decide on your size and make a rough box for a form. Then use four parts of sand to one part of cement, adding water until it is soft. Then fill the form and while the mixture is still soft force into it a shallow basin. For a pedestal, set a piece of tapered stovepipe upright in a small box, wiring it in place. This pipe should be of the height you desire the bath to stand. Put an iron bar or waterpipe in the middle to give strength and pour the cement into the pipe. When the cement has had time to set, the basin and the box can be removed from the bowl and the stovepipe taken from the pedestal. Now your birdbath can be put together.

There are many birdbaths of the pedestal type on the market. Those of high-fired terra cotta, marble or cast stone come in many attractive forms. Circular basins set in a series one above the other with a constant drip from the source of water in the uppermost to the lower ones are always a favorite with the birds. The larger birds bathe in the deeper basin below, while smaller birds enjoy the shallower ones above.

If you are on friendly terms at the near-by Museum of Natural History you may be able to secure a shell of the Giant Clam. Sometimes shells of this species weigh a hundred pounds and are used by the natives of the South Sea Islands as bathtubs for their babies. They are very smooth inside and should always have a layer of sand or gravel on the bottom. They can be used on the ground or mounted on a low pedestal.

It is a double lure for the birds if a feeding table is placed near the bath. Summer and winter a supply of crumbs, seeds and fruit should be placed on it. How pleasant for a water-soaked bird to know that breakfast is ready the moment his last feather is preened!

Many charming stories are told of birds and their love of bathing. The little hummingbird adores to flit through the fine spray of the hose, coming regularly all summer when the garden receives its evening shower. In the Far West, where the birds are more fearless than in the East, not only the hummingbird but the chestnut-backed chickadee, and Townsend's and black-throated gray warblers will come to bathe in the fine spray of the hose when it is directed toward the trees.

Shoffner in *The Birds' Book* says: "The most comical thing I think I have ever seen in bird life happened when a wandering party of crow black-birds discovered the pool in my garden one day in early fall. For fully ten minutes pandemonium held sway. Every 'mother's son' of them tried to bathe at the same time."

An amusing riot of this type often occurs when a bunch of young robins all try to get in a small bath at the same moment with perhaps tanagers and song sparrows anxiously waiting. How many times one stout husky robin will triumph and sit soaking, hunched up in the middle of of the bath, snapping viciously at any other applicant who may come near. Baby robins sometimes have to be taught to bathe, as is shown by the story told by Olive Thorne Miller in *The Bird Our Brother*. She says that one morning a mother robin tried to get her young one to go into the water. The youngster refused, seeming to be afraid. At last, after much coaxing, the mother flew away, and returned bearing in her beak a tempting earthworm. At once the infant began to beg and clamor for the morsel, but the mother alighted in the middle of the water dish, and, holding the worm in plain sight, stayed there until the unwilling youngster plunged in after it. Once in, he appeared to enjoy the wetting he received.

The catbird, like the song sparrow, loves the bath and will bathe in showery weather, though when the water begins to get icy he shies off. But not the song sparrow. If there is any water available he has his dip all winter long, as does that hardy Northerner, the evening grosbeak, which when it is far below zero will seek out a spot where there is an everflowing spring and spruce up his uniform of black and white and gold.

The birds of the flycatcher family often bathe a-wing, just as the swallows do. The kingbird dashes through the water and the phoebe often bathes and feeds at the same time. Mrs. Florence Merriam Bailey in her delightful *Birds of Village and Field* tells the following story of the least flycatcher or chebec: "The chebec was the pet of a lady who had many birds nesting in her shrubbery border. Almost every day through the summer when she would go out to water her garden in the evening the chebec would come flying in for a shower bath. He would sit on the fence saying 'chebec, chebec,' while she would spray him gently, then fly into the bushes and preen himself beautifully."

Miss Rhinelander of Sharon, Connecticut, tells how a goldfinch which she had raised from a nestling delighted in bathing in a bowl of water held in her hand. He first fluttered into it as she was taking it to him to drink. After that whenever she would say: "Now take a bath," he would fly to the edge, step in and bathe unconcernedly, not only when Miss Rhinelander was alone but quite calmly in front of unfamiliar spectators.

There is a world of pleasure in providing these drinking and bathing places for the birds. In summer the birds appreciate them highly and in winter often need them badly. In very cold weather a heated brick placed under a pan will keep the water from freezing for some time. What is much better is to install a small electrical heating-device in the bottom of the basin so the water can never freeze and there will be a constant flow. What better memorial could be erected for a bird lover than such a perpetually flowing fountain, cooling the thronging birds in summer and providing a source of life and hope in winter?

Chapter Nine

BIRD SONG

I lay suspended in a swaying net
Close-woven of the songs of birds;
The warp, the light yellow green
Of the vireo's constant, broken chant,
The woof, the robin's deep crimson note
Of harmonizing cheer,
Broken by the abrupt brown
Of the pheasant's staccato crow,
Accented by the harsh orange of the strident jay,
And a distant crow's discordant ebon call;
All interwoven with the tender rosy tones
Of song sparrows, far and near,
And brightened by the bubbling amber
Of the incessant wren.
—*Margaret McKenny.*

IN JUNE or July, either to lie in bed held in the magic net of song or, before the sun rises, to walk in the dusky woods or on the dew-wet prairies, is to hear an ecstatic, spontaneous expression of the joy of life comparable to no other earthly experience.

Few know of the rhapsodic outpouring of the dawn chorus. Many of us rise early to hear the birds' morning songs. But not early enough. By five or six o'clock on a June or July day, the chorus has died down and the birds have taken up the necessary duties of breakfast hunting, flitting restlessly from twig to twig or industriously scratching among the dry leaves on the ground. No, you must be out before there is a ray of light, by a little after two. It is still dark—not a peep from the dim shrubbery, except perhaps a soft quavery call from a little screech owl as it floats swiftly past on muffled wings. If you are on the prairie you will hear a faint "spe-e-e-d" and know that far overhead the nighthawks are coursing invisibly their tireless race through the air. But if you are in the garden or in bed drinking in the perfume of the lilac as it floats in the window, the first notes you will hear will be those of the tree swallows lisping their sharp sweet tones, more loudly and much more continuously than they do in the daytime. Then as the sky turns paler and the dawn wind breathes through the trees, a robin will wake and start his energetic "cheer, cheer, cheer," without a pause for breath between his notes. This is the signal for hundreds of other robins. You will feel that there cannot be so many robins in the world, for the air literally vibrates with their melody, which beats in waves on your eardrums. No bird can sleep now, and sparrows and wrens will weave their happy bubbling notes through the chorus and as the sun actually rises the tender, joyous song of the rose-breasted gros-beak will mingle with and then ascend above the diminishing chant of the robins.

By this time the garden, now revealed to you as if new-made, is seen sparkling in dew. The great white lilies stand breathing out their perfume, while bluer than the June sky the delphiniums tower above them; the fox-gloves, like magic wands, sway in the morning breeze, and hummingbirds flit from flower to flower.

Much has been written about why birds sing. There is, to put it as simply as possible, a distinction between bird calls, the regular song and the mating song. Bird calls are quite different from their songs and the young bird seems to have an inherited ability to interpret those notes which express alarm or warning. Then there is the bird's song itself, which by some scientists is considered merely an expression of animal exuberance, of surplus energy, an overflowing vital energy taking this form of muscular expression, just as babies smile and coo and lambs skip and baa because of physical well-being. The most extreme view of this is held by H. Eliot

Howard, who in *Territory in Bird Life* says: "Birds do not have ideas. The stimulus for song is an event, arriving somewhere, picking something up, being on a singing post, a change of wind, a noise." This interpretation shows how closely the intuitive conception of a poet may parallel the logical conclusion of a scientist, for long ago Lowell said of a bird that he "lets his illumined being o'errun with the deluge of summer it receives." That is, it sings, intoxicated by the pleasure of singing. This is just another way of coming to the scientist's conclusion that the bird sings because of superabundance of vital force.

This first type of song then has a three-fold purpose. First, an expression of physical well-being, a bubbling over of bodily energy. This would explain the songs of a well-fed, well-cared-for canary bird. Second, an explanation that generally receives credence today, is that the male, when he arrives in the spring, sings not only from well-being but in order to preempt territory for himself and his future family. He stakes out a claim, sets himself up in a certain tree or branch, and sings lustily as a determined announcement that all other birds of his kind must keep away from his territory. As Burroughs says, "the song is a sort of battleflag of the males, and when they unfurl it, if it is not a challenge, it certainly indicates that they have the 'fighting edge.' It is a notice to other males that this grove, or 'this corner of the field, is *my* territory, and I will tolerate no trespassing.' " Then, as the homesite becomes an established fact, the singing continues to attract the female, who usually arrives later than the male. Many of us have observed the intense activity of the male wren, working like mad to get ready, not one, but several possible homes, all the time casting his net of song skyward to snare a migrating mate that might heedlessly wing farther north. And third, this singing is intended not only to attract the mate and to charm her to choose him above all rivals, but also later to act as a stimulation to the young.

The third phase of singing runs imperceptibly into the mating song, that exquisite expression often given as a "whisper" song with half-closed beak, and seldom heard or known except to the close observer. This song often varies greatly from the everyday outflow of notes. For instance, we know well the ordinary optimistic lay of the song sparrow, who generally mounts to the top of some low willow or conspicuous brush heap and sings his characteristic notes, recognizable in all parts of the country. Then one day as we are walking along the edge of the woods we will be arrested by a song, so tender, so varied, so prolonged, that we can hardly believe it when we see, hidden in the midst of a bush, a song sparrow, visibly palpitating as he pours forth this series of notes differing entirely from his everyday song.

Other birds also, notably the mockingbird, catbird and purple finch, have "whisper" songs, which are most ecstatic expressions of joy in life or love, whichever you choose. Aretas Saunders says: "Is it not possible that both the beauty of songs and the ear to appreciate that beauty developed not from biological necessity but purely for the sake of the beauty itself?" The song sparrow seems to sing for the joy of singing, for certainly in the West he sings all winter long, not confining his silver lay to the breeding season. He thus seems to upset the theories of some scientists who hold that, as song is usually the attribute of the male, it is the result, as his brighter feathers are, at mating time, of his "maleness" or the result of the secretion of certain hormones.

John Burroughs speaks of birds like the goldfinches singing in chorus. He says: "In spring they have their musical reunions—a sort of sängerfest which often continues for days." In the West the meadowlarks congregate in great flocks in the fall and seem to have regular singing schools, for it is very easy to detect the efforts of the immature to imitate the golden rippling rapture of the older experienced singers. Often, too, the California purple finches assemble in the early spring before territories have been selected and long before mating has taken place. They sing in chorus, a song quite different from the usual rippling warble, which is as one observer has said, "like rolling something sweet under your tongue." It is also quite distinct from the prolonged canary-like "whisper" song, which is sometimes given from high aloft on an evergreen. From early spring the red-winged blackbirds join in a general liquid chorus. They evidently have community territorial rights, for they sing together quite amicably. Their songs suggest their cool retreats among the cat-tails on the shore of a little lake, their fluting echoing from shore to shore and their brilliant red and yellow epaulets glowing as they swing from reed to reed.

Usually the song expression is confined to the male birds. But, in a few species of birds both sexes sing. Both the male and female cardinal have their songs, often singing in answer to each other, but the male's song exceeds his mate's in beauty and strength. We have also the flight songs of such birds as the European skylark, celebrated by poets for hundreds of years, and in our own country that of the horned lark, the woodcock, the titlark and the black-headed grosbeak.

Another variation in song hard to explain beyond the love of song itself, is the fact that many birds sing at night. In May in the West, when all the garden is flooded with moonlight, when the cherry blossoms are so white that the boughs are laden as if with snow and the white rock cress sweeps like foam to the edge of the path, clear and sweet rings out at hourly intervals the song of Nuttall's white-crowned sparrow. The cat-bird sings his loveliest at night, while in the South the mockingbird seems to be intoxicated with the moonlight and sings hour on hour in the air heavy with the perfume of orange blossoms.

The observations of Anna Gilman Hill show how the morning chorus is affected by light. She has noticed that at her country place on the Hudson River the first notes of the robins always come faint but clear from the light area near the water. The music gradually spreads up through the trees until it reaches its culminating height in the garden beyond a grove of dark hemlocks. Mrs. Hill has also observed that on a dark and cloudy morning the chorus starts an hour or so later than the usual time.

We find, too, that rain affects some bird songs. A dawn chorus will quiet down and taper off suddenly if a shower falls at that time. Some birds sing more in sunny weather, though this cannot be said of the song sparrow that sings in the pouring rain. It is true that many birds join in a jubilant chorus after a storm, but it is also a fact that the robin also sings most emphatically just before a rain. We find, too, that some of our most gifted singers are the solitary birds, the hermit and wood thrush, the Townsend's solitaire, and the water ouzel of the rushing mountain torrents of the West.

Many bird songs can be imitated quite easily by human beings, often so successfully as to deceive the birds themselves, the chickadee having been known to change the pitch of his three notes into that of an imitation of a whistle. But the method of a bird's production of song is quite different from a human whistle. The apparatus which makes singing possible is the syrinx, which, located at the lower end of the windpipe, takes the place of the larynx of other animals. The shape of this syrinx, located deep down in his throat and combined with other vocal apparatus, varying in different species of birds, is of course inherited with other characteristics. But there is still much dispute as to whether the song is inherited or imitated. Many birds isolated from their kind never sing their own song; other observers have discovered that characteristic notes are given by birds even though they have never heard others of their own kind. The English sparrow, whose natural notes are through imitation a raucous chatter, when kept separate from its kind will imitate other birds and can learn to give the song of a canary with much more power and beauty than the bird it copies, due to the greater strength of its vocal cords.

Ornithologists who have made a study of bird language feel there is no doubt that birds do communicate ideas or give vent to their passing emotions in their notes and calls. These ornithologists claim it is easy in many cases to recognize such emotions and purposes as contentment, anger, alarm, surprise, scolding, coaxing, invitation to remain, etc. Certainly when we listen to some of the blue jays' and English sparrows' arguments, it seems easy to believe this. One observer of a caged English sparrow claims that it learned eleven different expressions, some directed to other sparrows and some to human beings. Others claim to have identified twenty-five different calls or notes in robins, each with a different meaning.

But to return to the birds in the garden, to those that will give us the pleasure of their glad notes and companionship as we watch them through the year. The best time to begin the study of their notes is in the winter. There will be only a few to learn, but with those well memorized it will be as if we were learning to recognize the individual instruments with their tonal qualities and peculiarities before we hear them combined in the full orchestra.

In the winter the brisk and cheerful chickadee will speak his name so clearly that even the purist who so intensely dislikes putting bird songs into words, has to agree that little else can be deciphered from that infectious greeting. In addition to the cheerful "chickadee-dee" we often hear the love song which seems to be used not only at mating time but as an expression of harmonious well-being. It is often spoken of as the "phoebe" call and usually consists of two or three tenderly sweet whistled notes, one high and one or two of a lower pitch. In the dead of winter the chickadee will respond to your imitation of this call, circling to your hand, ready to respond to the friendly overture of an outstretched lump of suet; and in the spring will come from afar, sometimes settling on your shoulder in answer to the irresistible lure of the notes of love.

Another winter bird is the blue jay, such a dandy in plumage and with such a harsh note; he, too, shouts his name "jay, jay," unmistakably. He has many notes, quite a vocabulary, which he certainly uses when he and his fellow rapscallions find a screech owl bewildered by daylight and gather in congress to cast vituperations on their indignant victim. Very little harm seems to come to the screech owl, unless he is partially deafened by the din. E. H. Forbush says the racket consists mostly of fuss and feathers—

bluff and bluster. The jay's winter notes consist not only of his called name, but of notes like a toy whistle and other strident ones, chattered as rapidly as a woodpecker's tattoo. He, too, will have a surprise for you after his instrument is tuned up for the spring chorus, though he will be very secretive about his attainments. When he is in love he has a most melodious warble or yodel, and besides this he is an accomplished mimic. P. L. Hatch says in his *Notes on the Birds of Minnesota:* "I heard such a mimicry of little birds as no language can describe . . . The notes fell in showers like dewdrops, almost inaudible, and were amongst the clearest, most delicate, sweet and melodious that ever found their way into a human ear."

Two other winter birds, the red-breasted and the white-breasted nuthatches, have distinct and rather unmusical nasal calls easily syllablized into "yank, yank." If white-breast consents to stay and nest in a box prepared for him, perhaps you may be observing enough to hear his seldom heard series of evenly pitched notes given only at mating time.

The junco will give you little but his rather wooden "tick" during the winter. Also an excited tittering note as a flock lights in a weed patch and eat together. As spring comes, before he leaves for his northern nesting place you may hear his tinkling trill, a series of the same tone, like the chipping sparrow's song but slower and less prolonged. He, too, has a soft sweet "whisper" song, seldom heard except near his nesting site.

If you are fortunate enough to have the song sparrow with you all winter, train yourself to know well his reedy chirp. It is very expressive and as you become accustomed to it you will know when it says "cat, cat," as well as if it were a shout in English. All winter in the West he sings daily, rain or shine; often in the East we hear a low and rather plaintive song on a mild day in January, and in March, while snow still lies in the northern fence rows the chorus of song rises. Even when the wind blows, silencing almost all other birds, the song sparrow will sing gaily from the shelter of the underbrush. Although there is a distinctive song sparrow intonation, which once learned will never be forgotten, the birds are great individualists in their singing. There is a distinctive quality of voice and rhythm to their song which Thoreau says is a reminder in Massachusetts to dilatory supper-makers: "Maids, maids, maids, hang up your teakettle—ettle—ettle." Really, the first three notes have a decided "cheer, cheer, cheer" quality, if we will condescend to put musical notes into letters. Aretas Saunders reports that each bird he has observed has seven or eight to twenty different songs in his repertoire and he has observed six hundred variations. In some sections the song sparrow is reported to start the morning chorus and during that concert to sing from six to eight times a minute.

Unless we are exceedingly fortunate in our situation, we shall have to distinguish the notes of our best-loved birds from the noisy gibberings of the English sparrow. As spring comes if we have sensitive ears we will be annoyed by his repeated "cheep," for his only way of expressing the urge of spring is by a more rapid repetition of that syllable in a harsh raucous tone.

Mingled with the din of the sparrows in many sections will be heard the notes of the starling. W. H. Hudson says these calls resemble clucking, squealing, sounds of snapping fingers or of kissing. Schuyler Mathews describes the notes as like the "twang of a Jew's-harp, the squeak of a rusty gate hinge, the cluck of a hen, and the rattle of a wire spring." It is true, though, that mingled with the medley are some eerily sweet whistles, very confusing to the student of bird songs.

By this time in the spring you will begin to hear such a multiplicity of notes, not only from your winter visitors but from spring migrants that you will need a comprehensive book on bird song—like Schuyler Mathews' *Field Book of Wild Birds and Their Music,* if your mind runs in terms of musical notations, or Aretas Saunders' *A Guide to Bird Song,* if you prefer diagrams. Keep a record and soon you will have notes of great value, for much is to be noted and observed especially about the "whisper" songs of some of our commonest birds. One thing you will soon discover. It will both help and hinder you if you are musically trained. It is true that birds sing roughly in accordance with our musical scale. But, like spoiled *prima donnas,* they don't worry about flatting or sharping frequently, oftentimes just enough to bewilder us sadly. And don't forget that individual birds in a species differ a good deal in their songs. In human songs, too, we insist that they begin and end somewhere, whereas a bird begins anywhere on the scale and ends anywhere. Also some of them, like the scarlet tanager and the yellow-throated vireo, sing double notes. When the wood thrush "turns three notes and makes a star," as Sara Teasdale puts it, it is very difficult for us to analyze that star. But if you find a bird's melodies some-times confusing especially when he gets very fast and florid, you will find that he nearly always is pretty much of a classicist in his tempo, and sticks to his 2/4 or 3/4 or 6/8, or whatever time he has set for himself, pretty carefully.

You will be surprised after your preliminary study of winter birds, how much more the songs of the old childhood favorites will mean to you. It is always a thrilling time when the first robin arrives; we know spring is here, or at least just around the corner. The robins are spring's advance guards; they are like the trumpeters who, by their flourishes from church towers or town squares in some Old World cities, announce that a music festival is about to begin.

The robin belongs to the thrush family and as we listen closely to his song, we can hear tones and undertones that show his kinship to those master singers, the hermit and wood thrushes. Parkhurst in his *Bird's Calendar,* says that "no other bird is able to give so many shades of mean-ing to a simple note, running through the entire gamut of its possible feelings." Nor is it only in the early spring that we find the robin so thrill-ing. Because of his great numbers in every part of the country, he gives volume and strength to the morning chorus, he heralds and welcomes rain if it is to come through the day, and softly and gently drops his rounded mellow notes at dusk. Individuals differ greatly in their song and again if you are fortunate and observing, you will hear the charming low notes rapidly repeated in a whisper with which he woos his mate. When said mate is won and safely incubating her eggs, he will, if at a safe distance from his nest, answer your imitations of these soft seductive notes.

Less positive and assertive than the robin, and less skilled as a singer, though in the refinement and melody of his tones showing his relationship to the thrush, the bluebird is heard even before the robin. His note is often lost in the morning chorus, but his lovely blue is always welcome. E. H. Forbush says there must be something wrong with the man who, hearing this brave and happy bird and seeing him fluttering and warbling, does not feel a responsive thrill. Both male and female sing, thus doubling in volume "their light load of song." In fall the notes are still lighter. Almost silently a hungry flock will strip your dogwood bush, then flit on southward, uttering a single plaintive note, a presage of winter.

As the migrants come through we hear the rather sad note, "a pensive whistle," of the white-throated sparrow. This is the song which in New England has given it the name of the Peabody bird, but which, according to the Canadians, is "Sweet Canada, Canada, Canada" as he crosses the border. His is a peculiarly rhythmical song, which unlike the song sparrow, he sings quite true to pitch. This song, lovely in intonation as it is, does not equal that given at his nesting site, where, as C. J. Maynard says, "the ledges of the mountain tops gleam in the brilliant moonlight, and the silvery beams are finding their way through the openings in the shadowy forest, illuminating the little glades which form the home of the sparrows." Here, both day and night, is the place to hear the plaintively beautiful song of the white-throat, called by the early settlers in Canada the *Rossignol* or nightingale.

Other birds which we will see and hear—during the year—are the bobwhite, the bobolink and the killdeer. Again to the prosaic-minded these birds say their name so positively that there can be no argument about their christening. The bobwhite is a quail and his clear and melodious whistle, though to the majority it seems to be "bobwhite," may say to you "more wet" or "ah wheat." It will be interesting to you to hear the variations in the call as you get familiar with it and notice that often there are extra notes at the beginning and at the end.

During migration the notes of the killdeer fall weirdly out of the midnight sky. These wild notes, though we often hear them near home, seem a part of the northern wastes. In defense of their nest or young, a pair will absolutely bewilder you with the incessantly reiterated "kill-dee, kill-dee."

The bobolink, who to some says "bobolink" and to others "spink, spank, spink," is paraphrased by Wilson Flagg as follows: "With a phew, phew, Wadolincon; listen to me, Bobolincon." This line is helpful to the beginner in suggesting the rapid, monotonous, and yet sweet moving quality of his song. And Nuttall tells of the morning chorus of the bobolinks, where sounds mingle like the noise of a distant torrent, becoming more distinct and tumultuous "till with the break of day it becomes their ordinary song."

One theory of bird song is that the birds most highly advanced biologically—that is, those highest in the evolutionary scale—are those capable of the greatest complexity and variety of song. If, as they have sometimes been classed by ornithologists, the thrushes are highest, this would seem to be true, except that the bluebird is a thrush and is far from a notable singer. But it is not only because of their complex musical quality that bird songs appeal to us. There is a great deal in association. To many the call of the flicker, with what Audubon calls his "prolonged jovial laugh," and others his cheery "wick, wick, wick," means spring as much as the carol of the robin. While the "quit, leave here" of the olive-sided flycatcher, a bird that is not classed with the songsters, means high fire-scarred forest lands topped with snow-capped peaks, reflected in the blue of a mountain lake; and the ringing "cock, cock, cock," of the pileated woodpecker instantly reveals a virgin forest of evergreens towering high in the morning mist.

128

The gay and bustling twitter of barn swallows and the rising amber bubbles of the wren mean happy country days, while that of the winter wren is part of the forest depths of the North or West. Burroughs' memory of our busy house wren is evidently not very happy, especially when he compares it with the winter wren: "The song of the house wren is rather harsh and shrill, far inferior as a musical performance to that of the winter wren. The songs of the two differ as their nests differ, or as soft green moss and feathers do from dry twigs and a little dry grass. A truly sylvan strain is that of the winter wren, suggesting deep wildwood solitudes, while that of the house wren is more in keeping with the noise and clatter of the farm and dooryard." Burroughs should have heard the winter wren in the depths of the Olympic National Park forest, where its rhythmic ripple mingles with the whistle of the varied thrush, now near, now far.

The eastern meadowlark is well-known and loved and one of its songs which another word-minded observer has translated as "Spring is here," is quite typical of his usual modulation. His commonest song has this melancholy droop, starting high and then falling to the last syllable. His tones, though capable of quite a little variation, are rather thin and wiry. But let us get a little west of Chicago and what a change! P. A. Taverner says in *Birds of Western Canada:* "The western meadowlark derives most of its well-earned fame from its voice which rings rich, full and true over the open fields and prairies. To the Easterner hearing the western meadowlark for the first time there comes a distinctly pleasant surprise. It is not a glorified eastern meadowlark song, but one entirely different . . . The song of the western meadowlark is a clear ringing whistle with an almost ventriloquist quality. It is longer and richer than the eastern, using several more notes and always ending on a joyous high note, redolent of the breadth and freedom of their prairie homes." On the prairie the western meadowlarks take the place of the robins in leading the morning chorus. At the first dawn ray their notes ring forth from the ground in such a gay triumphant chorus that you feel as if submerged in waves of melody. Donald Culross Peattie says: "A rapture of western meadowlarks."

The warblers, that vast concourse which saves our forest from a host of insect enemies, have songs very far from warbles. Most of their songs are light lisping tinkles or trills, difficult to put into any musical form. One of the best known is that of the ovenbird, whose "teacher, *teacher,* TEACHER, *TEACHER*" rings emphatically through the eastern woods. The notes of the redstart and the yellow warbler, the two warblers we are most likely to see in our gardens, will have to be studied as we watch the birds, attuning our ears to their variations, as will those of the flitting hosts we see during migration.

Among the small birds which flit restlessly through the foliage are the vireos. The red-eyed vireo upsets the scientists' theory by singing almost continuously spring, summer, and fall. Untiringly his sweet disconnected discourse weaves a pattern of song. E. H. Forbush says: "His singing is part of the game . . . He uses short phrases intermittently, but continually from morning until night." He sings a phrase, spies a worm, eats it, sings another phrase. Again the word-minded people have named him the preacher bird. "You see it—you know it—do you hear it—do you believe it?"—he repeats, happily, if monotonously. In the West the most frequently heard vireo is Cassin's. It flits from branch to branch singing— as one hearer humorously notes: "Sweetheart—sweetheart—come here— beat you me to it." All through August and September the invitation is heard when few other birds vouchsafe more than a chirping twitter.

The warbling vireo also keeps up a rolling hoop of melody. It resembles the purple finch's warble, but is more continuous and slightly more metallic in tone. Heard also quite as frequently in the autumn woods of the West as those of the vireos are the clear sweet notes of the tawny creeper—"a garland of song caught up at either end and made fast to the ether!" He sings as he works, traveling up and up the trunks of myriads of fir trees.

Chief singer among the small birds of the woodland is the ruby-crowned kinglet. Often during migration in the East we hear a bit of the preliminary song which, in its far northern nesting place, defies description for its exquisite vocalization. In the West both the preliminary try-out and the main theme are heard, and though there may be more spirituality in some of the thrush songs, there is an elfin other-world quality in the aria of the ruby-crown that makes it one of the most magical expressions of the vocal ability of birds. Although the ruby-crowned kinglet is of pygmy size, only about four inches long, the voice that rings out from that tiny throat has tones which may be heard far through the woodland. As you stand nearly at the top of the trail to the summit of Glacier National Park, the songs of the ruby-crowned kinglet float up a thousand feet or more, through the fleecy clouds below, intermingled with the mystic bell-like tones of the western hermit thrush.

This little bird shows a wren-like curiosity, and though apparently busy searching for insect eggs and singing its very heart out, it will, if you sit quietly at the edge of the woodland, approach closer and closer, inspecting you sharply, every once in a while flashing its ruby crown like a glowing coal of fire. And then, when you are so near, what a spray of fairy notes rises through the tenderly budded shrubs! W. L. Dawson says: "The bird often begins *sotto voce* with two or three high squeaks as if trying to get the pitch down to the range of mortal ears before he gives his full voice." Then, as if inspired he sings, higher, higher, sweeter, sweeter, the ravishing notes often rising beyond our register, too ethereal for human comprehension.

At some time or other every owner of an elm tree has seen the glowing orange of a Baltimore oriole as he and his mate look over the lacy tips of the limbs for a site for its pendent cradle. His note is a high clear whistle which later seems to blend into the more mellow flutelike mating song. E. H. Forbush says that the song varies much in tone and rhythm and that often birds have a song so individual that it can be recognized immediately on their arrival from the South. Schuyler Mathews says the oriole's song differs from the robin's because of its staccato quality, but as he busily looks over your elm tree for caterpillars he has a gentle, meditative soliloquy, not broken into emphatic phrases as is the red-eyed vireo's. Wilson says he sings "with the pleasing tranquillity of a careless ploughboy, whistling merely for his own amusement."

Another bird of the orchard is the rose-breasted grosbeak. On first hearing him perhaps you will think that you are listening to a robin who is a master singer. But listen closely and you will hear a tender warbling undertone and a finished ending never heard in a robin's song. Perhaps you may be astonished to come on a nest loosely placed in rather open shrubbery, and on it a rose-breasted male grosbeak taking his turn incubating the eggs and singing in indescribably sweet tones as he sits, aware of your presence, but steadfast at his post unless you approach too terrifyingly near. On the Pacific Coast the black-headed grosbeak sings the same tender cadence, prolonging the melody still further in its flight song as it circles over its territory, flying from fir top to fir top.

Another bird often confused with the robin or the grosbeak is the tanager. Listen carefully to the intonation. The notes are similar—"cheer-cheer-cheer-cheer," but entirely lacking in the robin's flute-like overtones or the tender pathos of the grosbeak. "Cheer-cheer-cheer-cheer"—he sings like a robin with a cold in its throat.

A trio of *virtuosi* consists of the brown thrasher, the catbird and that *maestro* the mockingbird. Of the same family, they all possess the power of mimicry. Taken in order of finished musical phrasing, the thrasher stands lowest. His notes are loud, clear and musical, but are sung with emphasis in disconnected phrases as if he were making a series of forcible statements, each one repeated. The catbird ranks next to the mockingbird in versatility and sweetness of tone, though often marring his song by his imitations of some harsh cry as that of the crested flycatcher, the squawking of a hen, or the call of a hawk. He often sings at night in the moonlight and then his flow of song is continuous. He has an exquisite "whisper" song which ap-

132

parently comes from afar, but in reality may be but six feet away in the old lilac bush by your window.

No proper southern garden is complete without its mockingbird singing among the magnolia blooms, pouring forth their sweet-bitter lemon perfume. Night and day he sings, mingling varying strains in a fascinating medley. He sings until his ecstasy arouses a faint answering chorus from among less energetic birds, then he will launch himself in the air, only to float down with fluttering wings near to his nest among the sweet olive from which rises a fragrance as all-pervasive and magical as his song.

The unequalled singers of the New World are the thrushes, the wood thrush, the veery, and the eastern and western forms of the hermit thrush; and the russet-backed, the varied thrushes and Townsend's solitaire of the West. Others, less well known are Alice's and Bicknell's thrushes.

More familiar than the hermit thrush of the East is the wood thrush. It is he that we are most likely to hear in the trees near the garden. E. H. Forbush ranks the song only second in musical quality to that of the hermit. The notes are sung more slowly and deliberately and there are bass tones which the hermit's song never possesses. It is "powerful, rich, metallic, with the vanishing vibrating tones of a bell."

To many the veery or Wilson's thrush, is only an eery voice at the twilight hour. Usually its chosen home is near a stream or lake. There is something curiously metallic about the tones which descend in volume and in pitch, until they seem to get beyond the bird's power of execution and quaver away into a series of rather off-pitch grace notes—"a spiral, tremulous silver thread of music."

A bird of the deep spruce forests of the mountain slopes of the West is the varied thrush, a robin-like bird, but lacking entirely the aggressive, nonchalant ways of our often too familiar robin. To be heard, not seen, seems to be this bird's desire, and to reach his ideal he not only conceals himself in the dense branches of a Douglas fir but to still further bewilder us throws his voice, sometimes high aloft, sometimes seemingly within a few feet. And that voice! A long drawn whistle, so full, so rounded, now deep and low, and then high with a vibrant piercing pathos.

Occasionally heavy snows will drive the varied thrushes to the garden, where they will eat shyly with the robins, song sparrows, chewinks and juncos. At times also they will linger late in the spring and then their long-drawn whistles will lead the morning chorus, floating high even above the insistent call of the robins. Scientists warn us not to read human emotion into bird song, but it still remains, that, as W. L. Dawson says: "There is no sound in the western woods more subtle, more mysterious, more thrilling than this passion song of the varied thrush. Somber depths, dripping foliage, and the distant gurgling of dark brown waters are its fitting accompaniments. . . . It is suggestive, elusive, baffling . . . it reminds one of antique china reds, or recalls the subdued luridness of certain ancient frescoes."

If the varied thrush is the bird of the deep spruce and fir wood and the deeply forested mountain slopes, the Townsend's solitaire is the voice of the mountain heights of the West. He, too, at long intervals spends a winter in a western garden. True to his name, he is always alone, but seems happy, helping himself to food which must have a strange flavor to his palate after the blueberries of his mountain home. He flits from bush to bush eating the berries of English ivy and holly and finishing the winter on the fruit of the rock cotoneaster. All through the winter he is silent, but seemingly out of thankfulness for the bounteous crop of cotoneaster berries, sometimes just before he leaves for the heights he bursts into a rippling song, a song which combines the rolling warble of the purple finch, the gay rhythm of the winter wren and the depth and volume of the wood thrush. This is just a foretaste of his full song which, before other birds begin their spring chorus, "ripples down the mountain sides, a silvery cascade of melody as clear and sparkling as the mountain brook, filling the woods and valleys with ringing music."

According to all students the hermit thrush stands pre-eminent as a

singer. His song has an ineffable sweetness and a spiritual quality unequalled by any other bird's. Professor Theodore Clarke Smith speaks of
the richness and penetration of his tones and says they have the reed quality of the oboe superadded to a flute's even tone. He continues, saying that
even heard from a distance the notes are fairly piercing, so full and vibrant
are they.

> "Then on the silence falls a fluted sound
> Melodious full and round . . .
> . . . a threefold chant of threefold intervals."
> —*Grace Denis Litchfield.*

W. L. Dawson says that the song of the hermit thrush is a thing apart,
that it is sacred, not secular music, a song that has developed for the sake of
the beauty itself. You feel certain of this when you stand high on the slopes
of the Olympic or Cascade Mountains of the West, with snow-capped
peaks above you, the far cloud-held ocean beyond you, and hear those notes
rise, pure, serene, ecstatic, telling of moonlight on far mountain slopes or of
a dawn through lonely mountain firs, a dawn washed clear of every trace of
earth.

Chapter Ten

CARE OF STRAY BIRDS

A HELPLESS bird on the ground! Yes, helpless, but does it need your help? "Stop, look, listen," should be your watchword when you see a bird fluttering in the grass or hear cries of distress from the bushes. Nine times out of ten if you move back out of sight but where you can watch, you will find that the parent birds, attracted by the hunger call, will be on hand to feed the forlorn young beggar just what he needs. Perhaps only a little while before he had been urged out of the nest so that he could learn to fend for himself. Watch quietly the next time you see an absurdly helpless baby robin. His mother will soon arrive with a wriggling worm and feed him and perhaps two or three other squawkers in nearby bushes. Many birds feed their young for some time after they leave the nest. Both robins and bluebirds feed their spotted-breast youngsters until they seem to be larger than their parents. Young song sparrows leave the nest early and are quickly herded under a brush heap or into a tangle by their anxious father and mother. The male oriole feeds the first set of young for some time after the female is incubating the second set of eggs. This is the time that cats reap a plentiful harvest, but in the garden for birds we shall presume that the birds will not have to contend with that alien enemy.

This is the time, too, when the mother bird seems to ignore everything else but the hunger call of her young and often you can have the thrill of holding young birds in your hands while the parents feed them. Occasionally the father or the mother is killed and then the remaining parent has a big job. Once, in the West, we watched a Shufeldt's junco nearly wear himself to a shadow as he fed two youngsters, insatiable in their demands when he was in front of them, but quite capable of picking up crumbs when his back was turned. A record has been kept of a house wren, who, when his mate was killed, was known to feed his young 1,217 times in the 15 hours and 45 minutes of daylight.

Of course there are cases when both parent birds meet with some disaster. Then, if you are properly philanthropic, you can adopt the young. But don't think that you have taken upon yourself an easy task. Let any one who has endeavored to supply enough angleworms to a baby robin, tell you how early the break of day seems when that unruly youngster sets up its pitiful hunger cry or rather demand, for food. And perhaps the man who fed his orphan red-shouldered hawks seventy pounds of meat will have something to say on the subject.

And insectivorous birds like wrens are still more difficult to deal with. Dr. A. A. Allen of Cornell tells how one whole family, including the maid and the butler, tried to feed a set of orphaned house wrens. Two men were detailed also to go to the woods and find grubs in rotten logs, but the wrens got hungrier and hungrier and at last gave up the ghost.

If we do take it upon ourselves to head a refuge home for birds, we do not have to depend entirely on foraging for food. We can supplement earthworms and cankerworms by raising maggots in liver or by rearing a few mealworms—a few tens of thousands, that is. To raise mealworms take a gallon earthen jar and fill it half full of cornmeal, oatmeal or bread crusts, adding some scraps of leather and raw potato for moisture. Drop in a number of beetles (*Tenebrio molitor*), and cover with wire screening and a woollen cloth. In a short time you should have a supply of larvae for your protein-hungry guests. We may also secure ants' "eggs" and prepared bird food from a dealer.*

An even simpler substitute is one part raw beef, free from fat; two parts scraped carrot; one part shredded wheat and three parts of crushed

---

* A fuller account of how to raise meal worms will be found in *Our Small Native Animals*, by Robert Snedigar, Random House, New York.

bird seeds. Hard-boiled egg may be substituted for the meat. This mixture should be moistened with white of egg and run through the coarse grinder of the meat chopper. As the mixture comes out of the chopper it looks like worms and can be broken into three or four inch lengths and fed to young birds. If possible, alternate each feeding with a natural food, such as a soft insect, a grub or a meal worm. Water should be supplied to very young birds by giving them a part of a blueberry, a raspberry, blackberry, or a strawberry, for this is the way the parent birds supply it.

In an emergency as when a nearly starved robin is brought in, scraped beef, liver, mashed hard-boiled egg or custard may be given, and the young bird immediately covered with a woollen cloth. Sometimes in the winter a nearly dead mockingbird may be found. A few drops of codliver oil will prepare the system for more concentrated food such as raisins or other dried fruits.

As it is against the law, without a special permit, to keep any of our wild birds, resident or migratory, except jays, crows, magpies or starlings, all other birds should be given their liberty as soon as they are able to care for themselves. The fate of a tame bird is usually a sad one, so as soon as possible stray birds should be turned loose to fight their own battles.

Jays and crows are quite easily raised by hand and become exceedingly amusing companions. If taken from the nest when very young they will transfer the child to parent attitude entirely to their owner, paying no attention to other birds, but fluttering their wings and begging for food only when he is present. Both crows and jays become very imitative and mischievous and presume greatly on their privileges in the home. One blue jay in Connecticut flew in and out of the house at will and after a number of pieces of silverware were discovered to be missing, a watch was kept on the jay. He was found to have a *cache* under the eaves and when it was raided the silver spoons were located and also an array of hair pins, matches, buttons and a gold thimble.

Allan Cruickshank says that a crow which he took from the nest when it was only two weeks old was completely conditioned to him in place of its parents and became his almost inseparable companion. The crow would accompany him on his walks and always watched carefully whatever he did. When he examined a flower or a leaf and then passed on, the crow would go to the same spot and tear the flower or plant to shreds, repeating this act time after time.

Frank Chapman Pellet in *Birds of the Wild* writes: "The most interesting pet which we ever had was a hawk. When cutting a near-by field of hay, the mowing-machine passed over the nest of a marsh hawk . . . Our youngster escaped without a scratch. He was a downy fledgling with brown feathers just beginning to show." Mr. Pellet goes on to say that the young hawk was fed on meat scraps and grew very rapidly. He soon flew about the yard, coming immediately when his name "Snappy" was called. He would fly onto the head or shoulders of any one he knew, showing not the slightest sign of fear. The chickens avoided him, but he never touched them. He lived on rabbits, mice and grasshoppers.

Occasionally a sick bird is brought to us. If there is no visible wound, it is much better to put it in a sheltered spot in the woods than to endeavor to care for it. It is usually hopeless to try to feed birds in this state, for a grown bird is often terrified by handling even to the point of death. Fortunately we seldom see sick or dying birds; they usually go quickly and easily as the food of hawks or owls.

Sometimes a bird may break a leg or wing by flying against a wire fence, a window or by striking an automobile. These injuries can frequently be cared for very successfully. If the bird is grown it will naturally be fearful of your approach, but occasionally if you are patient it will settle down and lie perfectly still in order to escape detection. Go to it quietly and with a quick move, cup it with your hand, grasping it firmly, but not too tightly, to prevent its wings from fluttering. In a moment or two it will become quiet; it can then be lifted and carried. If the leg is broken, allow it to extend down between the fingers. If on examining it you find the break is a bad one, amputate the leg with a snip of sharp shears. One-legged birds frequently survive for some time, though it would seem kinder to put an end to such a hazardous existence. If the break is not serious, put miniature splints on the leg or wing, fastening them firmly with a soft bandage. Then with a cloth tie the wings down and put the bird in a cage which should be put in a shaded spot, out of drafts. Put a saucer of water and juicy fruit near the bird, also seeds, mashed hard-boiled egg or a bit of custard. Forcible feeding is seldom successful. If the bird is to live it will find the food. When it is thought that the bone is set, the bandages should be removed and the bird given its liberty out of doors.

The curious case of a stray bird which, instead of being adopted, adopted a family, is told by Alice Earle Hyde, who has a summer camp on Mount Tom Pond in Connecticut. Mrs. Hyde writes that she and her two young grandsons, John and Jerry, were eating breakfast on the porch when they noticed an ovenbird walking down the path toward the house. He was full grown but evidently a young bird. Up the steps he hopped, across the porch and under the table and chairs where he walked about picking carelessly at crumbs. From that time on this fearless bird made his home on the verandah, never leaving it except for a few minutes. He showed no fear of the family nor of visitors. He would stand in front of Mrs. Hyde as she sat painting, cocking his head and listening as she talked softly to him. He even ate bread crumbs out of a saucer with a parrot and a tame chipmunk, his beak often touching that of the parrot or the nose of the chipmunk. He also broke bread with a tame wood rat which lived in a near-by woodpile.

As September drew near Mrs. Hyde feared that "Spooky," as her grandsons had named him, would not develop the migrating instinct, so arrangements were made to have him cared for over winter at the New Canaan Bird Sanctuary. But this care was not required, for Spooky's confidence was for once misplaced. One morning he did not appear and after a search was found near the back of the house with the crown of his head gone. He had evidently tried to fraternize with a weazel.

In Vancouver, British Columbia, Mr. Charles E. Jones, who from childhood longed to have intimate contact with birds, has developed a gigantic outdoor aviary. Here he has hundreds of birds which nest and bring up their young almost as if they were in the wild. He has netted quite an area of land and has made a scientific study of the food of each species and feeds the young in conjunction with the parents from the moment they appear out of the shell. In this way the young are conditioned to human beings as well as to their parents and grow up without fear, flitting about the heads and shoulders and taking food from all who visit "The Bird's Paradise."

This is not an experiment which would be practicable or desirable generally. It naturally means a breaking up of the balance of nature, for of course, the birds have no check except old age, or disease, which is quite likely to develop under such conditions. It is much better through proper planting to build up a natural environment where one ecological factor supplements another and a reasonable balance of all types of life may be obtained.

Chapter Eleven

MIGRATION AND BIRDBANDING

Oh, let your strong imagination turn
The great wheel backward, until Troy unburn,
And then unbuild, and seven Troys below
Rise out of death, and dwindle, and outflow,
Till all have passed, and none has yet been there:
Back, ever back. Our birds still crossed the air:
Beyond our myriad changing generations
Still built, unchanged, their known inhabitations.
A million years before Atlantis was
Our lark sprang from some hollow in the grass,
Some old hoof-print in a tussock's shade,
And the wood-pigeon's smooth snow-white eggs were laid
High, among green pines' sunset-colored shafts . . .
                                        J. C. Squire.

FOR how many thousands of years has man dated spring and fall by the inevitable arrow of wild geese piercing the mists as it wings unhesitatingly North or South? We know how ancient is the lineage of birds, for their fossilized remains have been found in the upper Eocene deposits of France and England and these remains show that the birds of forty million years ago are almost identical with those of today. Back and forth the flocks have sped, sure, confident, over the ages, led by the marvelous migratory urge, and this ancient impulse, this inexorable regularity, makes us think more than anything else of how little man's progressive civilizations have counted in the evolution of animal life.

Donald Culross Peattie asks: "What can it be, this homing instinct, that brings the birds back to us every year? That brings the wrens and

AMERICAN REDSTART

MALE, FIRST BREEDING PLUMAGE   FEMALE, BREEDING ADULT
                                      MALE, BREEDING ADULT

PALM WARBLER

BREEDING ADULT   JUVENAL PLUMAGE

OVEN-BIRD

JUVENAL PLUMAGE (NESTLING)   BREEDING ADULT

Scale about one-half

swallows to the very same nests around the house and barn? That leads the carrier pigeon home across a hundred, five hundred miles?"

Many generations of philosophers have pondered on the problems of migration. Aristotle knew the swallows migrated, but knew not where they went. Speculations, wild, or nearer the mark, went on through the centuries. In 1703, C. Morton, an English nature student, wrote a pamphlet in which he set forth very learnedly his theory that the birds went every fall, either to the moon, or to "some invisible aerial island fixed above our atmosphere." Even at that time of credulity, this theory was thought by other naturalists to be an "ingenious but chimerical account." But only a little later Gilbert White of Selbourne wrote that he was sure that the swallows hibernated in the mud of some of the lakes of southern England. For many years this theory received credence, while in many parts of Europe peasants still think that the cuckoo becomes a hawk in winter.

We now know, since man has explored the four corners of the earth, where many of our birds winter and where they breed in summer. One of the results of systematic observation has been the tracing and charting of the great migration trails. It has been learned that some birds like robins, grackles, red-winged blackbirds, and woodcocks go little if any south of the United States, while others like the bobolinks and tanagers go as far as Brazil. Another remarkable variation is that many birds go south by one route and return north by another. For instance, the Connecticut warbler goes south along the New England coast, through Florida and thence to South America, but on coming back in the spring veers west from Florida and follows the Mississippi valley north to its nesting-grounds in Canada. It has been learned, too, that great mountain ranges often present insurmountable barriers. The birds of western Alaska do not cross the mountains but migrate south in a narrow pathway along the sea-coast, while birds in eastern Alaska, among them the little blackpoll warbler, may cross the entire continent to Florida, and then fly over the Caribbean Sea to their South American winter haunts. Another strange fact is that millions of birds, among them many species of frail warblers, go to Central and South America over the water route, directly across the Gulf of Mexico. They prefer this perilous passage to the longer route through Texas, or from Florida to Cuba, through the Lesser Antilles, and thence to Yucatan, though on these routes they would have stopping-places where they could rest and feed.

A new theory of why the birds use the various flyways has been brought forward by the aviator, Captain Neil T. McMillan. He feels very strongly that birds unconsciously take advantage of the flow of air currents and ride with the wind just as the skilful aviator does. Oftentimes when the pilot sets out the wind near the earth may be blowing contrary to his course, but he knows that usually by rising a few thousand feet he will strike a current of air flowing in the direction he wishes to go; knowingly or unknowingly the birds do the same.

Captain McMillan points out also that just as the interchange of land and sea breezes tend to equalize the temperature through the day, so in spring and fall the warm air rushes north or south to equalize the temperature over all the earth. At these times we have our great storms and also our great north and south waves of birds. These voyagers fly through the air at their usual rate of speed plus that of the wind and as they are part of the air current progress peacefully along as if they were in a calm. Oftentimes the greater part of their progress north or south is due greatly to the propelling force of the wind.

This would explain why migrating birds sometimes arrive in the face of a "norther," having apparently had to fly faster than the wind. We think of this snow coming from the north, but it is really the result of moist warm air rushing in from the south meeting cold air from the north which causes the moisture to be precipitated in the form of snow. The birds fly in on the high warm air current, only to land at their nesting sites in cold and sleet. This, according to Capt. McMillan, is the reason that birds appear promptly in spring on their usual dates in spite of the unfavorable local weather conditions; they are following the rhythm of the equinoctial storms, those great equalizers of the earth's temperature.

But even though we know something of the great airways and where many of our birds go in their vast travels, only theory explains this inexorable necessity, this inborn urge to travel twice a year over land and sea, leaving the plentiful supply of food in the tropics for northern regions, still cold and desolate, and again leaving their nesting sites, as swallows, orioles and nighthawks do, when insect food is at its maximum. We may speculate endlessly and still the birds come and go. Nothing can stem that tide which has surged back and forth through unknown ages. As James Rorty says in *Bird Music*,

> . . . when the white-throat's quiver of song
> Is shaken on the wind that blows
> A rippled path across the thawing lake,
> Halt if you will that clear annunciation . . .

To the casual observer it would seem as if storms and the destructiveness of man would have some effect on bird life as a whole. Storms often take a terrific toll of the smaller weaker birds. Doubtless thousands of warblers perish each year as they endeavor to pass over the Gulf of Mexico, and lighthouses are a death trap for many more. In a wet snow storm over Minnesota, longspurs in migration, were forced down and perished by millions. A "norther" in New England some years ago almost wiped out the bluebirds.

Man, too, occasionally destroys a whole species, as he did when he killed off the passenger pigeons——seen by Audubon in a flock so vast that it was estimated to have contained over two billion individuals, and of which he wrote: "the air was literally filled with pigeons; the light of the noonday sun was obscured as if by an eclipse."

But still in spite of storm, in spite of man, the remaining billions of birds make their flights. Each spring and fall the tiny hummingbird flies over thousands of miles of land and sea, and still the Arctic tern travels twice a year his eleven-thousand-mile journey from nearly pole to pole.

At the present time there are several theories of migration; though we have no definite proof that any of them are true. All migrations must be considered as having gradually developed through ages of time, the result of trial and evolution on the part of the birds. What seems to us an established fact now may be something in a process of change too gradual for us to notice, having perhaps taken thousands of years to reach its present point of development, and perhaps tending toward a different phase in the future. An interesting adaptation is seen in the migration of the bobolink. This bird, because the irrigation of farmland has made it possible for it to nest in what was formerly a desert area, is gradually spreading westward, having even reached eastern Washington and British Columbia. Naturally the pioneers in this movement have to cover new territory, but in spite of this added mileage, they return eastward each fall to the Atlantic Coast and take the old bobolink flyway to South America.

One theory of the cause of migration is that once the birds were congregated in the tropics and as they became too numerous, portions of them flew north to nest, eventually returning when cold weather set in. The other, more widely accepted theory, is that before the first glacial period, when the climate of the whole world was warm, even tropical as far north as Alaska, birds were widely distributed over the earth's surface. Then, because of a slight tilting of the earth's axis, the climate of the world grew colder, the polar icecaps crept down, pushing the birds toward the Equator. Later, as the glaciers receded during a warm period, it is thought that the birds followed the ice farther and farther northward, generation after generation, eventually reaching their ancestors' original birthplace. But, as in the meantime the climate of the earth had changed, they found a distinct difference between summer and winter in their northern breeding places, and knowing of the happier lands of the tropics, they returned to them each fall before the advent of cold.

Recently students of evolution have suggested that the migratory impulse, like other attributes of animal and plant life, developed as a mutation of certain individuals, suddenly, not over a long period of time. Only thus, they assert, can such a phenomenon as the flight of the golden plover from Alaska to the Hawaiian Islands become intelligible. This theory like the others, is far from sufficient to account for the complexities and regularities of bird migration.

Added to the mystery of what impelled birds to migrate in the first place, there remains the equally puzzling enigma of what spark sets them off on their journeys year after year. Whatever the stimulus, it must occur with great regularity, in order to account for the almost time-table accuracy with which the migratory movements of some birds can be dated. Climatic conditions, like temperature and barometric pressure, are too haphazard to base it on, as are the fluctuations of food supply. For a time scientists enthusiastically acclaimed the experiments of Dr. W. Rowan in Canada, who spent much time testing the effect of the shortening period of daylight on the reproductive structure of captive birds. It was found that as the days grew longer the production of sex hormones increased, and the puzzle seemed near solution until some one pointed out that near the Equator, where most of the birds winter, the days are all practically of the same length.

Perhaps future study of glands will make clear that there is a rhythm of the reproductive urge quite aside from any change induced by light. But even if this solved the problem of the spark that sets the rocket off, we would still have to endow the birds with an additional sense, that of direction, to enable us to explain how birds find their way over trackless seas, or how some young birds that leave the north before their parents, can find unerringly, the old ancestral trails. Scientists in Europe have been investigating the effects of terrestrial magnetism. It is suspected that birds may be sensitive to magnetic influences and be guided by them.

Another interesting fact to observe about migration, is that some of the groups of birds move by day and some by night. Swallows, which are insect eaters, move by day, and it will be seen by looking at their charted trails that they follow the longer land routes, going two thousand miles farther than the birds that cross the Gulf of Mexico. Other day-fliers are robins, grackles, swifts and crows. Hawks also fly by day, as do the jays and even the hummingbird. The warblers and a number of other small birds always travel at night, resting and feeding during the day, though generally moving onward slowly in the direction of their goal. Sometimes during a heavy migration all night long the air is full of the peeping notes of hordes of warblers, vireos, thrushes and flycatchers. On a night when the moon is full, through a telescope, the black silhouettes of birds may be seen to pass for hours across its bright disc. One observer estimated that he saw nine thousand birds pass in an hour. Ducks and geese travel by both day and night and often at sunrise on the West Coast, if there is a line of clear sky near the horizon, you can see an inky stream pushing steadily northward toward the nesting grounds in Canada and Alaska.

But to return to the birds in the garden. Before we have observed them through many seasons we cannot help but notice that our berry-bearing shrubs and well-placed baths bring many strange birds to our homes, birds that appear each spring and fall and are there for only a short time. These are the migrants, stragglers that have stopped for a brief rest, and which nest farther north and winter farther south, and no matter how attractive our sanctuary is, cannot be persuaded to linger with us long. These "travelers" are always welcome, and observation of them adds greatly to the fascination of bird watching.

One need not be a "collector" of specimens to add a great deal to our knowledge of birdlife. Much is to be done in the field of observation. Accurate, scientific study of birds in America commenced only in the nineteenth century when Audubon, Wilson and that strange character Rafinesque, recorded their observations of a wilderness, unbelievably rich in bird and animal life. Since then has followed an era of exploration and study, financed by scientific bodies, eager to have complete collections of specimens in their museums.

Side by side with the trained naturalist has grown up the amateur bird lover, who, rather than read the ponderous tomes of the scientist, prefers to observe the fluctuations of bird life in his own garden and thus gain first-hand knowledge. And, if he takes careful notes, recording his observations carefully and accurately, his account of birds passing through his hundred-foot garden can be of real value to the professional ornithologist.

Some day as you are watching the birds in your garden you will see that one has a band on its leg. Another day, perhaps a neighbor, knowing your interest in birds, will bring you a dead bird with a leg bracelet. On removing the band you will see that there is lettering on it, "Notify Biol. Surv. Wash. D. C.," and then two sets of numbers. This band should be sent immediately to the Chief of the Biological Survey; you will be notified of where the bird was banded. Here has been opened up to you a new and fascinating branch of bird study, that of birdbanding.

The earliest birdbanding we know of was done as sport. In the days of falconry, a peregrine would bring down a heron but not kill it. His noble owner would put an inscribed band on its leg and set it free again. Perhaps next day the lord of a neighboring domain would take that heron, read the inscription and thus a community of sport was enjoyed.

In 1710 a great gray heron was taken in Europe; on its leg were several bands, one apparently having been placed on it in Turkey. This is the first definitely dated European record of birdbanding. In America the first birdbanding was done by Audubon who, in 1803, put a tiny twist of wire around a phoebe's leg and found that the same bird returned the following spring. With that as an example one would have thought that long before the twentieth century American ornithologists would have used this method to help solve some of the mysteries of the age-old riddle of migration, but many years passed before scientists followed the lead of the genius, Audubon.

The first systematic birdbanding was done in Denmark in 1899 by a schoolteacher, Professor C. C. Mortensen. His success encouraged Dr. Leon Cole, Howard H. Cleaves, and S. Prentiss Baldwin to begin the work in this country. Later Jack Miner in Canada did much to interest both the public and scientists in banding ducks and geese. He had a record of a forty per cent return of all the birds he banded. The enthusiasm of these men and the published results of their work brought about the formation of four regional birdbanding associations, which take in all of North America, north of Mexico. The interest was so great and the task of keeping the records became so vast that in 1920 the United States Biological Survey took over the care of the records and now directs the work.

An amusing story is told of the first bands secured by the Biological Survey. The bands were made in England and the British stampers having no knowledge of our governmental departments, translated the inscription into a culinary recipe and much to the scientists' chagrin inscribed on the bands: Wash. Boil. Surv.

Thus birdbanding which started with the work of amateurs, has developed into an accepted scientific pursuit. There are stations scattered all over the country reporting to the headquarters in Washington. Each station is run at the bander's expense, and the amount of his equipment depends upon his ingenuity and his purse. While the larger stations, banding thousands of birds a year, naturally produce a larger number of scientific reports, valuable information has come from "home garden" stations run with a few traps but much industry. The National Association of Audubon Societies is doing extensive banding in their numerous sanctuaries, and the work is also carried on by the members of the expeditions which it sends out far afield.

At first birdbanding was largely confined to nestlings, but gradually as interest grew it was found that still more information could be secured by banding adult birds. This necessitated using traps which would not

BOBOLINK

MOLTING MALE
JUVENAL PLUMAGE (NESTLING)

MALE, BREEDING ADULT
FEMALE (AND FALL MALE)

WESTERN MEADOWLARK
ADULT MALE
JUVENAL PLUMAGE

EASTERN MEADOWLARK
ADULT MALE

Scale about one-half

harm or unnecessarily alarm the birds. The first trap used was the trap recommended by the Department of Agriculture for the capture of the obnoxious English sparrow. Later more elaborate types followed, many of them designed by S. Prentiss Baldwin, whose work aided greatly in the efficient handling of small birds. At the present time most of the traps are made of wire mesh and have automatic doors released by a spring; others have a funnel entrance. Those of the latter type are rectangular with a central funnel of wire which leads down to the ground where there is food or water. The bird climbs down and once below the mouth of the funnel can not find his way out; it is then easy to capture him by shooing him to a collecting cage held against a sliding door on the side of the trap. Other traps have doors controlled by springs so delicately poised that even a hummingbird can release them. Still others have doors operated by a cord that can be worked from the house or some other point of observation. After the birds are in the collecting cage they are carried to the house or some other safe place and the bands are fitted on their legs. These bands are furnished, with complete instructions, only to persons that the United States Biological Survey considers completely competent and reliable. Indiscriminate banding is not encouraged, the permits being granted now only to those who wish to carry on a scientific study of some special species, or to those that are in a position to band species about whose migration little is known.

Of course birds will come only to places where all the surroundings give them a feeling of safety and where they can get food and water. This is why even a small garden, if it is a well-conducted sanctuary, may be a very valuable birdbanding station. If observations have been made of the favorite foods of various species, it will be easy to place in the traps a tempting bait. One very successful bander has learned that in the fall pokeberries are very alluring, as are also the fruits of false Solomon's-seal. The same person has developed an elaborate system of overhead pipes, ending in petcocks which will let the water tinkle out, drop by drop into a dish just below the funnel or other trapping device.

Birds are not greatly alarmed by the experience of being trapped and banded. This is shown by the number of times some of them return to the traps. E. W. Nelson tells of a chipping sparrow that returned fifty-four times. Great care should be taken in placing the bands on the legs to see that the edges meet exactly, for an uneven joining might catch in a string or briar and mean entanglement with a tragic ending. Often birds after being banded will lie on the palm of the hand as if hypnotized for a few minutes, then spring away, perhaps only to fly a few feet and then stop to sing or to take a bite of food. This certainly shows that the momentary fear they experience on being caught has no lasting effect.

It may be easily seen how much we can add to our knowledge by banding. We may know by our observations through the binoculars when the first catbird arrives or when the cheery juncos desert our winter hospitality, but only by capturing a banded bird on its way through the garden can it be determined where that particular bird came from, how long it took to get there, and whether it is the same bird that was banded the year before. Banding is a method of studying the lives of individual birds, and there is almost no limit to the aspects of bird life upon which banding can throw light. Some banders analyze their records to see how birds organize their flocks. For instance, whether the white-throated sparrows travel in family groups or not, or whether all members of a colony of red-winged blackbirds go south together. Other students take detailed notes of the change of plumage of the birds they catch and thus assist the museum ornithologists.

An interesting way of studying migration is the founding and study of a tree swallow colony; a few properly built boxes erected in the open will attract many of these birds. An example is at the Austin Ornithological Research Station on Cape Cod, where a colony of over a hundred pairs of tree swallows was established in six years. Fascinating questions are being answered by both amateurs and professionals who have undertaken such projects. Do the same birds mate more than one season? What are the marital relationships? Where do the young birds go the next year if their natal colony is over-populated? Does a bird return to the same box on successive years, or how far away does it nest, and is there a territorial law governing this? An inspiring example of work of this type has been done by Mrs. Margaret Nice, whose observations of song sparrows are acknowledged by scientists all over the world as an outstanding contribution to our knowledge of bird behavior.

Perhaps the key to the secrets of migration or other puzzles may be found by you or some other garden lover, if by suitable planting the birds have been brought around and you bring to bear upon these fascinating problems a mind unclouded by other people's ideas about them. Always remember that, rightly used, a garden is as much a laboratory as any room set aside for research in a museum or university, and from it may come contributions to the sum total of human knowledge as important as those from any scientific institution.

Chapter Twelve

BIRDS ON THE COUNTRY PLACE

O N AN estate of some extent, there are usually fields surrounded by hedgerows, and what a boon these hedgerows are, not only to the home gardener, but to the farmer. They furnish food and cover to many species of birds, not only to those of the orchard and garden, but also to those which make their homes in the woods and fields. If in outlying fields, the red cedar climbs in thick ranks on the hillside sloping south, and if hemlocks or other evergreens partly clothe the northern slopes, then ideal protection is found for any of the birds that stay through the snows of winter, or in spring or fall, for any migrants which may arrive to help them in their good work.

Greeting us on those nostalgic days of early spring, as we walk through the fields, watching as in childhood for the first early flowers, comes the sweet yet melancholy note of the meadowlark. "Spring is here," he calls from a tall tree or a near-by fence post, and "Spring is here" another answers not far away. His song, as Mrs. Mabel Osgood Wright says, has a "breezy sound, as fresh and wild, as if the wind were blowing through a flute." The falling note in the end gives a melancholy cadence, strangely at variance with the real nature of this handsome, lively bird, who arrives from the South, ready for business, the minute he strikes the old familiar fields.

Smaller than a bobwhite, the meadowlark may be known by his bright yellow breast, barred with a black crescent, and the white feathers at each side of his short tail as he flies.

The nest is always on the ground, well concealed; usually arched over.

It is very hard to find, for the birds seldom light at the site, but have little runways in various directions, through which they come and go.

There is no bird more worthy of protection than the meadowlark. It is practically harmless and takes nothing that is of any use to man except a few small grains and seeds. During the winter it may eat a few of the wild fruits in the hedgerow, but in summer most of its food is made up of enemies of the farm and garden, insects and allied forms.

When one reads the list of pests that are destroyed by this bird one marvels that any one worthy of the name of sportsman could raise his gun to bring down such a morsel of flesh. Grasshoppers are eaten in such quantities that their destruction makes an appreciable increase in the hay-crop over the whole country. Caterpillars, the cotton-boll weevil, and the alfalfa weevil, the army worm, and many cutworms are also destroyed.

The killdeer, though allied to the shorebirds, frequents upland fields. "Killdee, killdee"—its sweet, keen note rings out at earliest dawn, as it runs on tripping feet near some little pond. No other cry seems more in harmony with the open, removing us in spirit far from the turmoil of so-called civilization, even though it rings over a ploughed field or the golf links. Killdeers are exceedingly handsome birds, about ten inches in length, with double black belts across their snowy upper breasts. And how the female resents an intruder in her domain, be it man, dog, or horse! Up she will fly, with an agonized cry, right in the face of the horse if he is near the nest, in order to change his path entirely; while with man or dog, curiosity will lead them to follow an abject cripple, trailing a 'broken' wing or leg and uttering most pitiful cries of distress. Then, when the enemy has been decoyed far away from the nest, up will flit the supposed cripple, whole of wing, glad and free.

But besides the amusement and pleasure afforded by this lovely bird in our walks over the fields, we know that its economic worth has been absolutely proved. The killdeer is one of the most valuable birds to the agriculturist and should be protected in every way. Of particular interest to the estate owner are the quantities of the larvae of salt-marsh mosquitoes that it devours. It eats also grasshoppers, ticks, ants, bugs, caterpillars and beetles. Among other pests are the alfalfa weevil, clover-root weevil, cotton-boll weevil, billbugs, horseflies and cotton cutworms. An amusing story is told by T. S. Roberts, author of *The Birds of Minnesota,* of a killdeer that having secured a particularly long and juicy earthworm, was about to be robbed of it by a companion. The bird lay the worm down and sat on it until something distracted its companion's notice, when it then ate the succulent meal in peace.

The killdeer lays its eggs in a slight depression in the ground, some-times unlined, sometimes carelessly lined with stems and bits of grasses or bark, or little shells or stones. It is placed in the open, on beaches or in open fields.

Another of our shore birds, which chooses the hilly pasture for nesting sites, is the upland plover. This plainly colored bird, in soft shades of gray and tan, has been ruthlessly hunted in the past and because of its destruc-tion estate owners have lost thousands of dollars through the ravages of insects. It is now protected in this country by the Migratory Bird Law, but it flies to Argentina for the winter, where it has no protection, and is there shot for the market. Because of this fact it may be exterminated as the passenger pigeon and the Carolina parakeet were, and this once familiar bird of the fields will no longer greet us in spring with its loud, clear whistle and its curious dance flight. The farmer, too, will lose a valuable ally in keeping down grasshoppers, sawfly larvae, horseflies, cattle ticks, and the various weevils, wireworms, white grubs and cutworms.

Suavely groomed in fawn, which, if you approach near enough, you will see is touched with purple iridescence on the breast, the mourning dove is another of the farmer's or estate owner's best friends. So similar to the extinct passenger pigeon is this bird that it has often given rise to claims that the pigeon has been seen again. The passenger pigeon is gone forever, but, as the mourning dove does not nest in vast flocks, thus invit-

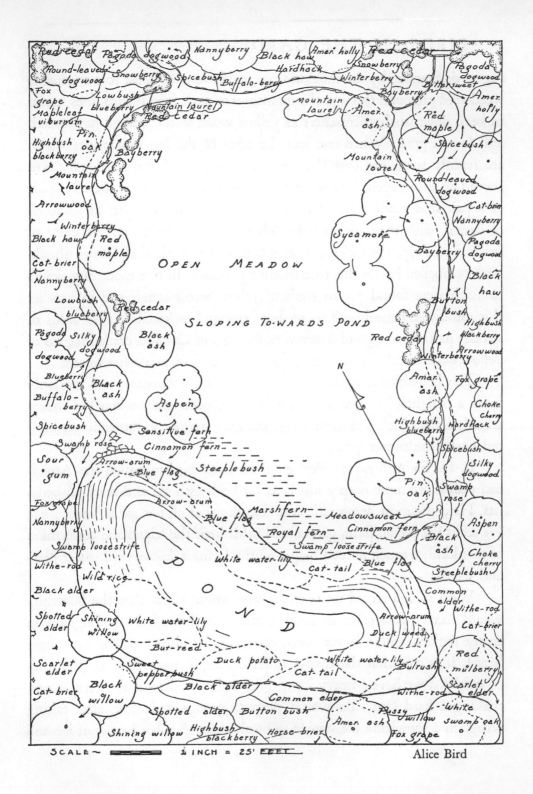

ing its destruction by the thousand, we still have it with us. It is a valuable weed-seed eater and through the quantities of such food it consumes, tends to keep down such encroachers as yellow wood sorrel, orange hawkweed, and foxtail grass. When one sees the acres of the last two plants which are rapidly spreading over the country, one sees why this friendly bird should be encouraged. One woman did object though to the friendly spirit of a pair that made a nest on her windowsill and woke her at "screech of dawn" with their melancholy "oh woe, woe, woe-oe-oe." In spite of her loss of sleep, the following records from the Biological Survey should have reconciled her to this true friend's presence. In one mourning dove's stomach were found 7,500 seeds of yellow wood sorrel, and in another this astonishing meal: 4,820 seeds of orange hawkseed, 2,600 seeds of slender paspalum, 950 of hoary vervain, 120 of Carolina cranesbill, 50 of yellow wood sorrel, 620 of panic grass and 40 of various other weeds!

The bobwhite is another valuable asset on the estate, and certainly he is a delightful companion on a late afternoon walk when his cheery whistle echoes back and forth across the field where the sumac heads burn red under the sunset glow.

E. H. Forbush says: "Perhaps there is no bird to which the American people are more deeply indebted for both esthetic and material benefits. He is the most democratic and ubiquitous of all our game birds . . . He seeks the home, farm, garden and field; he is the friend and companion of mankind; a much needed helper on the farm; a destroyer of insect pests and weeds;———"

With such a record to its credit, one would think that the bobwhite would receive protection in every State. But through New England in many regions where it was once common, its cheery call is no longer heard. It is true that the coveys suffer during a particularly cold winter, especially if we have a heavy snow, followed by a thaw and then a freeze, making a hard crust. Bobwhites sleep in groups and often after taking refuge in a snowbank are unable to break through a hard crust of ice and thus a whole covey is wiped out. But, even so, the hunter's gun does the most damage. In Ohio, the bobwhite was placed on the songbird list and rapidly increased in number when before it received protection it was not holding its own.

When one thinks of the pleasure that this bird's presence gives and its great economic value, it seems as if the hunter and gourmet should forego their fleeting pleasures. Judd states that sixty different weeds are represented in its food, including buttonweed, smartweed, sheep sorrel, ragweed, crab grass, pigeon grass, pigweed, tick trefoil, and wild peas. It destroys also potato and cucumber beetles, cotton worms, chinchbugs, locusts, grasshoppers and weevils of many kinds.

Bobwhites nest in the open and the young are ready to run the minute they pop out of the eggs. When disturbed the female gives the alarm note and the young "freeze" so successfully that they are usually indistinguishable in the grass. A covey often sleeps in what is called a "bomb" formation, tails together and bodies forming a circle. In this way there are always some birds to face the source of danger, and to give the alarm to the others if any enemy should appear. Then if alarmed the covey "bursts" into the air with a most disconcerting "whirr" of wings.

Everything should be done to encourage the bobwhite on the estate, and much can be done to help the coveys through a hard winter by providing food and shelter. Piles of brush may be placed against poles built up in tepee fashion and ears of corn and sheaves of wheat hung inside, or sheaves of wheat may be tied on trees in the woodland so that the grain may be above the snow.

E. H. Forbush advises cutting weeds as soon as ripe and storing them until a heavy snow storm comes. Then they should be carried to a sheltered spot to the south of an evergreen grove or a shrubbery thicket and laid down to the depth of about a foot. The pile should be made of alternate layers of brush and weeds, and the whole capped with evergreen boughs, then it should be weighted with rocks. The bobwhite will be delighted to find this shelter and will feed on the weed seeds and any grain that may be provided. A platform of small logs set two feet above the ground and covered with brush makes an excellent shelter. Corn shocks left standing with an opening opposite the direction of severe storms also serve as refuges and feeding stations.

Quail also frequent fields of small grain or weedy gardens. Buckwheat, millet, popcorn and various peas may be planted in waste corners and left standing to attract them in the winter. Soy beans are a great favorite, both with quail and other upland birds, and their planting adds to soil fertility. Cobs of corn driven on spikes on a board provide a good method of feeding. Provide grit in the shape of sand or very fine gravel, for this is necessary for their digestion. With a little care and protection the farmer may greatly help in the preservation of this valuable bird.

Another game bird making a valiant fight for existence is the ruffed grouse. In early days, unsuspecting and tame, but now wary, yet steadily decreasing in numbers, this prince of our game birds should be assisted in its struggle for existence by greater protection.

Once the ruffed grouse, a valuable ally of the farmer, was common over the northern and eastern parts of the United States, but with the advance of agriculture, there is less and less forestland for it to breed in. Fortunately it does not ask for a vast acreage, and a stretch of natural woodland on an estate can become an excellent sanctuary. This is especially true if the hedgerows of which we have spoken surround the outlying fields and there is natural ground-cover in the woods.

In summer the ruffed grouse's food consists very largely of insects. It eats quantities of grasshoppers, crickets and locusts. It also devours caterpillars (including cutworms), ants, beetles, also bugs, including leaf and tree hoppers. The vegetable food of the ruffed grouse consists of practically all kinds of wild berries, and also wild nuts and even mushrooms. A list of the food eaten, given in Forbush's *Useful Birds and Their Protection* and largely compiled from a Biological Survey Bulletin of the grouse and wild turkeys of the United States, by Dr. Sylvester D. Judd, is quoted for the benefit of those doing planting to encourage the presence of this characteristic American bird. As this publication is now out of print, the insertion of the list here may serve a useful purpose for those who desire to increase the numbers of this fine game bird: Nuts or Seeds: Hazelnuts, beechnuts, chestnuts, acorns. Seeds of tick trefoil, hornbeam, vetch, hemlock, pitch pine, maple, blackberry, lily, beggar's-ticks, chickweed, sheep sorrel, sedges, violet, witch-hazel, avens, persicaria, frostweed, jewelweed. Buds, Blossoms or Foliage: Poplar, birch, willow, apple, pear, peach, alder, hazel, beech, ironwood, hornbeam, blackberry, blueberry, spruce, arborvitae, Mayflower, laurel, maple, spicebush, partridgeberry, sheep sorrel, heuchera, chickweed, catnip, cinquefoil, buttercup, speedwell, saxifrage, live-forever, meadow rue, smilax, horsetail rush, azalea, false goat's-beard, dandelion, cudweed. Fruit: Rose hips, grape, smooth sumac, dwarf sumac, staghorn sumac, scarlet sumac, poison ivy, partridge berry, thorn apple, cockspur thorn, scarlet thorn, mountain ash, greenbrier, hairy Solomon's-seal, smooth Solomon's-seal, black raspberry, raspberry, domestic cherry, cultivated plum, wild black cherry, wild red cherry, elder, red elder, black haw, nannyberry, mountain cranberry, snowberry, feverwort, black huckleberry, black alder, flowering dogwood, bunchberry, cornel, silky cornel, pepperidge, mulberry, bittersweet, manzanita, barberry, Virginia creeper.

An interesting fact about the ruffed grouse is that it is immune to the poison in mountain laurel and in sheep laurel, but that people eating the flesh of birds which have been feeding on buds and leaves of these shrubs may become violently ill.

There is nothing more a part of our forest life than the grouse's spring drumming, and it is always an exciting experience and a day long to be remembered when we come unexpectedly on a female with young in the summer. Sometimes, after a warning call to the babies to scatter and hide, she will fly at you hissing and squeaking like a rat, every feather a-bristle. Again she will limp away, apparently most pitifully crippled with a broken leg and wing, trying to lure you from her young. Step carefully, for the young may be right at your feet.

If we have marshy lowlands and alder thickets on the estate, we may be fortunate enough to have a few pairs of that distinctive bird, the woodcock. Colored the warm tans and browns of fallen leaves in the tangles where he loves to hide during the day, the woodcock may entirely escape attention. When flushed, he will fly a short distance, then sink to the leaves not far away, his color blending so with his surroundings that it is practically impossible to distinguish him. The female, also trusts so to this protective coloration that she will sometimes allow herself to be stroked as she sits tight upon her nest.

The eyes of the woodcock are set high in its head, evidently so that when it is probing in the mud for its favorite diet of earthworms it may look backward to watch for an enemy. It has a long bill, the upper half sensitive and capable of being moved like forceps to pull out its prize from the mud.

In eastern New York, the countryman believes that when the woodcock flies low across the road that it is a sure sign of rain. As this largely nocturnal bird would be much more likely to be flying on a dull cloudy day, it is, perhaps, a safe bet that rain is not far off.

The woodcock is most memorable, though, for its flight song during the time of courtship. Just at dusk, rising in spirals from sixty to two hundred feet, he flies upward and upward giving vent to a long series of ecstatic cheeping twitters, only to plunge at last headlong to the ground with a nasal "peent." He then may march, all feathers spread, in front of his (we hope) properly impressed lady love, only to rise again, silhouetted dimly against the faint afterglow in the western sky. Every farmer and estate owner should guard the woodcock as a treasure. The greater part of its stay from May to November it remains in the lowlands, probing with its sensitive bill for earthworms, but it also destroys many larval insects, such as those of wireworms, horseflies and crane flies;

at times in summer we may find it in the pastures and even in the vegetable garden eating cutworms and white grubs with our old friend, the robin.

So a part of the countryside is the ring-necked pheasant, its miniature crow, like the sound of a child's metal whistle, ringing out all through the spring, that it is hard to think that less than two generations ago it was unknown in our fields and woods. Introduced first into Oregon from China in 1881, it is well established in both the West and the East, and is now a lordly game bird in many of our States, being quite common in the warmer parts of New York and New England.

It is always a risk to introduce a foreign species and generally unwise. The ring-necked pheasant is no exception and is not considered desirable by all persons. Many complaints come from farmers because where fields are near the birds' breeding places, as flocks congregate during the season closed to hunting and pull up a planting of sprouting grain, peas, corn and even potatoes. It has also been accused of being an enemy of our native grouse and bobwhite.

But it seems that the "ring-neck" has come to stay. The handsome cocks parade openly in our fields and their sober-colored mates often marshal their broods, with an admonitory "keck, keck, keck" right on the edge of the shrubbery border. While during the winter they often come to the feeding station to share the grain which has been scattered on the ground.

Often on the estate or farm there are lakes, ponds, marshy spots or swampy woods where migratory ducks and geese may stop to rest or feed on their way north or south. A few species may even nest if the conditions are favorable. If such wet areas do not exist they may be created quite easily if there is a small stream or spring. One way is to dam a stream and flood a low section of land. This has been done in the Pleasant Valley Bird and Wild Flower Sanctuary in the Berkshires. Pike's Memorial Pond is one of the most attractive spots in the area and few know as they look out on the placid stretch of water that it has been in existence only since 1931.

Dr. George Wallace, warden of the sanctuary, says that it is now a nesting haven for semiwild ducks and geese and, because of the well-chosen planting of sheltering evergreens and fruit-producing shrubs, its shores produce fine nesting sites for a great variety of song birds.

Another way to produce shallow ponds is to introduce beaver. They help greatly in restoring environmental conditions of the past and so bring back much of the wild life formerly existing in the region. This has also been done at the Pleasant Valley Sanctuary and Dr. Wallace says that where the beaver have worked, a rather insignificant alder thicket has been transformed into a veritable haven for interesting bird and plant life. The flooding naturally kills some of the trees but this only adds to the interest as the dead stubs soon become fine nesting places for that gayly plumaged treasure, the wood duck, and also for smaller birds such as the valuable woodpeckers and tree swallows. And in the fall, decoyed in by the semi-wild breeders, black ducks seek refuge along the shores, often followed by mallards and an occasional pintail or teal.

Mr. William Carr, director of the Trailside Museum at Bear Mountain, says that the beaver introduced into that part of the Hudson Highlands have produced a great change both in bird and animal life, many species being seen that were entirely absent a few years ago. The beaver have helped establish a permanent water table and thus assist tremendously in the control of forest fires. On the edge of the ponds dammed by the busy engineers, he says both wood ducks and wild mallards now nest, and various herons, bitterns and other birds attracted by such wet spots are becoming more common as the years advance.

If there is no hunting on the estate, migrating wildfowl soon learn that there is a spot where they can have safety and food. They fly high above any gunshots from surrounding land and settle down peacefully, sometimes in great numbers. Of course it is always best to build up the natural food plants, but in times of stress grain should be supplied and it is remarkable to see how tame these ruthlessly hunted birds become in a place where they are protected.

It is thought probable that in the past more species of ducks nested in the Northeastern States than do so at the present day. But due to spring shooting the breeding stock was wiped out, and now we have few species nesting with us except the black duck, the wood duck and the blue-winged teal. We may materially aid in the increase of these species by building up a suitable environment for them. Wild mallards are now nesting on Long Island, but it is thought that they are the progeny of birds formerly held in captivity. Or another theory is that some of these breeding mallards and also other species may be the descendants of disabled pairs that nested because they were unable to migrate.

Much can be done through planting to make an area suitable for ducks and other water fowl. Of course many ducks will settle to rest among the reeds of an open marsh, but planting taller cover near the edge of the marsh will provide a feeling of security. Also if the water area is of some extent there are many plants that can be set on the margin or in the water itself which will help to supply food all through the year.

If the land has been cleared, restore the landscape to the harmony of the past by planting native trees and shrubs. They will produce natural cover and there is much less danger of their becoming weedy and spreading unduly than if certain exotics are used.

Among the trees of larger growth, the red maple, *Acer rubrum*, thrives in low land and will soon become established near the edge of a lake. It is one of the first trees to bloom in the spring, its bright red blooms welcoming the early arrivals from the South, while in the fall its brilliant scarlet foliage heralds the autumn migration.

Equally at home in the damp soil is the pin oak, *Quercus palustris*; its drooping limbs produce protective cover, it has fine autumn coloring and its acorns are eaten by ducks.

With the roots almost in the water, a thicket of spotted alder, *Alnus incana,* will make secure hiding places for black ducks and mallards, while on the landward edge of such a thicket should be planted that member of the holly family, often called black alder, *Ilex verticillata.* Its red berries, make a blaze of color seen from afar in the fall.

Another shrub that can be massed around the margin of the pond is the buttonbush, *Cephalanthus occidentalis.* The mallard takes delight in its seeds. While the elderberry, *Sambucus canadensis,* which thrives in moist ground, is always lovely in flower and carries fruit that is exceedingly attractive to birds. The highbush blueberry, *Vaccinium corymbosum,* also furnishes food.

The various reeds and rushes on the edges of ponds make ideal nesting spots and hideaways for many ducks, while plants which grow on or under the surface of the water produce food for many species. At the end of the book are lists of trees and shrubs for marginal planting and also of plants that will grow in the ponds.

During migration in the Eastern States, you may be able to identify ten or more species of ducks and also flocks of geese on your ponds. Among those that you will be most certain to see is the mallard, which comes early and stays late. It often lingers in protected areas all through the fall, and, if it stays after the migration urge has passed, will remain all winter if there is an open spot of water and food. Frequently mallards collect in flocks and feed in the cut-over grainfields.

The mallard is quite like its descendant, the domestic duck of our barnyards, but smaller. The green head and white ring on the neck of the male make it easily recognizable. The female is a modest brown bird, sharing with the male, however, the white-bordered blue beauty spots on the wings.

It is quite easy to tempt these handsome birds to our ponds. It is a pleasure to watch them, and in addition we may know that if they nest with us we have excellent mosquito eradicators in our midst. Not long ago, Dr. Samuel G. Dixon, while Health Commissioner of Pennsylvania, used

ORCHARD ORIOLE

BREEDING MALE, FULLY ADULT

FEMALE   MALE, FIRST BREEDING PLUMAGE

BALTIMORE ORIOLE

FEMALE

MALE, BREEDING ADULT

IMMATURE MALE, FALL

Scale about one-half

mallards in keeping down mosquitoes in swamps not practicable to drain. He wrote in an article in the Journal of the American Medical Association that the ducks devoured the larvae and pupae of mosquitoes ravenously, seeming to prefer them to any other food. Mallards also eat fish fry, grasshoppers, mice, snails, leeches, angleworms, aquatic insects, frogs, toads, and salamanders. The greater part of their food though, is vegetable and consists of sedges, grasses, wild celery, duckweeds, pondweeds, smartweeds, acorns, wild millet, coontail, wapato, wild rice and waste grain. Proper planting, supplemented by judicious feeding of grain will keep the mallard with us.

Mallards make a bulky nest of leaves and grasses, heavily lined with down from the breast of the female. It is usually placed on the ground near water, well hidden in tangled grasses or rushes. Occasionally, though, a nest is found farther upland and it has been reported that abandoned nests of crows or hawks have been used.

It is interesting to note that the loud quacking we hear from the rushes is all done by the female. The drake contents himself with a reedy croak and lets the duck do all the talking.

Another duck that nests in the Northeastern States is the black. It is quite like the mallard in shape, but is sooty brown, with the feathers lighter-edged, especially on the neck and throat; the beauty spot lacks an upper white margin, but the lining of its wings is white. It is found in the waters of sloughs and slow marshy streams. Its nesting habits are similar to those of a mallard, but it has been known to conceal its nests in the lower branches of a bushy evergreen.

If the mallard is a valuable tenant because of its destruction of mosquito larvae, the black duck pays rent by acting as a consumer of weed seeds. In spring its diet runs more to meat than to vegetables, consisting principally of the larvae of water insects, tadpoles, mussels, leeches, minnows, earthworms, and even toads, salamanders and small mammals. But in the fall you will find your planting appreciated, for then, nuts and berries, grassroots and vast quantities of weed seeds form the greater portion of the black duck's menu. As with the mallard the duck is the talkative member of the family. When alarmed she shouts "Quack—quack—quack—," very resonantly. This alarm note is heard also when a snapping turtle pulls one of her young under water. But in spite of handicaps she generally manages to raise a fine set of youngsters.

Spring will bring us that jeweled beauty, the wood duck. The drake is the most gorgeously colored of any duck in America, if not in the world. It is even more beautiful than the Mandarin duck so widely pictured in the art of the Orient. Its backward falling crest of iridescent purplish-green, its white throat and cinnamon breast are unmistakable. In the past it was common in many localities; once its habits were as well known to the country dweller as those of the blackbird and the robin. But its gentle, unsuspicious nature, combined with its conspicuous coloring, nearly brought about its extinction. It was ruthlessly hunted wherever it nested until a few years ago when it came under the protection of both State and Federal laws. Now it is slowly coming back and proper planting and the provision of nesting sites will aid in restoring this bit of pure beauty to our woodlands. The dark brown female is also crested.

A swampy woodland, not an open marsh, is the type of place selected by this duck for its summer home. And here the value of our planting comes in, for the wood duck's food is largely vegetable and consists not only of seeds, but of the tender green growth of many plants on the edge of the water or in it. It enjoys eating duckweeds and pondweeds, and the seeds of grasses, sedges, water lilies and skunk cabbage and will canvass the woodland margin for acorns, other nuts, wild grapes and berries.

The wood duck's natural preference for a nesting site is a hollow in an old dead tree. It has been known to use the abandoned hole of a pileated woodpecker, but it will nest also in a barrel or a box fastened in a tree. Many stories have been told of the female carrying the young down to the water, but it is generally thought now that the babies, like bits of fluff, tumble lightly to the ground and then follow their mother to the pond, occasionally over quite a distance.

The three ducks described are the kinds we are most likely to have nesting with us, but there is always the probability that we may have the pleasant surprise of seeing such a delightful duck as the blue-winged teal or even a shoveller, as the latter are now breeding in Maryland. The creation of an artificial lake at Pymatuning in Pennsylvania has added since 1934 eight species to the list of breeding ducks in that region.

Other interesting birds which might nest in such refuges are the Canada goose, pied-billed grebe, and the Florida gallinule.

Chapter Thirteen

NATURE'S BALANCE KEEPERS

THE gardener as well as the farmer should know how beneficial hawks are in the scheme of nature. Dr. John B. May says: "It is evident that hawks play an important role in nature or they would not be found in such large numbers of species, and so widely distributed, but until a comparatively few years ago man had very little conception of what that part might be." Unfortunately, as he points out, in the many myths that have sprung up about them in different countries, they have often been used not only as symbols of courage but of rapacity, and through the years popular prejudice has been built up against them. The word "hawk" has come to have a sinister meaning. The villain of the play has a "hawklike" profile and the eye of a "hawk" is always baneful.

It is true that hawks are meat eaters. But so is man. It is true that hawks occasionally prey on game birds and sometimes on our most delightful song birds. But is man, with that powerful weapon, the modern gun, the only creature that has the right to kill a duck or a grouse? Except in a pioneer country he has no actual need of these birds for food, while the hawk needs to eat them in order to exist. And as for the song birds, if all that were hatched each season were allowed to live the earth could not support them! Checks on the too rapid increase of birds are necessary parts of the scheme of nature. In the case of the song birds, though we may shudder to see a sharp-shinned hawk pursue a junco or song sparrow before our eyes we must realise that the apparently murderous bird is only helping to preserve that mysterious equation called, so glibly, "the balance of nature." That very junco or song sparrow may have been unwary because of disease or because of some physical defect which would cause it to be unfit for the struggle for existence.

As to game birds we are likely to blame their decrease on anything but the right cause. Dr. T. S. Roberts says, in *The Birds of Minnesota:* "Man is unquestionably the worst enemy of wild life and is he not striving to lay the blame, for at least a part of the havoc he has wrought, where it does not rightfully belong? In unsettled and sparsely-settled regions, where hawks and owls are undisturbed, game and non-game birds are more abundant than in settled regions just as was the case in former times. The fault today lies chiefly with the great body of organized sportsmen. With rare exceptions they cannot with equanimity view the loss of a small part of *their* game, that the greater good may be served. All predators are classed as 'vermin,' an opprobrious epithet that has been defined by Dr. Pearson, when used in this connection, as 'any wild creature that kills something that you want to kill!' To conserve and protect simply to destroy later is Conservation in only a limited and selfish sense."

To many gardeners as well as to the farmer all hawks are "hen hawks" because our father or our grandfather called them that, and when a number of "hen hawk"-minded men get together, as in a legislature, then laws are passed against hawks in general. These birds are classified as "vermin" and a bounty is offered for their destruction. Against no other branch of wild life has this popular prejudice been so virulent and widespread. Against nothing else in nature has man lifted a more violent hand.

Especially during migration has this persecution been most pernicious. Often at these times hawks fly in vast companies; especially is this true of the broad-winged hawk, a species of great value to the farmer. Yet Dr. Roberts in *The Birds of Minnesota,* tells how the broad-wings were shot one year in numbers over four thousand in one day as they passed over some of the villages of his State. So strong was the prejudice against these birds that the farmers thought that they were doing a righteous act in exterminating these "vermin."

No one is more bitter in hawk prejudice than the poultry or game raiser. Near their farms hawks have been killed to an outrageous extent. Gamekeepers especially have become absolute fanatics on the subject. To them the only "good" hawk is a "dead" hawk. Naturally, certain bird-eating hawks are attracted to places where there is a concentration of bird life. But if both the poultry- and the game-raiser would protect their runs by enclosing them with wire netting, they would not need to fear even there the few hawks that do prey upon birds, or the few immature birds of the more beneficial species that might be tempted by the easily obtained food. In a few States such as California, the gamefarms have protected runs and suffer no "depredations" from hawks or owls.

Not many years ago Pennsylvania farmers, as well as the hawks and owls, suffered greatly through a law passed to give a bounty on all birds of prey. Nearly a hundred thousand dollars was paid out in bounties, and it has been estimated that nearly four million dollars was lost through grain destroyed by mice, rats, and insects, which increased with great rapidity because not kept in check by their natural enemies. Throughout the United States as a whole it is estimated that the annual loss from rats and mice is five hundred million dollars. If the hawks and owls that prey upon these harmful rodents are exterminated, not only will agriculture suffer increased damage, but many regions will be impoverished for game through increased rodent consumption of vegetation.

The United States Department of Agriculture has pointed out that the killing off of the birds which prey upon them has been the greatest factor in the increase of rats, mice and other destructive rodents. It states that rats destroy more poultry and game, both eggs and young chicks, than all the predatory birds and wild mammals combined, and yet some of the natural enemies of rats are persecuted almost to the point of extinction. It advocates a repeal of all bounties on predators.

It is true that in some States the majority of hawks are afforded protection by law. But that law is seldom enforced. No one ever reports the shooting of a hawk. "Only a hen hawk"—and the matter is dismissed. The story is told of the farmer who saw a hawk fly into his poultry yard. He rushed into the house, brought out his shot gun and blazed away. The hawk fell and a huge dead rat fell too. The rat had doubtless been responsible for all the farmer's chicken losses.

Only within the last few years has the prejudice against birds of prey somewhat abated. This has been due chiefly to the efforts of the United States Biological Survey and the National Association of Audubon Societies. The Biological Survey has brought to the public through publications written by Dr. A. K. Fisher and W. L. McAtee the results of the examination of stomach contents of birds of prey. These examinations have proved beyond a shadow of doubt the beneficial status of the majority of the hawks. Through the Audubon Societies, popular feeling has been aroused, not only through spreading knowledge of the economic worth of these birds but also of their esthetic value as a part of the beauty of nature. Dr. George Miksch Sutton dwells on this value: "Our deepest, most sincere reasons for protecting wild life are not, after all, based on economic values. If you can make the public sense the need of these magnificent creatures in every one's experience, the preservation of birds of prey which are now too rare, will become an important and fascinating feature of the wild life conservation movement."

After extensive studies, scientists have come to the conclusion that even in areas where there is a concentration of bird life, it is a mistake to interfere with natural checks. In one sanctuary it was only after great losses among young ducks that it was realized how dangerous it is to interfere with nature. In this case, in order that the ducks might breed and increase in peace the skunks were trapped, and it was found that the ducklings were being destroyed by snapping turtles. This was due to the fact that there were fewer skunks to keep down the numbers of the turtles by devouring their eggs, and, of course, there were soon many more turtles to pull the young ducks under the water and devour them.

BIRDS IN THE GARDEN

This experience shows how disastrous it is to upset the balance of wild life. In the bird sanctuary an equal disturbance might result if every hawk were killed. There would be such a rapid increase in meadow mice that every ground-nesting bird would fail to bring off its quota of nestlings; while the weaklings of other birds, which would have lived because of the absence of hawks, would die from food shortage or disease, or the hardships of migration. On the other hand, it would be a great mistake to dispose of all the meadow mice by poison. Their own natural enemies are their best checks. Richard Pough in the National Association of Audubon Societies' Leaflet *Enter Hawk—Exit Mouse* says: "Because they are native species these mouse-eating predators (hawks and owls) are naturally present wherever meadow mice occur, unless they have been killed off by man. It is usually only when these predators have been persecuted, as a result of the mistaken idea that they are harmful, that mouse populations rise to unnaturally high levels . . . Therefore during periods of mouse abundance, if the 'natural enemies' of the mice have not been too greatly reduced by unwise 'vermin control campaigns,' the number of mice caught tends to be greater than the number raised, until the population is reduced . . . It is this continued 'see-sawing' up and down of an average population level that is a true 'balance of nature,' and it can only be preserved through the conservation of all kinds of native wild life, each variety of which plays a part in some important balance such as the balance between the meadow mouse and its 'natural enemies.' "

In the ordinary course of things nature is a great adapter and is ever trying to keep things at the same level. Every year many individuals are sacrificed. The nature student has to face this, realizing that the species will carry on. Joseph A. Hagar, State Ornithologist of Massachusetts, says in an article entitled *We Need More Realism in Conservation:* "If nature has on hand next spring as many mated pairs of any species as she had this spring, she has achieved her goal of species perpetuation."

The hawks which we are most likely to see about our garden or country

174

PINE SISKIN

INDIGO BUNTING
MALE, BREEDING ADULT
FEMALE, BREEDING ADULT
MOLTING MALE

AMERICAN GOLDFINCH
WINTER
MALE, BREEDING ADULT
FEMALE, BREEDING ADULT

Scale about one-half

place may soon be recognized by the bird-student and as we learn to look at them without fear or prejudice there will quickly come to us an appreciation of the grace of their soaring flight and an admiration for their fearlessness and indomitable spirit. The majority of them are of great value to the horticulturist and should be protected at all costs.

Belonging to the falcons—those birds which played such a conspicuous role in the age of chivalry—the delightful little sparrow hawk is one of the first of the hawks likely to come to the attention of the gardener. According to W. L. McAtee of the United States Biological Survey, the sparrow hawk is almost exclusively insectivorous except when insect food is hard to obtain, and should be called the grasshopper rather than the sparrow hawk, as it eats quantities of grasshoppers and crickets, besides white grubs and caterpillars.

This little hawk, reddish above and buffy below, with a chestnut crown on his bluish-gray head, is not much larger than a robin. Like the tree swallow, it has adapted itself to the ways of civilization and now nests quite frequently in a hollow tree on the village street, or in a birdbox in the garden. It is not only one of the most beautiful and brightly colored of the hawks, but one of the most useful. If, some morning, we hear its noisy "killee, killee" in our garden, we may know that we are sheltering the foe of not only insects but of meadow mice—those destroyers of tulip bulbs and girdlers of trees. Perhaps during the nesting season it may take an occasional song bird, but even then its prey usually is an English sparrow, which certainly we can spare without a pang.

Sparrow hawks certainly add great interest to the open fields in the East and to the prairies in the West. Quite fearlessly they often perch on dead snags or fence posts watching for their prey. Suddenly spying a slight movement in the grass, they will launch out and hover for a moment with quivering wings before descending upon a hapless cricket, grasshopper or mouse, or sometimes prey as large as a half-grown striped gopher.

The hawks that we are most likely to see soaring overhead on a summer's day are the *Buteo* or buzzard hawks. They are heavy, sluggish birds having long, round-ended wings, and when flying show a tail spread like a fan.

Though the average farmer still persists in calling them "hen hawks" and blazes away at them whenever he gets a chance, hawks of this class have been proved by actual examination of stomach contents to be largely beneficial to agriculture.

One of the most frequently seen, the red-tailed hawk, sails aloft on almost motionless wide-spread wings and with wide-spread red tail, or sits on some high, dead tree waiting patiently until it spies its prey of field mice, ground squirrels, or other small rodents.

E. H. Forbush says that in hunting, these hawks circle slowly and drift at great heights, often up among the clouds. When with its keen, far-seeing eye one detects the movement of some fat meadow mouse below, it will nearly close its wings, and rush head foremost through the air, falling like a hissing meteor from the clouds until it sees a convenient tree-top, when with spread wing and tail it checks its flight and alights gracefully on some dead projecting limb, ready to fall instantly to the ground at the next quiver of a grass blade.

The red-tail usually nests in forests, but occasionally in small patches of woods near villages. The nest is placed from twenty to eighty feet up and is usually well concealed, sometimes by twigs covered with green leaves. Its calls include a high-pitched whistle and a spluttering note like escaping steam.

Another hawk commonly seen in many parts of the Eastern States is the red-shouldered hawk. Of course, because of hawk prejudice it is not seen as often as formerly and certainly not as frequently as it should be near every farm. It is not as likely to be seen circling aloft in leisurely circles as the slightly larger red-tail, but more often perches on a bare stub. It may be recognized by the bright reddish-cinnamon shoulder patches. The nest is often found in trees in wet woods, and frequently it is built at no great distance from houses. Never as high as the red-tail's, quite often it is in plain sight. Spring after spring the red-shoulder will return to the same spot and both male and female work at nest building.

Dr. John B. May says that the red-shouldered hawk is a decidedly beneficial species as at least 65% of its food consists of small rodents and it prevents the too great increase of snakes that destroy the eggs and young of ground-nesting birds. Its note is a clear jay-like whistle.

On an estate where there is much rough, wooded land, the broad-winged hawk may be found nesting on the hills and occasionally near our homes. Although usually placed up to ninety feet high in trees, its nests may be found at lower levels.

The broad-wing is a small hawk, about the size of a crow, but appearing larger because of the wide spread of its wings. Its broad, square-angled tail crossed by a broad pale band near the middle as seen from below, is an excellent identification mark. This is another beneficial hawk that should be recognized and protected. Its food consists of snakes, toads, shrews, red squirrels, moles, mice, grasshoppers, crickets, May beetles, earthworms, caterpillars and only occasionally a small bird. Its note is very like the wood pewee's, but louder and more emphatic without the melancholy cadence.

The broad-wing sometimes flies very high, and, almost among the clouds, sails back and forth with the air currents. At times though, it skims over the tree tops or near the ground seeking the "small fry" that constitute its menu.

Over meadowland we may expect to see the delicately proportioned, graceful marsh hawk, gliding like a gull through the air, coursing tirelessly back and forth by the hour—even carrying on its love affairs aloft. It may be easily recognized by its white rump, and long wings and tail.

Unlike most of its relatives, which usually nest high on trees or on cliffs, the marsh hawk, the American representative of the harriers, builds its nest on the ground not far from water.

The food of this hawk varies greatly according to the region where it is found. There is no doubt that part of its food consists of small birds. Dr. A. K. Fisher thinks that its value is so great as a destroyer of rodents that the fact that it destroys some birds should be overlooked. But due to unforgivable ignorance, the farmer and sportsman shoot it down at sight, regardless of the fact that it preserves an enormous quantity of grain, thousands of forest trees, and innumerable game bird nests by keeping in check meadow mice, squirrels, and other small rodents.

The three hawks that we may expect to take regular toll of birds in the woods and garden are those classed as the "blue darters," the sharp-shinned hawk, the goshawk and Cooper's hawk. Their characteristic actions are quite the contrary of what the average person thinks of as hawklike. They do not usually soar in sweeping circles high in the air. They have short, rounded wings and long narrow tails, and, instead of spying their prey from above, fly over and through the shrubbery and pounce on a bird sometimes before your very eyes.

Only slightly larger than the sparrow hawk, the sharp-shinned hawk is easily distinguished from the little falcon because it is heavily cross-barred below and instead of bright cinnamon, is grayish-blue above. Its wings are short, broad and rounded, while the sparrow hawk's are true falcon shape, long, slender and pointed.

All the actions of the sharp-shinned hawk are entirely different from those of the more peaceable little falcon who sometimes nests quite amicably in a box in the garden. The sharp-shinned nests in trees, sometimes in pines, but usually in deciduous timber. And from the underbrush of the woods it comes out on its forays, pursuing its prey in quick, short flights. It lives chiefly on small birds, but because of its own size it can do little harm to game or poultry, other than chicks. It at times eats grasshoppers, mice and harmful insects, and though, to us, who can see but such a small part of nature's drama, it may seem cruel, it is merely conforming to the behavior pattern of its species, and must be considered one of the useful checks against over-production of the smaller species it preys upon. Moreover it is steadily diminishing in numbers due to the ruthless manner in which it is shot particularly during migration. It should be given protection from extermination as it is part of our native wild life.

The largest of the "blue darters" is the goshawk. It is larger than a crow and sometimes has a wing spread of forty-seven inches. It is light slaty-gray above, only the marsh hawk being lighter in color. It is a powerful and bold bird, breeding in the Far North and appearing in our territory only in the winter when driven south by shortage of food. On such incursions, the goshawk preys heavily on grouse and poultry, but in Nova Scotia and New Brunswick, where it summers, it seldom attacks the ruffed grouse which flourishes in these regions except where there is excessive shooting. It feeds extensively on rabbits which do much damage to trees in the forest and orchard and always need a check on their over-abundance. It also eats many red squirrels, known to eat game birds' eggs. This bears out what Richard Pough says, "that as long as plenty of mice and other rodents are available . . . hawks and owls, will not seek further for food. Game birds and most of the other kinds of wild life we would like to see undisturbed by predators are, if healthy and well fed, fairly hard for them to catch. Most predators, therefore, are perfectly satisfied to live on easier prey such as mice, as long as they can be obtained."

On the Cooper's hawk, a larger edition of the sharp-shinned, must be laid much of the blame for the evil repute of hawks in general. It breeds throughout the Northeastern States and it undoubtedly does eat many game birds and unprotected poultry. Like the sharp-shinned, though it may occasionally be seen flying overhead, it generally darts suddenly on its prey from cover. J. T. Nichols finds that "there is a subtle difference in the character of the flight between the two, the sharp-shinned giving the effect of buoyancy and the Cooper's of momentum." It has a peculiar "cuck, cuck, cuck," call and all the smaller birds seem to know when that note is heard that the cold wind of danger is blowing, for silence is their only answer to that buccaneering signal.

Even if a few unwary birds are taken by this hawk, it is only performing the part which nature assigned it before man came along with his domestic fowls and game farms, the latter designed to make up for his own rapacity in over-shooting game. Even now Cooper's hawk is undoubtedly a check on the spread of disease among ducks, grouse, and quails, for weakened and diseased individuals naturally are the most easily captured, while it also preys upon the less alert and cautious of the small birds of the hedgerows.

One of the handsomest of the hawks, the duck hawk, is the representative on this continent of the noble peregrine falcon, the bird trained abroad in the Middle Ages for the famous sport of hawking or falconry. It is a little larger than a crow, dark slate gray in color with a black cap and black "moustaches." It is so rare that we may view without too many qualms the daring assaults of the few which eat jays and smaller birds as well as some of the shore birds and water fowl. Like the Cooper's hawk, it is only playing its part gallantly; unfortunately though, occasionally it preys upon the "meat" which man considers belongs to him exclusively, and then it falls before his gun.

The duck hawk will not be seen near our gardens unless, strange to say, we are in a city and have a roof garden or a terrace. It is very interesting to know that sometimes in winter duck hawks take their stands on the tops of large buildings in New York, Boston, Philadelphia, Chicago, San Francisco, and probably other large cities, and from there descend precipitately upon the hordes of pigeons, starlings, and English sparrows all of which can well be spared.

Though hardly a bird of our gardens, the bald eagle, related to the *buteonine* or buzzard hawks, might be seen floating over some of the larger wooded estates. That is, we might see it if this majestic bird, our national emblem, had not been one of the greatest sufferers in the campaign against predators. When young, it is often killed for a hawk, and when that mistake is realized it is then thought to be a golden eagle. This is because for the first four years of its life its distinguishing white head and tail have not yet developed. Including this grand bird in the unthinking slaughter of so-called "vermin," shows definitely that as a people we are without sentiment in the best use of that word. We have done irreparable damage in almost eliminating this symbol of majesty from our wild life. Dr. John B. May says: "This magnificent appearing bird is an inspiration to all observers and of great esthetic interest, as it soars easily high overhead on widespread pinions, or perches apparently in deep thought, on the jagged summit of some great dead tree beside the shore of a wooded lake or an inlet of the sea."

The bald eagle is very rare now except perhaps in Florida, British Columbia and in some parts of Alaska. You might think that in Alaska that land of fish and game, the bald eagle could have found sanctuary, but in that territory persecution has reached its height. Every year thousands of dollars are paid out in bounty on the receipt of majesty's severed feet. And all because the bald eagle eats a small portion of something that man, that mighty being, lord of all he surveys, wishes to keep for himself. It is true that the bald eagle eats salmon, but the greater portion of it is carrion, for the Alaska salmon, after spawning, dies and then is food for whatever creature finds it. And even if the eagle took a few salmon before their death, what of the enormous salmon canneries which do away with millions of live salmon? Has the decrease of salmon in the Alaska waters been due to the bald eagle or to man's greed? For thousands of years the bald eagle had eaten salmon and was still eating it when the first fisherman marveled at those now seemingly mythical runs of fish, those countless silvery hordes which fought their way up the rapids of the unpolluted rivers.

The newspaper stories of the fierceness and the rapacity of the eagle are fictions of the grossest character. It is really a rather slow, sluggish bird and according to W. L. McAtee of the United States Biological Survey, lives largely on carrion, but it does occasionally eat ducks and other water-fowl. But as part of our wild life it is of inestimable value and as it is our

BIRDS IN THE GARDEN

National Emblem a federal enactment should protect it in every State and Territory that it may be preserved before its majestic soaring flight over lonely mountain crags is only a memory, a part of our traditions, as are the stories of the vast, sun-darkening flights of the passenger pigeon.

Chapter Fourteen

BIRDS IN THE CITY GARDEN

THE twitter of the barn swallow, the bubbling song of the wren—how those that are shut in cities miss them if they have known the joy of childhood in the country. Too many times bird song to the city dweller means the harsh chatter of English sparrows or the monotonous moan of pigeons, neither natives of America. But even barriers of wood and stone cannot prevent the true nature student from pursuing his hobby. Astonishing records of the number of birds observed have been made in the tiniest of backyards and often the rarest species are seen in Central Park, that green pulsing heart of New York City. In answer to the question: "Where can I learn to know the birds?" The enquirer will be astonished to know that one of the best places is in a city park which has a planting of tangled shrubbery. Here, during the spring and fall you may see rare warblers without even using a glass—birds, which in the country would be lost among the branches of taller trees. The explanation is this, that many of our smaller birds, particularly the warblers, travel at night, and after a long flight are attracted by city lights and come to rest in the wide open spaces of the parks. Here, surrounded by the crags of the skyscrapers, they are thankful to find themselves in the safe haven of trees and shrubs. They see nothing tempting farther ahead, and instead of traveling slowly toward their north or south goal by flitting from grove to grove, as is their custom in the country, they are glad to remain a number of days in a land of abundant food.

Let us go one morning in early May to Central Park. The sun has not yet risen and fog still lingers. We are in the "Ramble," where the paths climb up and down and there are miniature ravines with streams trickling through them, gradually making their way to a small lake. Let us take a seat on this outcropping rock which looks down on a little stream, and where we can look into the branches, only lightly veiled by pale green unfolding leaves.

The sky lightens and from all about rises a chorus of joyous chirps. "A wave of warblers came in with the fog," we whisper to a friend new to the city, as proud as if we are responsible for the phenomenon.

And as the first rays touch the delicate green foliage we see every tree is full of warblers, as gayly colored as butterflies, their plumage a mosaic of gold, crimson, azure and black. Perhaps some of them have come as far as from South America and they are so joyous at finding a haven and so eager for food after the long journey that they utterly ignore our presence, often coming quite near to us.

Look, within three feet, a black and white warbler circles that dwarf wild cherry precariously rooted in a crevice of the rock. And there beyond a blue-gray myrtle warbler shows the yellow spots on wings, rump and head, while his white throat swells with the thin, quick, "check, check," in answer to the notes of hundreds of his brothers in near-by trees.

A blue jay calls and six of the cerulean dandies follow one another through the silvery branches of the beeches growing on the knoll before us. A sharp "quick, quick" and a rose-breasted grosbeak gives a few preliminary notes of his tender warble. He lights above us and his rosy breast glows in the morning sunlight. We see a hermit thrush making his way through the dead leaves, his tail as red-brown as if it had been singed by a hot iron; and through that leafy tangle near the stream an ovenbird walks primly along, picking her steps as mincingly as a proper Victorian maiden. And, yes, not far off on the other bank is a northern water-thrush! See the yellow line over the eye and the way he wags his tail and teeters up and down with ridiculous little curtsies. He is a true warbler but prefers the rich foraging along streams, rather than the effort of flitting through the tree

184

tops, and this has gained him the name of water thrush or water wagtail. Like the brook whispering around stones, rises a few notes of his spraylike song.

"Oh, look above," you whisper, "hear the lazy drawling "zee, zee, zee." Yes, it is a black-throated blue warbler." We rise and stand, looking directly up at his snowy breast and black throat. He is distinctly blue, black and white—clean-cut and tailor-made.

We walk on slowly. On every side are other quiet strollers. We cannot call them loiterers for they are all there with a definite purpose and are all armed with a badge of fellowship—a pair of field-glasses. The sun is well above the buildings beyond Fifth Avenue now, but still the busy travelers search for food. We walk out in the open. "Oh, quick, in that red cedar!" you tell your friend. And there, within ten feet of us, going confidently about his own affairs, is a magnolia warbler—we note the yellow throat, blue-gray back, yellow rump and yellow breast lined with black. "Why, it is as exquisite as a swallowtail butterfly!" your friend exclaims.

A note like a robin's but more guttural, and there in the yellow-green of a sassafras tree are several brilliant scarlet tanagers, their startling tropical color never losing its novelty to northern eyes. We pass through an open grassy part of the Park and see an old apple tree, so covered with pink and white blossoms that not an inch of its scarred and gnarly branches is visible. A movement, and weaving in and out of the fragrant blooms we see a Cape May warbler with his "tiger-pattern" of yellow and black.

We now turn toward the "Point," a narrow bit of land which extends into a little lake. A brown creeper lights at the foot of a tree almost at our feet and goes up the trunk, propping himself with his tail and probing with his slender bill for his breakfast. We whistle his song, but he ignores it, preferring to reserve his lovemaking for his northern nesting place. Central Park is merely a roadhouse on his journey, and he is late as it is.

What is that group looking at so intently? Some one with the true "camaraderie" of the naturalist beckons to us and we hurry quietly up.

185

And then we gasp—it can't be true! But the notes are unmistakable and we can see his orange-yellow head gleaming in the sun. It is a prothonotary warbler! Utterly oblivious of the interested spectators, this seldom-seen wanderer from the southern swamps flits from twig to twig, singing and eating. Ludlow Griscom says that in the early days of observation in Central Park the excitement caused by the unexpected arrival of this bird brought a number of converts to the cult of "bird watching."

Nine o'clock and the office calls. We reluctantly turn our way toward the subway entrance, lingering to watch a ruby-crowned kinglet flit through the wistaria draping a dead stub leaning over the water, and to have the joy of seeing a Blackburnian warbler light up branch after branch of the "witches'" brooms on a hackberry tree. Just as we leave the "Ramble" we pause at the sound of a whistle and are carried in spirit to the cool ravines of the White Mountains as we listen to the wistful song of the white-throated sparrow.

Central Park has not the mystical charm of the untouched wilderness, but its very situation in the heart of one of the greatest cities in the world gives the experience of bird watching in its midst an unreality, a romantic quality—brings to it a feeling of adventure which is lacking in a trip in the country. We share the delight and happiness of the little adventurers more intimately. Their fearlessness makes us feel closer akin to them in this sky-scraper-barred park than we do when they are more aloof from us in the open country.

Not only do the trees in the parks extend a welcome to the birds but trees in any part of the city seem to have an irresistible lure for them. In various parts of the city of New York, especially in the older sections, we find gardens behind the forbidding brownstone fronts, delightful little retreats where trees and shrubs thrive in spite of soot and reflected heat. And year after year these little court-yards are the haven of many a wing-weary wanderer. Many are the delightfully intimate experiences with birds which the owners of these gardens have known. It seems as if one were dreaming when the notes of a song sparrow float in through the window of a city apartment. But you know that you have heard truly when you see him scratching busily under the privet bush or venturing a bath in the basin placed so conveniently near the feeding shelf.

And then to look out into the branches of the ailanthus and see the gold of an oriole—one year an oriole was so intrigued with the food prepared for him that he lingered all winter in a garden in Greenwich Village. In the autumn a flock of juncos foretells snow, and perhaps a woodcock may float in, as brown as the fallen leaves among which he conceals himself. And when a robin appears in the spring! This bird, quite taken for granted as a herald of spring in the suburbs or in the country, is greeted as a long-lost friend and welcomed as a returned adventurer in the city.

Nothing can dramatize the joy of the visit of migrating birds more vividly than the experience of Miss Holder and Miss Bohmfalk—who for fifty years have lived in one house in the heart of Manhattan. Back of it is an open space where not only the hardy ailanthus trees thrive, but also a few plums and cherries, while privet, forsythia and rose-of-Sharon make lower, sheltering cover. Miss Holder writes:

"Last October, a bunch of black alder berries, *Ilex verticillata,* was sent us from Maine. Hermit thrushes on their southbound journey, had already stopped to pay us a visit and we placed a large bunch of the berries in a tall tin vase, (filled with water so it would not tip) on the paving-stones about eight feet from the kitchen door which is on a level with the yard. Another bunch was placed on a stone garden table which stands near the kitchen window.

"It did not take the birds long to discover the berries. They came— one, two, sometimes even three at a time, sitting in the branches, at first a little wary and then growing bolder and bolder. And then more and more came. We felt that they must be sending out messages to other thrushes that might be in the neighborhood. We have hermit thrushes in our yard at migrating season every year, perhaps four, five or six at a time, with perhaps a few wood thrushes with them. But last fall I counted at least fifteen and there may have been more.

"We noticed that the hermit thrush could consume but three berries at a time while the wood thrush ate five. After having picked their quantity, they flew away, and later returned for more. Back and forth the feasters flew until by noon there was not a berry left on either of the big bunches.

"But, the birds still lingered looking over the bare branches hopefully, so I took a fresh branch from the library, intending to place it out of doors. It was thick with berries and the thought occurred to me as I was dressed inconspicuously in black, that if I held the branch in my hand the birds might come to me. I stood close to the door jamb, and I think the birds must have known that this was a friendly house, for after flying toward me and away several times in order to survey the situation, to my astonishment, one took courage and lighted on my branch! I was so delighted that I feared he could feel my heartbeats through the ends of my fingers! He did not eat right away—he sat there holding me with his eye. I was distinctly on trial and I did not dare to move so much as an eyelash. The lovely brown of his back was so beautifully smooth, and it was interesting to see at such close range how the "speckles" on his breast are made—not just flat spots, but the tips of tiny soft feathers. After this breathless interval he plucked a berry and flew off.

"Then another came. I continued to stand rigidly still—a second flew to my branch, then a third, and then a fourth! But there was not room for the last one—he lighted on the back of one of the others and flew right off. I thrilled with the sensation of weight when the third bird lighted— the weight of a bird!

"And so they ate most of my berries!

"But it was cold out of doors, so I placed the vase with the branches inside the kitchen door. I wondered whether by any chance I could have the pleasure of bringing the birds into the house. I then stepped back about a dozen feet into a doorway and waited to see what would happen. It happened soon. They came—one, two, three—in and out, a regular traffic—and they ate the berries from the branches on the mat, within the door.

"I felt that this had been quite an achievement, and as the berries were nearly gone I set the vase outside the door. I was tired from the excitement, so lay down on a couch in the corner of the room. When I awoke I found that the birds were flying toward the glass panes in the upper half of the door. I felt they were trying to get in. Perhaps I might have the joy of entertaining them again. This time there were no berries inside and I really didn't mean to tease them, but I opened the door and stepped back. In they came, one after the other, round little bodies hopping on slender legs—a little parade. Since there were no berries on the mat they went in search of them. They hopped around the kitchen. They pattered on the linoleum, they lighted on the rungs of the chairs, on the edge of the kitchen table, all of which were near the door. Then not contented with this survey they lit on the washtubs, the full width of the room away.

"We have an old-fashioned kitchen range, a big one, in which there was a fire that day, because, as I told you, it was cold; and as the birds hopped in that direction they spread themselves toward the warmth. There were eight in the kitchen at one time! Eight shy hermit thrushes within a room! Then I began to be anxious lest they go too far within four walls, so I walked gently toward them and out of the door they hopped. Then, so they would not feel cheated, I gave them another thickly berried branch and closed the door. I noticed, however, later in the afternoon, when the berries were all gone, that one or two of the birds were flying toward the panes in the door.

"Fortunately my friend with whom I live was an eye-witness of this experience, otherwise I might be accused of spinning a yarn."

For nearly a century in New York and other large cities, birds which have missed the parks and the scattered planting behind the high buildings, have had to fly over miles of desolate roofs, as forbidding as mountain crags or a desert. But now within the last few years roof gardens have come into existence. What a joy it must be to the birds to find these gardens, sometimes as much as a city block in extent, where both trees and shrubs hold out welcoming branches.

One of the most extensive of these roof plantings is on the eleventh floor of Rockefeller Center in the middle of Manhattan Island. Here, what are called the Gardens of the Nations have been built between the sky and the busy streets below. These gardens have been laid out with great labor and ingenuity, and are typical of the work of many lands. We see English, Spanish, Italian, Japanese gardens. There is a wild garden, too, with a trickling stream, and a vegetable garden surrounded by fruit trees, whose blossoms in spring, lure the bees from the near-by hives.

The following account of birds seen in the garden is taken from the observations of Henry Mlott:

Hundreds of birds come to the Gardens of the Nations, both fall and spring. Often for days in April a hermit thrush picks his way fastidiously through the shrubs of the Japanese garden, while yellow-bellied sapsuckers play their familiar game of hide and seek behind the trunks of the trees which shade the paths. The tiny kinglet searches for insect eggs on the weeping willows and often a gusty spring storm brings in a rain of gayly-plumaged warblers, that flutter delightedly among the flowering crabs and cherries. Not long ago two screech owls stayed a number of days, while jays often streak stridently through the branches.

Last spring a catbird, instead of searching diligently through the shrubbery for some long-lingering berry, every day took his stand boldly on the wellhead in the Spanish Garden and sang his melodious medley. He would sing a while and then flutter to the Japanese Garden, only to return again to his singing-post. On investigation it was found that he had a larder all to himself, a tent caterpillar's nest on one of the supposedly pestfree ginkgo trees!

Two years ago a fall gale brought to the Gardens of the Nations a belated whip-poor-will. So exhausted was the wanderer that it had to be nursed by one of the attendants for several weeks. It lived royally on a diet of scraped calves' liver and was kept warm every night with an electric pad.

In a corner near the wild garden is an aviary where tropical birds are kept. This cage seems to act as a magnet for the migrants. They flutter toward the caged inmates, seeming to try to get in as if they would rather share the imprisonment than continue the long journey north or south.

The following list could doubtless be greatly amplified if an interested ornithologist would station himself in the Gardens for detailed observation, but it serves to show that vegetation is the prime attraction for the birds and that they will find it, even if it is on a roof.

blue jay	robin
screech owl	veery
brown thrasher	hermit thrush
yellow-bellied sapsucker	wood thrush
downy woodpecker	golden-crowned kinglet
junco	myrtle warbler
whip-poor-will	Nashville warbler
catbird	black-throated green warbler
	black-throated blue warbler

List of Birds Seen in Central Park During 1939

Compiled by members of the National Association of Audubon Societies

Jan. 1-5—herring gull	Mar. 7—horned grebe
pheasant	Mar. 10—fox sparrow
downy woodpecker	bluebird
duck hawk	Mar. 12—purple grackle
sparrow hawk	Mar. 15—bronzed grackle
Jan. 6—robin	Mar. 20—white-throated sparrow
Feb. 15—chickadee	flicker
Feb. 20—tree sparrow	Mar. 23—hermit thrush
Mar. 5—junco	Mar. 25—woodcock
song sparrow	cowbird

BIRDS IN THE GARDEN

Mar. 25—purple finch
  goldfinch
  swamp sparrow
Mar. 27—greater scaup
Mar. 28—field sparrow
Mar. 29—wood duck
Apr. 2—chipping sparrow
  white-breasted nuthatch
  brown creeper
Apr. 10—black-crowned night heron
  black duck
  phoebe
  red-winged blackbird
Apr. 12—green-winged teal
Apr. 15—osprey
  yellow-bellied sapsucker
  golden-crowned kinglet
  myrtle warbler
Apr. 17—brown thrasher
  laughing gull
  pine warbler
Apr. 18—rusty blackbird
Apr. 19—towhee
  blue-headed vireo
Apr. 20—green heron
  lesser scaup
  ring-billed gull
  mourning dove
  nighthawk
  yellow palm warbler
  savannah sparrow
Apr. 21—blue jay
  black and white warbler
Apr. 22—American bittern
  house wren
  winter wren
  ruby-crowned kinglet
Apr. 23—crow
  blue-gray gnatcatcher

  Western palm warbler
  cardinal
Apr. 24—least flycatcher
  black-throated green
    warbler
  Northern water-thrush
  Louisiana water-thrush
Apr. 25—ovenbird
  loon
Apr. 27—catbird
  chestnut-sided warbler
  veery
  redstart
  white-eyed vireo
Apr. 28—parula warbler
Apr. 30—kingfisher
May 2—yellow warbler
  rough-winged swallow
  chimney swift
  Lincoln's sparrow
  spotted sandpiper
  prairie warbler
May 5—crested flycatcher
  warbling vireo
  olive-backed thrush
  sharp-shinned hawk
  barn swallow
May 6—Cooper's hawk
  Baltimore oriole
  solitary sandpiper
  Nashville warbler
  gray-cheeked thrush
  Northern yellow-throat
  indigo bunting
  black-throated blue warbler
  black-poll warbler
  magnolia warbler
  wood thrush
  orange-crowned warbler

192

May 7—blue-winged warbler
      Cape May warbler
      wood pewee
      Canada warbler
      scarlet tanager
      yellow-breasted chat
      orchard oriole
      rose-breasted grosbeak
      black-billed cuckoo
May 8—worm-eating warbler
May 10—great blue heron
      pigeon hawk
      kingbird
      yellow-bellied flycatcher
      Wilson's warbler
      blackburnian warbler
      yellow-billed cuckoo
May 11—hooded warbler

May 12—white-crowned sparrow
      semipalmated sandpiper
May 13—red-eyed vireo
      red-breasted nuthatch
May 15—Brewster's warbler
May 16—bay-breasted warbler
May 17—golden-winged warbler
      bobolink
May 18—yellow-throated vireo
      Acadian flycatcher
May 19—fish crow
      meadowlark
      ruby-throated hummingbird
May 20—red-headed woodpecker
May 22—mourning warbler
May 25—whip-poor-will
      olive-sided flycatcher
May 26—tree swallow
Sept. 15—dickcissel

Lists of Birds Observed in Gardens in New York City

Birds seen by Miss Holder and Miss Bohmfalk, 221 East 52nd St.

Scarlet tanager
Rose-breasted grosbeak
Chewink
Fox sparrow
Slate-colored junco
Chipping sparrow
Song sparrow
White-throated sparrow
Baltimore oriole
Blue jay
Great crested flycatcher
Kingbird
Hummingbird
Flicker
Yellow-bellied sapsucker

Robin
Hermit thrush
Olive-backed thrush
Wood thrush
Ruby-crowned kinglet
Golden-crowned kinglet
Chickadee
Red-breasted nuthatch
White-breasted nuthatch
Winter wren
Yellow-throated vireo
Myrtle warbler
Black-throated blue warbler
Yellow warbler
Black and white warbler

193

BIRDS IN THE GARDEN

Redstart
Canada warbler
Wilson's warbler
Yellow-breasted chat
Northern yellow-throat
Kentucky warbler
Northern water-thrush

Ovenbird
Palm warbler
Black-throated green warbler
Black-poll warbler
Blackburnian warbler
Chestnut-sided warbler
Magnolia warbler

Birds seen by Edson Burr Heck at 117 West 11th St.

Woodcock
Flicker
Yellow-bellied sapsucker
Blue jay
Phoebe
Chickadee
Scarlet tanager
Hermit thrush
Olive-backed thrush
Robin
Towhee
Junco
White-throated sparrow

Fox sparrow
Song sparrow
White-breasted nuthatch
Blue-headed vireo
Black and white warbler
Yellow palm warbler
Myrtle warbler
Nashville warbler
Black-poll warbler
Magnolia warbler
Black-throated blue warbler
Redstart
House wren

Chapter Fifteen

HUNTING WITH A CAMERA

I N THE far-off days of the caveman if one did not hunt, one starved. It was either hunt or be hunted, and thus the hunting urge, through the desire for self-preservation, became ingrained in man. After thousands of years, life and the struggle for existence became less strenuous and in civilized countries man no longer had to pursue and kill for food. But to-day there is a theory that just as the human embryo shows the various stages of man's evolution, so the child repeats his psychic development through the ages in the years from babyhood to maturity. It is interesting to conjecture about the forms that the primitive urges take. Certainly in every mother's son of us there remains a remnant of the hunting urge.

We no longer have to kill to live, nor do we have to pursue animals in order to secure them for food, but the old urge to hunt still lingers, carried through childhood, through adolescence and into maturity and is shown in the popularity of various sports such as fox-hunting and fishing. This urge is often so modified that the sense of achievement takes the place of the primitive thrill of the kill. Thus a child may early substitute the pleasure of skill in marksmanship for the actual hunting of small animals. Later he may become an explorer or strive to attain trophies in such competitive sports as golf or polo. The less active types may become connoisseurs or collectors of art objects, books or jewels. Others, more creative, may become research workers or poets, ever in pursuit of elusive realities or intangibles. All of us rise to hunt every morning and go to bed at night with the chase unfinished. Always we are striving to capture the unattainable perfection, whether it is in pleasure or in work.

BIRDS IN THE GARDEN

The prime hunter through the ages has been the artist, tracking down and making records of beauty. Since the caveman delineated with marvelous fidelity on the walls of his cave the animals pursued in the chase, in every age and in every country there have been gifted ones who hunted with artist's tools rather than with the weapons of the chase. And now in this scientific age the camera has been given us, a new weapon with which to pursue our quarry.

Still, as of old, the wilderness lures us. We are drawn to the woods and mountains in pursuit of the animals and birds which once stood only for food. Now we see them with new eyes. We still wish to hunt, but only because of a consuming desire to know more of these creatures' lives and of their value in the scheme of nature. Put a camera in the hands of a child and let him stalk his prey. He will have all the thrill of the chase and develop much more skill than if he had only to sight along the barrel of a gun. The primitive urge of the chase will be satisfied; and his trophy will be the picture which can be admired by his parents and friends. He will be launched on a career of nature study, one of the most satisfying of pursuits, one never ending in satiety, for so immense is the variety of objectives that there is always a new phase to be studied, a new goal to be attained. The knowledge which will be gained is the most satisfactory investment which can be made in this world's goods, an investment never ceasing to return a manifold percentage.

There are few of us who do not long to have a pictorial record of interesting experiences with birds: the first time the wrens nest in the new box, the chickadee when he feeds from your hand, the harassed robin answering the hunger call of her young, her beak dripping worms—all simple happenings in the garden, but giving us keen delight and doubly dear when we have captured the moment by our own photographs.

The question of cameras is such a big one that it cannot be discussed in detail here. Fairly good pictures can be secured if an ordinary camera is used with care, but of course much better results can be obtained with

196

finer equipment. But no one should be deterred from photographing birds because of the difficulty of the undertaking. Often charming pictures have been taken with very inexpensive cameras. The greatest necessity is patience and then more patience. Otherwise the same rules apply as to any other type of photography. We cannot take a snapshot of a young bird in a dense shady thicket and not expect to have a blank or an underexposed film, or at best a confused pattern of vines and leaves with a most inconspicuous subject; and neither can we expect to picture a bird in flight without speedy lens and a fast shutter.

Cameras range in price from a few dollars to many hundreds, and all types may have added to them lenses costing much more than the camera itself. They vary in type from the small box with a set focus for everything beyond four or five feet, to the miniature with a shutter speed of 1/1200 of a second. But if only a box camera is available, it can be equipped with a moderate-priced portrait attachment which will enable you to get within a few feet of your subject and with a time exposure get good pictures of such stationary objects as nests with eggs. You more than likely will take better pictures in the end and run less risk of bitter disappointments if you work up from an easily managed camera to the more complicated instruments. And remember a good light meter is invaluable.

A little more expensive, and with the addition of portrait lens, capable of taking very good pictures, are the various folding roll-film cameras. Some of them are set-focus, others have to be adjusted according to the distance; the best results with near-by objects can be secured when the number of feet from the object to be photographed to the lens is carefully measured and not merely estimated.

In both the foregoing kinds of cameras the subject to be photographed is located in the finder. This often results in an unsatisfactory picture because of the distance between the finder and the lens, and if more accurate detail and placing are wanted on close-ups we must turn to the film-pack type. These cameras have the film in a frame which fits in grooves in the back of the case. This film-pack case can be removed and a ground glass in a frame slipped in its place. When the shutter is open an image is seen on the ground glass and the bellows can be racked in and out until every detail is in sharp focus. Then the ground glass is removed, the shutter closed, and the film-pack replaced, and *after* the protecting slide is removed the exposure is made. These cameras often come with double or triple extension bellows, thus enabling you without the aid of a portrait lens to come within a few inches of the object to be photographed.

Next in order are the reflex cameras. With these you may see an image through a hood at the top of the camera. This image is thrown upward from the lens by a mirror. It has the advantage of being rightside up and is bright when the lens is wide open, but as is the case with the film-pack camera, becomes dim when the opening is made smaller in order that greater depth of focus may be secured.

Although almost all nature photographers swear by this graflex type of camera, the shutter mechanism is complicated, and almost all of them are large and heavy which makes it difficult to carry them on long trips.

A later type is the twin reflex. These cameras are small and compact, only a little larger than the true miniatures. You see a distinct image through a focusing opening at the top. This image is thrown up from the upper lens which is mounted directly above an identical lens on the front. The picture is taken through the lower lens, and though it may be necessary to stop down, the image seen through the upper lens still remains clear even after the exposure is made. The disadvantage of these smaller cameras is that they carry only roll-film to which many photographers object as a whole roll has to be developed in order to know whether a certain picture is good, while with the film-pack, one negative may be developed at a time.

The miniature camera is becoming more and more popular for nature photography because of its small size and consequent portability. But for work with birds the standard lens on these cameras has such a short focus that it results in a very small image on the film, often so small that even an enlargement would not bring out a good picture. And so, for work with birds in flight or at some distance from the camera, a long focus lens is a necessity, and this is a very expensive accessory. For close work at nests this would not be essential, and here again just as good results could be attained with a camera costing much less than a miniature.

Of course the new color films add greatly to the artistic possibilities of the work. If you can afford it color photography is certainly worth experimenting with. As yet it is expensive and difficult to make prints in color, but the films can be cut up and mounted as slides and make beautiful projections. Fine work is being done also with the small motion picture camera. Remarkable studies of birds' home life and their flight can be made in both black and white and in color.

If you are feeding birds on a shelf at the window during the winter you will often get some excellent subjects for pictures. The camera can be placed on the shelf behind some evergreens and focused on a certain part of the tray. A strong black thread can then be attached to the shutter release, run under the partly raised window and operated from the room. When the bird alights and is in profile over the area in focus the negative can be exposed and often you will secure an excellent portrait of such confiding birds as chickadees or downy woodpeckers outlined against the snow.

Later in the year the feeding shelf on the edge of the shrubbery is a good place for other studies. Here again very good pictures may be secured by the inexpensive cameras, especially if they are equipped with a portrait attachment. The camera can be concealed behind branches and, just as at the window, the shutter opened and closed by remote control, that is by a thread or string attached to the release, and operated by a person concealed at some distance. The camera should be carefully and firmly set, either on a tripod or fastened on a branch by a clamp which can be secured at a photographic supply store.

Sometimes unless there is thick cover in which the photographer can conceal himself, a good blind plays its part. A shelter of boughs is easily made. This bough shelter is the simplest type to use for woodland pictures. Cut three small trees, tie them together at the top, then force their bases into the ground and cover them with boughs or bark. This produces a natural effect quickly accepted by the birds. An umbrella also makes a good portable blind. The handle should be fastened to a sharpened stake which can be driven into the ground. Other blinds can be made of a packing case or a pup tent. In these a bench or folding chair may be placed, for often it is hours before our "prey" is in proper position or correctly lighted. All of these blinds should be disguised with boughs or brown or green burlap or canvas. If cloth is used be sure to fasten it securely so that it will not flutter in the breeze. Dr. A. A. Allen says he finds that if two persons set up the blind and one leaves that the birds, not being able to count, presume that all danger is past and soon resume their activities.

If you want to photograph birds feeding in a more natural setting than a shelf, set up a dead limb and place on it tempting bits of food, such as suet, sunflower seeds, meat, or that titbit, so greatly loved by so many birds, the black walnut kernel. The catbird will come very near to you in pursuit of its favorite delicacy, the raisin. Sunflower seeds glued to the bark will keep chickadees or nuthatches busy for some time while they work to crack the shell.

Frequently amusing pictures can be taken if the blind is located near the bird bath. Oftentimes there are fierce battles over precedence, and if the belligerents can be caught at the right moment we have made an enlightening record in bird psychology.

Of course pictures of nests and eggs are quite easily taken, for there is no question of movement. They are more interesting if we can get the parent bird near by, but of course that would mean a quicker exposure. Nests are usually in the shade, and boughs may be bent back and tied while we are working. But under no circumstances should they be cut

away. The foliage acts as protection from sun and rain and also as concealment from enemies. And remember, eggs are easily chilled or overheated.

Pictures of the young in the nest are much more difficult to take, but
are so interesting that they are well worth trying for. The nestlings, when
very young, snuggle down in the nest, out of sight, or if a little older,
breathe so quickly that they are in constant movement. When they are a
little older they can be placed in a row on a near-by bough. That is, if you
have that essential quality of the bird photographer, patience and more
patience. To get a row of teetering birdlings all posed for the camera would
certainly have stumped Job, himself. But happily, this is the time when the
parents are most fearless, ignoring all else but the hunger cry of their
young, so that often the nestling may be held in the hand while the parents
feed them. Of course the young birds should never be exposed to the hot
sun or kept from the nest very long, and the surroundings should be disturbed as little as possible, for fear that cats, skunks or jays may follow
your trail.

Fortunately, even though pictures which we secure after hours of
patient waiting may not be masterpieces, to us they contain much more
than can be seen by the eye. When we look at them we smell again the
fragrance of the garden and the woods, hear the ripple of the near-by
stream, and, though in the picture we see only the young birds in the nest,
we can hear again the flute notes of the wood thrush as he sings hidden
deep in the foliage.

Chapter Sixteen

SANCTUARIES

THE word sanctuary means a place of refuge. In ancient times a criminal sought refuge in a temple or a church to escape from his pursuers. But even then he had to go through certain forms before he received protection. And now, though we speak of our gardens as bird sanctuaries, they are often far from perfect places of refuge, for, of course, no bird can receive complete protection; it always must be subject to the various checks which maintain the delicate balance of nature.

Nicholson, in *Birds in England,* says a sanctuary should be an area where birds can live undisturbed, and where only one ecologic factor has been removed—man. That is why in this day and age the wilderness areas of our great National Parks are more truly sanctuaries than any other place in the world. Here, the thrush may sing in peace, the hawk take its legitimate quota, the eagle soar undisturbed—one factor balancing another through years of scarcity and years of plenty.

But this type of sanctuary is far outside the experience of the ordinary person, and to appreciate the life of the wilderness we must, as Thoreau did, know and love the life of our dooryard and our immediate neighborhood.

When the white man came to America he came to a vast wilderness. The Indians were so few in number that they were practically a part of the wild life, but the white man with superior tools caused an almost immediate change. Forests were felled, fields were cleared and planted, and little by little the wilderness retreated. In the case of smaller birds this was no hardship, for few birds live in the forest. Many species welcomed the coming of orchards and the shrubby tangle of second growth, and increased in number.

But ever as the white man advanced westward he left destruction behind him. The last lonely buffalo of the southern herds was killed in the middle of the nineteenth century, ducks were shot in enormous numbers, both spring and fall, the vast flocks of passenger pigeons were wiped out of the sky, and through lack of knowledge of their place in nature as well as through unthinking prejudice, our valuable predators, hawks, owls and eagles suffered enormous losses in their ranks.

But in the midst of the shooting and chopping, railroad building and tunneling, there were a few thoughtful people who studied and watched, and *feared,* and because of this fear did something to stay the devastating waste.

In 1884 William Brewster of Massachusetts suggested that the American Ornithologists' Union form a Committee for the Protection of North American Birds. This Committee was formed and from it grew the National Association of Audubon Societies, with the avowed object of preserving wild birds and animals. Since then these Societies have done a vast amount to influence public opinion, not only in regard to the necessity of preserving wild life, but in awakening young and old to the beauties of nature. And through the efforts of the Junior Audubon Societies, educational work is being done in the schools of almost every State in the Union.

From the work of the Union's Committee on Migration and Distribution of North American Birds, developed the Biological Survey which was founded in 1885 and is now recognized as the leading wild life agency of the country. Through advocacy of the Biological Survey and its supporters, the great national system of bird refuges has been established. Fortunately at the beginning of the twentieth century Theodore Roosevelt, that great lover of wild life, became President, and on March 14, 1903, he created by Executive Order the first National Bird Reservation. This was Pelican Island in the Indian River in Florida. Since then area after area has been set aside, and by 1933 the Biological Survey had acquired by Executive order, by gift, or by purchase 99 bird refuges.

Since then, through the increased interest in the conservation of our national resources, stimulated and aided by President Franklin Delano Roosevelt, emergency funds have been made available, additional areas have been purchased and our wild life refuges now number 248. There are 232 in the United States and 16 in Alaska, Hawaii and Puerto Rico. In the 1938 report of Ira N. Gabrielson, Chief of the Bureau of Biological Survey, the number and extent of the national wild life refuges administered by the Bureau are as follows:

	Number	Acres
Migratory water fowl refuges (including easement refuges)	140	1,537,298
Refuges for other migratory birds	60	917,332
Wild life refuges (mammals and other forms) . . .	10	4,062,894
Refuges chiefly for non-game birds	28	105,537
Big game reserves and ranges	10	5,027,297
Total	248	11,650,358

At the present time the areas where we are endeavoring to preserve wild life are divided into Federal, State, Audubon, Municipal, and Private Sanctuaries or Refuges. Even before the first national refuge was established, some of the states had set aside similar preserves and now over 30,000,000 acres are under State control. Through gifts and purchases the National Association of Audubon Societies now own outright 26,353 acres and lease or occupy by the consent of the owner over 230,000 acres more.

Since the primary object of the sanctuary and warden work of this Association is to extend protection to species of birds threatened with extinction, it is not its policy to accumulate large acreages requiring maintenance. A group of nesting roseate spoonbills, for example, may move from one area to another, depending on the condition of feeding grounds, or for other reasons, and the Association desires to post and patrol the *locale* where they are at the moment, and of necessity must follow them from one place to another. So it is with most of the birds whose welfare is the chief concern of the Association.

But these figures are merely impressive as they show the awakening of a people who not many years ago considered robin pot-pies a delicacy, shot game birds ruthlessly in both spring and fall, and paid fabulous prices for egret plumes torn from bleeding birds while the young were left to starve in the nests.

Undoubtedly the greatest step forward in bird preservation was the passage of the Federal Migratory Bird Treaty Act in 1918. This law, giving effect to a treaty between the United States and Great Britain on behalf of Canada, with exceptions under certain conditions, protects chiefly insectivorous birds and certain designated water birds that migrate between the United States and Canada; specifically names for protection the band-tailed pigeon, cranes, swans, and most shore birds, the wood duck and eider duck; and defines migratory game birds subject to shooting in prescribed seasons. The shooting season of migratory game birds is limited to not more than three and one-half months in any given zone and all spring shooting is abolished. The treaty was effectuated also by the Migratory Birds Convention Act of Canada, and thus for the first time in American history Conservation was recognized as an international affair, a thing of vital interest to all people and all nations. A similar treaty with Mexico ratified in 1937 was given effect by an amendment to the Migratory Bird Treaty Act. The authority of the United States over migratory birds while they are in this country, now has a dual basis—Canadian and Mexican treaty obligations—and the three countries are linked in co-operative efforts to extend protection to wild life in general. The Canadian Treaty provided Federal protection for 350 species of birds, and the Canadian and Mexican Treaties together for 449 species.

The awakening of the public to the necessity of Conservation has been slow and it has taken decades to secure the passage of adequate protective laws. We know that enforcement of laws can come only through our co-operation and more and more and more are we coming to realize that only as our children are taught to understand and appreciate conservation of our natural resources will they work to preserve their valuable heritage of wild life. And this is where the smaller municipal and private song bird sanctuaries prove of the greatest value. Through them the community becomes conscious of birds and thus the way is opened for bigger projects that should preserve the species in danger of extermination.

The Federal Wild Life Refuges can only be listed in this book, but a few words about the smaller sanctuaries in various parts of the country will show how widespread the interest in Conservation is becoming.

In the heart of the City of Oakland, California, is Lake Merritt, a Wild Fowl Refuge, one of the first State Game Refuges to be set aside. This is a natural salt-water lake containing over 150 acres. Here, where tall buildings almost shade the water and trolley cars are within a stone's throw, may be seen in season hundreds of diving ducks and dabblers, wild geese and other water birds, such as herons, gulls, coots and cormorants. Here they eat and rest, either in the water or on the shore, fearless of the public or the sound of passing motor-cars. It is estimated that between five thousand and eight thousand ducks winter in this refuge. Grain is fed them, the City Park Department defraying part of the expense, and the rest being paid for with contributions by the public through the purchase of grain in small bags.

Farther north on the Pacific coast, in Seattle, Washington, a part of Lake Washington and the land adjoining, has been made a State Game Preserve, and at one place a feeding station for ducks is maintained through private generosity. Thousands of ducks congregate there all winter and sometimes as much as forty-five tons of grain are put out in one season. When these water fowl take flight it is a marvelous sight.

One of the earliest of the song bird sanctuaries established by private

WOOD DUCK

ADULT MALE

ADULT FEMALE   MALE IN ECLIPSE

Scale about one-fifth

funds was Birdcraft Sanctuary at Fairfield, Connecticut. The late Mabel Osgood Wright was the founder, carrying out the wishes of her father, Dr. Samuel Osgood Wright, who often spoke of his estate as a bird sanctuary. Careful management has built up a large nesting population, and a small museum adds greatly to the interest. There is a resident keeper.

Outstanding in educational work among the sanctuaries maintained by private funds is the Pleasant Valley Bird and Wildflower Sanctuary of Lenox, Massachusetts. It was originally sponsored by the Lenox Garden Club, but is now maintained by private membership fees and has a resident warden. The land now owned amounts to over four hundred acres of wood and marsh. Artificial ponds have been made and the work of introduced beavers has resulted in the flooding of other sections, thus adding to the variety of acreage suitable to bird life. One hundred and fifty-nine species of birds have been recorded in the last ten years, and at the 1939 spring nesting census it was found that there were four hundred nesting pairs, representing seventy species.

Peacefully situated in almost the center of the village, the New Canaan Bird Sanctuary is the realization of one woman's dream, which after her death was brought to complete fulfillment by the devoted work of her brother assisted by altruistic friends. Although there are only eighteen acres in this sanctuary, there is a great diversity of terrain, woodland and marshland being bordered by open shrubby growth containing excellent nesting sites. A definite planting program to build up the environment so that it may support more bird life is being carried out by the Association through the work of a warden.

At Oyster Bay, Long Island, New York, is the Roosevelt Sanctuary, a memorial to Theodore Roosevelt. The development of this area shows how proper planting can increase the bird population in an area not eminently suited to bird life. The original tract of land was waterless, and covered with an almost uniform growth of locust trees. Water was brought in, in some parts the trees were cut entirely and grassy spots developed, while many species of berried shrubs and vines were planted and soon made a thick undergrowth for cover and nesting. Dead or dying trees, usually quickly removed by the trained forester, were left standing and thus furnished natural nesting places for woodpeckers and bluebirds. Within ten years the nesting population was doubled, reaching a density of twelve pairs to an acre. This sanctuary is maintained by the National Association of Audubon Societies, which has established on it a museum and nature trail.

One of the largest of the refuges administered by the National Association of Audubon Societies is the Rainey Wild Life Sanctuary. It embraces about twenty-six thousand acres bordering the coast of Louisiana 140 miles west of New Orleans. It is the winter refuge of tens of thousands of wild ducks and geese. This land was given to the Audubon Association by Mrs. Grace Rainey Rogers as a memorial to her brother, Paul J. Rainey, and its upkeep is endowed.

A remarkably fine waterfowl refuge in the Middle West is that developed by the Chicago Park Department. This refuge is in Jackson Park, just south of the Field Museum.

Twenty acres of the East Lagoon has been fenced in and the water is kept in the proper condition by the inflow from five pipes, while a small water-wheel in motion keeps the water from freezing in winter. The water and edges of the land have been planted with suitable food plants. On the shore and on the islands trees and shrubs were placed; these not only bear edible fruit but act as shade and cover.

To this refuge thousands of ducks come through the year. It is an excellent example of a municipal refuge, and won national recognition in the 1935 Refuge Contest.

An outstanding example of what can be accomplished through the initiative of one person who is a true conservationist is the Hawk Mountain Sanctuary. This is the first sanctuary in the world for birds of prey.

The Hawk Mountain Sanctuary is in the Kittatinny Ridge in eastern

Pennsylvania. Here, for years, so-called sportsmen had gathered and shot down migrating eagles and hawks by the thousand. It has been estimated that from 3,000 to 5,000 hawks were killed annually at this point. Richard Pough, in Bird-Lore, tells of what he saw before the land became a sanctuary: "Over 100 men, armed with shot-guns and rifles, were seated among the rocks. Every Hawk that came by was greeted by a barrage of shot. Many suddenly collapsed, to travel no more. Others went into dizzy spins and dropped among the rocks on the mountainside far below.

"A long scramble took me down to where the Hawks were dropping and I found that a large percentage were not dead but only 'winged,' or wounded in some other way. Many showed signs of having suffered for days before starvation and thirst claimed them. Those still alive—and there were many—would try to hide among the rocks. Failing to do that, they would spread out their wings and fall backwards. With fear in their blazing eyes, they tried to fight me off with their talons. In a small space, on that day, I picked up over 100 birds, and the total dead easily ran into the thousands. Nothing that flew by was being spared and I found a Blue Jay and a Flicker among the Hawks."

Then in 1934, Mrs. C. N. Edge, Chairman of the Emergency Conservation Committee, leased Hawk Mountain including two square miles of land, and overnight the slaughter was abolished. The property is under the direction of the Hawk Mountain Sanctuary Association, and now where the noise of guns made the peaceful autumn days hideous, hundreds of quiet bird students through their glasses watch the migrating hosts fly southward. Eagles, ospreys, marsh hawks, goshawks, and all the other magnificent gliders, utterly oblivious of the carnage of the past, now sail peacefully down their ancient airway.

Chapter Seventeen

DESCRIPTION OF BIRDS SEEN IN THE GARDEN AND THE COUNTRY PLACE

This list is arranged for the beginning student, and that is why the order is alphabetical, not according to the AOU Check List.

Blackbird, Red-winged, *see Red-wing*

Bluebird, Eastern

Length 7 inches; male, bright blue above, cinnamon below; female, similar, but duller; young, mostly brown with speckled breast; nest of grass in a hole in a tree, post or bird-house; eggs, pale blue, nearly white.

Bluebird, Mountain

Length 7 inches; male, sky blue above, paler blue on head and breast; belly white; female, grayish, blue showing on wings and tail; young brownish with speckled breast; nest in old woodpecker holes in stubs, in cliffs, or in nesting boxes; eggs, pale blue, occasionally pure white.

Bluebird, Western

Length 7 inches; male deep purplish blue above, running under chin; with a chestnut bar running across breast and shoulders; below, rich chestnut red; female, similar but duller; young brownish with speckled breast; nest,

in woodpecker holes, in natural hollows in stubs, or in nesting boxes; eggs, uniform pale blue.

Bobolink

Length 7¼ inches; male, mainly black; nape creamy-buff, shoulders and lower back white; female, young and male birds in fall and winter, yellowish-buff with dark stripings on crown and upper parts; nest on the ground in grass; eggs, gray, marked with brown and dusky.

Bobwhite

Length 10 inches; male reddish-brown above with darker brown mottlings; below mostly white with dark markings; female similar but duller; nest, on the ground among grain, grasses or bushes; eggs, white, often stained with brown.

Bunting, Indigo

Length 5½ inches; male bright indigo blue above and below; female dingy brown; young brownish, softly striped below; nest of grasses, dead leaves, and pieces of bark, on the ground or in a crotch of a bush; eggs, whitish marked with brown.

Bunting, Lazuli

Lenght 5½ inches; male bright blue above; ruddy-buff and white below; female and young rusty-olive above, whitish below; nest of grasses, dead leaves and bark; eggs, pale blue, occasionally dotted with reddish-brown.

Canary, Wild, *see Goldfinch*

Cardinal, Eastern

Length 8¼ inches; male with a crest, all red, except for a black patch around the bill; female with a crest, brownish with slight tinge of red and large red bill; young brownish; nest, loosely built of twigs, bark-strips, grasses, etc.; usually low in vine, bush or tree; eggs, whitish, spotted and dotted with some shade of brown.

Catbird

Length about 9 inches; male dark gray above and below, top of tail and head blackish, chestnut under tail; female similar; nest of twigs or small sticks, bark or rootlets, placed in a bush or vine; eggs, dark, greenish-blue.

Cedar-bird, *see Waxwing, Cedar*

Chat, Yellow-breasted

Length nearly 7½ inches; male, above green; breast and throat yellow; female similar; nest of grasses, leaves and bark in crotch near the ground; eggs, white, marked with brown or lilac.

Chebec, *see Flycatcher, Least*

Cherry-bird, *see Waxwing, Cedar*

Chewink, *see Towhee, Red-eyed*

Chewink, Spotted, or Spurred, *see Towhee, Spotted or Spurred*

Chickadee, Black-capped

Length 5¼ inches; male, grayish above with black cap, whitish below with black throat; female and young similar; nest of moss, feathers or other soft materials placed in natural hollow in tree, occasionally in hole dug out by the birds in a decayed stub or in a nesting box; eggs, 6 to 10, white spotted with reddish-brown.

Chickadee, Chestnut-backed

Lenght 4¾ inches; male with back and flanks reddish-brown, crown and throat dark brown; below white; female and young similar; nest lined with fur, feathers, or other soft material and placed in a hole in a stub or a nesting box; eggs, pure white, sprinkled with reddish-brown dots.

Chickadee, Hudsonian

Length about 5 inches; similar to Black-capped Chickadee, but darker; cap grayish-brown instead of black; throat patch grayish; sides touched with reddish-brown; nest of moss and fur in hollows of trees, or stubs; eggs, white, spotted brown.

Chickadee, Oregon,
See Chickadee, Black-capped

Creeper, Brown
Length 5½ inches; dark brown above, marked with whitish; under parts white; female and young similar; nest of bits of bark, dead wood and moss placed behind loose piece of bark or cleft in a tree trunk; eggs, grayish-white, spotted with brown.

Crossbill, Red
Length about 6 inches; male, dull red; female and young greenish or yellow; bill with tips prolonged and crossed; nest, of twigs and grasses, usually placed in coniferous trees; eggs, green or greenish-blue, spotted brown and lavender.

Crossbill, White-winged
Length about 6 inches; male rosy red with white wing-bars; female yellowish or greenish with white wing-bars; nest usually in coniferous trees, of twigs and grasses lined with moss and rootlets; eggs, bluish-green or white, marked with brown and lavender.

Cuckoo, Black-billed
Length nearly 12 inches; male grayish brown above, white below; small white spots on tail feathers; female similar; nest loosely constructed of sticks and placed in a vine, bush or low tree; eggs, greenish-blue.

Cuckoo, Yellow-billed
Length about 12 inches; male above olive-brown, reddish on wings; white below and large white spots on ends of inner tail feathers; nest a collection of sticks in a bush or tree; eggs light greenish-blue.

Dove, Eastern Mourning
Length nearly 12 inches; male, upper parts grayish-blue, shaded brown; lower parts pinkish-purple with sides of neck iridescent; female similar but duller; young grayer than female, with white edges to feathers; nest a platform of sticks placed at moderate heights in trees; eggs two, white.

Duck, Common Black
Length 22 inches; male and female, very dark sooty brown with silvery white underwing surfaces, head a lighter brown; metallic blue patch on wings; nest on the ground near water; eggs, grayish-white to greenish-buff.

Duck, Mallard
Length 23 inches; male grayish above with a green head and white ring around the neck, and a reddish breast; speculum or beauty spot on the wing, purple with white bars; female mottled brown but showing the beauty-spot; nest, on the ground in high grass or reeds; eggs, dirty-white.

Duck, Wood
Length 18½ inches; male, dark above with a crest with green and purple iridescence; light below with ruddy breast; female, dark brown, with crest and white space near the eye; nest in hollow stumps or trees or in nesting box; eggs, buffy or creamy-white.

Eagle, Bald

Length 33 inches; adult, dark brown or black with white head and tail; young, all dark brown; nest, made of sticks, very large, usually in tall, isolated trees; eggs, white, often stained yellow.

Eagle, Golden

Length 30 inches; adult dark brown with back of neck of golden buff and a dark tail; young are dark with a white tail with a black band; nest, of sticks on cliffs, or sometimes in tall trees; eggs, dirty-white, usually spotted with brown.

Finch, California Purple

Length about 6 inches; male suffused above with reddish-purple, below white; female and young olive-brown above, heavily streaked with darker brown; white below, also streaked with brown; nest of twigs, grass and rootlets set in coniferous trees; eggs, greenish-blue, marked with brown or black spots.

Finch, House

Length 5-6 inches; male, above, brownish gray, rosy or orange-red on head and rump; below, white streaked with brown, throat and breast reddish; nest in bushes or trees, sometimes in crannies about buildings, made of leaves, rootlets, ravellings etc.; eggs bluish white or pale greenish-blue, marked with black or brown.

Finch, Eastern Purple

Length 6 inches; male, reddish-purple or "crushed raspberry"; female and young, olive-gray, streaked with darker; nest, of grass, rootlets and fibers, usually in coniferous trees; eggs, greenish spotted and scrawled with brown and black.

Flicker, Northern

Length 12 inches; male brownish above, light below with round black spots, with black band across breast, red bar across the nape, white rump; under surface of wing and tail feathers yellow; black "moustache" mark; female similar but without the "moustache" mark; nesting hole in dead tree or in a nesting box; eggs, glossy white.

Flicker, Red-shafted

Similar to Northern flicker, but with red "moustache" mark on male, usually with red mark on nape and with under surfaces of wing and tail red; nest in dead tree or in nesting box; eggs glossy white.

Flycatcher, Least, or Chebec

Length about 5½ inches; dull olive above, lighter below, a white eye ring and two white wing-bars; nest of wood fibers, rootlets, etc. placed in the crotch of a tree, 5 to 40 ft. up; eggs white.

Flycatcher, Northern Crested

Length 9 inches; olive-brown above, throat and upper breast gray, underparts yellow; nest in abandoned woodpecker holes, in hollow trees, or in nesting boxes; eggs, creamy or reddish, marked with scratches and lines of purple and lavender.

Flycatcher, Olive-sided

Length nearly 7½ inches; above dusky olive; below, throat, part of the breast and middle of the belly yellowish-white, rest of the underparts dusky; nests of moss and twigs near the end of a limb about 25 ft. up in an evergreen tree; eggs purplish-white, spotted with reddish-brown.

Gnatcatcher, Blue-gray

Length 4½ inches; blue-gray above; whitish below with a white eye ring and long white-bordered black tail; nest interwoven of fine strips of bark, grass, etc., and covered with lichens, placed on branch usually 30 feet up; eggs, bluish-white, marked with various shades of brown.

Goldfinch, Eastern, or Wild Canary

Length about 5 inches; male bright yellow with crown, wing and tail black; female brownish-yellow above, wings and tail dark brown, grayish-white below; young, much like the female; male in winter like female but retaining black wings and tail; nest, a down-lined cup of grass and moss in a tree 6 to 40 ft. up; eggs, bluish-white.

Goose, Canada

Length 23-39 inches; both male and female, brownish above with black head and neck with white patch under the chin; underparts light and occasionally dark as the back; nest on the ground in grassy spots, occasionally in old hay-cocks or even in a deserted nest

in the top of a tree; eggs, greenish or buffy-white.

Goshawk

Length 22 inches; blue-gray above, pearly gray below; a long tail, a black cap and white line over eye; nest in trees; eggs, white, marked pale brown.

Grebe, Pied-billed

Length 13½ inches; grayish-brown, darker on head and back; throat patch and rounded bill, black; nest, a heap of matted reeds or flags, among reeds or water brush; eggs, dull white, stained with brown.

Greenhead, *see Duck, Mallard*

Grosbeak, Black-headed

Length about 8 inches; male, head, face, wings and tail with a saddle across the shoulders, black; white patches on wings and tail; below tawny to lemon-yellow; female, brownish, striped; nest of twigs, stalks and rootlets in bushes or trees; eggs greenish blue marked brown and lavender.

Grosbeak, Eastern Evening

Length 8 inches; male, yellowish with black wings, tail and crown; yellow bar on forehead, white patch on wings; female grayer; both have a large greenish-white bill; nest of small twigs lined with bark and rootlets; eggs, pale bluish with dark markings.

Grosbeak, Pine

Length about 9 inches; male, above and below gray suffused with rosy or scarlet; female and young, grayish, suffused with rusty yellow over head and rump; both have a large heavy bill; nest of twigs and rootlets in coniferous trees; eggs, light greenish or blue, marked with brown.

Grosbeak, Rose-breasted

Length about 8 inches; male, above black with patches of white on wings, rump and tail; breast rose-red; below pure white; female dull olive-brown, striped above, below white, sharply striped; nest, poorly built of twigs, rootlets or even weed-stalks, in tree 5 to 20 ft. from the ground; eggs, pale blue, marked with brown.

Grouse, Ruffed

Length 17 inches; reddish-brown and gray with soft black feathers around neck making a "ruff"; tail broad, many-barred; nest, on the ground lined with leaves; eggs buffy or yellowish white occasionally spotted with brownish.

Hawk, Broad-winged

Length of male nearly 16 inches; above, grayish brown; below, heavily barred with red-brown, throat white; tail with two or three broad white bands; length of female nearly 17 in.; nest in trees, 25 to 50 ft. up; eggs white, marked with brown or buff.

Hawk, Cooper's

Length of male 15½ inches; above, slaty-gray, wings short and rounded, tail long, with black bars; below, barred with reddish; length of female 19

inches; nest in trees, 35 to 50 ft. up; eggs, bluish-white, sometimes spotted brown.

Hawk, Duck

Length of male 16 inches; above, bluish slate color, cheeks black and back barred with black; below, creamy-white, barred and spotted with black except breast; wings pointed; length of female 19 inches; nest, on cliffs usually overlooking water; eggs, creamy-white, marked with brown.

Hawk, Marsh

Length of male 19 inches; above, gray; below gray and white, lower breast and belly spotted and barred with reddish-brown; tail gray barred with black; rump white; length of female 22 inches; nest on ground in or near a marsh; eggs bluish-white.

Hawk, Red-shouldered

Length of male about 17 to 23 inches; above, brown; shoulders reddish; below, white, cross-barred reddish brown; tail fanlike, black narrowly barred with white; length of female 19 to 24 inches; nest in trees 30 to 60 ft. up; eggs dull white, blotched with brown.

Hawk, Red-tailed

Length of male 19 to 22½ inches; above, brown mottled with gray, tail fanlike, reddish-brown with white tip; below almost white; length of female 21 to 25 inches; nest in trees 30 to 70 ft. up; eggs dull white, usually marked with brown.

Hawk, Sharp-shinned

Length of male 10 to 12 inches; above, slaty-gray, wings short and rounded, tail long with black bars; below reddish-brown, barred with white; length of female 12 to 14 inches; nest in trees 15 to 40 ft. up; eggs bluish-white or buffy, marked with brown.

Hawk, Sparrow

Length of male 10 inches; above reddish brown barred with black, top of head ashy blue with chestnut crown patch; cheeks and throat white, tail reddish brown; wings long and narrow; below creamy, belly and sides spotted black; length of female 9 to 12 inches; nest in a hole in a tree, or in a nesting box; eggs creamy-white to reddish, marked with the same color.

Hummingbird, Black-chinned

Length nearly 4 inches; male, above, dull metallic bronze green; wings dusky purplish; lateral tail feathers purplish-black; gorget, squarish, velvet black; a white collar edged with metallic violet; remainder below, whitish; female, dull metallic bronze green, throat sometimes dusky; nest, beautifully made of cobwebs and down, saddled on a branch; eggs, white.

Hummingbird, Ruby-throated

Length 3¾ inches; male rich metallic bronze green above; below dull white with throat patch of ruby-red; female and young greenish above, dull white below; nest an exquisitely formed, softly lined cup saddled on a branch and finished with lichens held together

with cobwebs; eggs white, about the size of pea beans.

Hummingbird, Rufous

Length 3½ inches; male brick red above with greenish iridescence on crown; throat and gorget fiery red; female and young greenish-bronze above, white below; nest a cup covered with moss and lichens; eggs, pure white.

Jay, Blue

Length 11¾ inches; sky blue above with a conspicuous crest; nearly white below with a black necklace around upper breast; nest in trees, of twigs and rootlets; eggs, olive-green, or brownish, marked with brown.

Jay, Canada

Length 12 inches; soft gray with white forehead, face and throat, and black cap; nest large and deep, of twigs and fibers, thickly line with feathers and fur, placed in coniferous trees; eggs, white, spotted with brown.

Junco, Oregon

Length 6¼ inches; male, head and breast black, white below, back and flanks reddish chestnut; female similar but duller; young browner, streaked; nest of grasses, mosses and rootlets, on or near the ground; eggs white, spotted with brown.

Junco, Slate-colored

Length 6¼ inches; male mostly dark or light gray, white below; female similar but lighter; young, browner and streaked; nest of grasses, mosses or rootlets, on or near the ground; eggs white, spotted with brown.

Killdeer Plover, *see Plover, Killdeer*

Kingbird, Arkansas

Length 9 inches; light gray head, breast and back; tail almost black; concealed orange crown spot; below yellow; nest well built of weed-stalks, grasses, strips of rags or string, and lined with plant down and rootlets, about houses, in eave-troughs or downspouts and sometimes in bird-houses; eggs, white or creamy-white, spotted with brown.

Kingbird, Eastern

Length about 8½ inches; very dark gray above, crown and tail nearly black; below white; wing and tail feathers edged with white; a concealed orange or vermilion spot on crown, shown when excited; nest large, made of straw, rootlets, string and feathers and placed in trees, sometimes on a building; eggs, white, spotted with umber.

Kinglet, Golden-crowned

Length about 4 inches; yellowish-green above; dull white below; crown of black, lemon yellow and orange, prominent white line above the eye; nest a ball of moss and feathers in evergreen tree; eggs, white, thickly specked with buffy spots.

Kinglet, Ruby-crowned

Length about 4 inches; yellowish green

above; dull white below; crown of male with concealed spot of bright red shown when excited; nest half-hanging in evergreen tree, of moss and strips of bark, lined with feathers; eggs, dull white or buffy, speckled with reddish-brown.

Mallard, *see Duck, Mallard*

Mallard, Black,
See Duck, Common Black

Martin, Purple

Length about 8 inches; male, deep lustrous blue; wings and tail dark brown, tail slightly forked; female, brown above, purplish on head and back, forehead and throat grayish; nest in hollow tree or bird-house; eggs white.

Meadowlark, Eastern

Length 10¾ inches; above brownish, streaked; below chiefly yellow with black crescent on breast; tail short, outer tail-feathers white; nest of grasses, on the ground in a field, usually arched over; eggs, white with brown spots.

Meadowlark, Western

Length 10¾ inches; similar to Eastern Meadowlark, except in voice which is rich, ringing and joyous, instead of having the melancholy cadence of the Eastern bird's; nest of grasses placed in thick grass or weeds in slight hollow in the ground overarched with dried grasses; eggs, white, marked with cinnamon brown or purplish.

Mockingbird

Length 10½ inches; gray above, white below, white patches on wings and tail; nest, of coarse twigs, weed-stalks, etc. in small trees or bushes; eggs, pale greenish or bluish, marked with brown.

Nighthawk

Length 10 inches; patterned in rich dark brown and silvery grays; long tail and long wings, the latter showing beneath a conspicuous round white spot when the bird is flying; nest none; eggs laid on a rocky ledge, the bare ground or a graveled roof; eggs, dull white, marked with brown.

Nuthatch, Red-breasted

Length about 4½ inches; above bright bluish-gray, crown black, tail feathers marked with black and white; below, chin and throat whitish, lower parts rusty or deep buff; a white stripe above and a black line through the eye; female similar but duller; nest in hollow tree or bird box; eggs, white or creamy, speckled with brown or lavender.

Nuthatch, White-breasted

Length about 6 inches; above slate-blue, with crown, hindneck and shoulders, black; below including face, white; female similar but duller; nest in a hole of a tree or bird-box, lined with leaves and feathers; eggs, white or creamy, marked reddish-brown or lavender.

Oriole, Baltimore

Length 7½ inches; above, including head, neck, wings, and tail, black; below, yellow or vivid orange; wings marked with white; female and young much duller; nest a deep pouch woven of tough fibres, often hanging from limb of an elm; eggs, bluish-white, scrawled with brown or black.

Oriole, Bullock's

Length 8¼ inches; male a rich golden orange with bib, crown, line through eye, back, wings and part of tail, all black; female olive above, dull orange below; nest a long bag of woven plant fibers and down hanging from a branch; eggs, smoky-white, streaked and spotted with black or brown.

Oriole, Orchard

Length about 7½ inches; male similar to Baltimore oriole with orange replaced with rich reddish brown; a black tail; female an even dull green; young male like female but with a black throat; nest woven of green grass and hanging from a crotch; eggs, bluish-white, marked with brown or black.

Oven-bird

Length about 6 inches; above, olive-brown, crown, dull orange; below, white streaked with dark brown on the breast; nest, large, on the ground, made of grass, weed stalks, rootlets and leaves, opening on the side like an oven; eggs creamy white spotted brown or lilac.

Owl, Acadian, *see Owl, Saw-whet*

Owl, Barn

Length 18 inches; general color reddish-buff; below lighter; facial disk heart-shaped, no ear tufts; eyes black; nest in trees, banks, in barns, steeples or towers; eggs, white.

Owl, Saw-whet

Length about 8 inches; head round; above brown; below white, streaked with brown; nest in holes in trees, natural or abandoned homes of woodpeckers or squirrels; eggs, white.

Owl, Screech

Length about 9½ inches, head, eared; two color phases, brownish-white or gray and brick red; nest in hollow trees, occasionally in nesting boxes; eggs, white.

Partridge, *see Grouse, Ruffed*

Pewee, Wood

Length 6½ inches; dull olive and whitish; nest carefully made of fibers and rootlets, covered with lichens and fastened on a limb, 10 to 40 feet up; eggs creamy-white marked with dark spots at the larger end.

Pheasant, Ring-necked

Length 30 inches of which 16 inches is tail; head green; above, intricate markings of various colors; throat and neck, black; foreneck and breast coppery-red with metallic luster; collar of white; a long purple and green tail banded with black; female, mostly brown with long tail but no white collar; nest of leaves, grasses, etc., on the ground under clump of grass or a bush; eggs dull gray or buff.

Phoebe, Eastern

Length about 7 inches; above, dull olive-brown, head blackish; lighter below, sides and breast shaded blackish; tail notched; nest of mud covered with moss, lined with grass or feathers, placed on a beam of a building or bridge, under the edge of a bank or ledge of rock, in a cave, occasionally on a nesting shelf; eggs white.

Plover, Killdeer

Length 10½ inches; grayish above; white below with two black breast-bands; in flight showing a golden-red tail; nest, usually none; eggs, spotted, on the ground.

Plover, Upland

Length nearly 12 inches; above, light tawny-brown with dark markings; breast and sides tawny streaked blackish; belly whitish; nest in the open, in a hollow in the ground; eggs, creamy, speckled dark brown.

Quail, *see Bobwhite*

Redbird, *see Cardinal*

Redpoll, Common

Length about 5½ inches; above dusky, with bright red crown-cap and suffusion of pink on the rump; below, chin and throat, blackish, breast tinged with pink, belly white, sides streaked with dusky; female similar but without pink and more heavily streaked; nest of grasses, leaves, plant down, etc., in low tree or clump of grass; eggs, white tinged greenish or bluish, spotted reddish-brown.

Redstart, American

Length about 5½ inches; male, above

lustrous black; bright orange patches on wings and tail; belly white; female similar but without black; nest, small, compact in upright fork of small tree; eggs, whitish with fine markings.

Red-wing

Length 9½ inches; male, black with red epaulets edged with buff or yellow; female and young, brownish, heavily striped below; nest, near water, well-made of grasses and fastened to rushes or grasses and occasionally placed in a bush; eggs, pale bluish with dark markings.

Reed-bird, *see Bobolink*

Rice-bird, *see Bobolink*

Robin, American

Length 10 inches; male, above dark grayish-brown; black on tail, head and throat, the latter lightened with white dashes; below brick-red; female similar but duller; young with breast spotted black and flecked with white; nest of grass, leaves, rootlets, etc. usually with an inner cup of mud, lined with fine grass, in fruit or shade trees, near or on houses, or on a nesting shelf; eggs, blue.

Siskin, Pine

Length 5 inches; above, streaked olive-brown; below lighter; wings suffused with yellow; nest of twigs and rootlets lined with plant down, placed in coniferous trees; eggs, bluish-white, spotted reddish-brown.

Solitaire, Townsend's

Length 8 inches; gray with outer tail feathers white; nest, of sticks and weed stalks, in hollow in rock or bank on upturned root of tree; eggs, grayish white, spotted pale brown.

Snowbird, *see Junco*

Sparrow, Chipping

Length 5 to 5½ inches; above brown, streaked; crown bright reddish-brown; black line through eye; breast light, unspotted; young with breast, sides and top of head streaked; nest in a bush, vine or tree, carefully made and lined with hair; eggs, bluish, spotted at larger end.

Sparrow, English

Length 6½ inches; male, above streaked chestnut and black with crown gray; throat and breast black; female, above, streaked olive and brown, below dull olive or white; nest an untidy, bulky structure placed on awnings, buildings, in trees or in nesting boxes; eggs, whitish, marked with brown or black. (*Not a true sparrow; it is now classed as a weaver finch. An undesirable introduced species.*)

Sparrow, European Tree

Resembles the English Sparrow, but marked with a large black spot behind the eye.

Sparrow, Field

Length 5½ inches; crown and back reddish-brown; below gray, whitish wing-bars; nest on ground or in low bush; eggs white finely spotted with brown.

Sparrow, Fox

Length 7¼ inches; above reddish brown; below, white, heavily striped reddish-brown; nest of coarse grass lined with fine grass, moss or feathers; eggs, pale bluish, speckled or blotched with brown.

Sparrow, Song

Length 6½ inches; above brown, streaked darker; breast and sides whitish, spotted, the spots massed in a splotch on center of breast; nest of grass, rootlets and leaves, on the ground or in bushes, rarely on nesting platform; eggs, white marked brown.

Sparrow, Tree

Length about 6½ inches; above streaked brown and lighter; top of head reddish-brown; below, grayish, white on belly, an indistinct black spot on center of breast; nest of rootlets, grasses, etc., on or near the ground; eggs pale gray or greenish blue spotted with reddish brown.

Sparrow, White-crowned

Length nearly 7 inches; back striped, seal-brown and gray; crown black with prominent white stripes; below white; nest of grass and fibers; on the ground or in a low bush; eggs, pale greenish-blue.

Sparrow, White-throated

Length 6¾ inches; above, brown streaked with black, a white stripe above the eye; pale gray below with a white throat patch and white belly; female similar but duller; nest of grass, rootlets and moss, on the ground or in low bush; eggs, pale, heavily spotted.

Starling, European

Length 8½ inches; above, greenish-purple with metallic luster, feathers tipped with yellowish spots; wings, tail, and underparts, brownish-gray edged with buff; bill yellow; in winter, whole bird heavily spotted; nest, of grasses, twigs, etc., in buildings, hollow tree or bird box; eggs, pale bluish.

Swallow, Barn

Length nearly 7 inches; above dark blue, tail deeply forked, forehead chestnut; below, throat and breast chestnut, belly buff; nest of mud, feathers and straw, plastered on a rafter in shed or barn, or on a nesting shelf; eggs, white, spotted brown.

Swallow, Cliff

Length about 6 inches; above bluish, forehead cream-white, rump, light chestnut, tail square-ended; below, throat chestnut, other parts whitish; nest of mud, usually flask-shaped, placed on sides of cliff, on barns, or under eaves; eggs, white, spotted with cinnamon.

Swallow, Tree

Length nearly 6 inches; above dark blue, tail slightly notched; below white; female duller; young, above, brown with faint collar across upper breast; nest in hollow tree or bird house; eggs, white.

Swallow, Violet-green

Length 4¾ inches; above, bottle-

221

green, washed with violet and bronze, rump and tail violet; below, solid white, extending almost across rump; female similar but duller; young ashy-brown above; nest, of dried grasses with or without feathers, in crevice of cliff, or in bird box; eggs, pure white.

Swan, Trumpeter

Length 65 inches; a white bird larger than the whistling swan; nest of grass and moss lined with down, on the ground; eggs, soiled whitish.

Swan, Whistling

Length 55 inches; white, with yellow or orange spot in front of the eye; nest of grass, moss, etc. lined with down, on the ground; eggs, soiled whitish.

Tanager, Scarlet

Length about 7 inches; male, all scarlet, except black wings and tail, in fall like female; female, greenish above, yellowish below, wing and tail brownish; young like female; nest of twigs and straw, usually in lower branches of large tree, sometimes in the orchard, occasionally as high as 20 ft.; eggs, light greenish-blue, marked brown and purple.

Tanager, Summer

Length about 7 inches; male bright rose-red all over; female, above olive, below yellow; nest of leaves and strips of bark, near end of limb 20 feet up; eggs, bluish-white or greenish-blue marked with brown.

Tanager, Western or Louisiana

Length 7 inches; male, bright lemon-yellow, with crimson head, black saddle, wings and tail; in autumn only spots of crimson on head; female and young, dull yellow green with brownish wings and tail; nest of twigs, rootlets and moss, in trees or bushes; eggs, pale greenish-blue to deep blue, dotted with lavender and greenish.

Teal, Blue-winged

Length 16 inches; male, dull-colored above, white crescent in front of eye, large chalky-blue patch on fore edge of wing; female, brownish, streaked; nest on the ground amidst grass; eggs, buffy or creamy.

Thrasher, Brown

Length nearly 11½ inches; above reddish-brown; below white, streaked or spotted with black; wings barred with white; nest of twigs on the ground, brush pile or low bush; eggs, white or greenish, spotted reddish-brown.

Thrush, Alice's, *see Thrush, Gray-cheeked*

Thrush, Gray-cheeked, or Alice's

Length about 7½ inches; above, including tail, grayish brown, cheeks gray; below, white with breast heavily spotted brown; nest, large, constructed mainly of mosses, in low bushes or on the ground; eggs, greenish-blue, spotted rusty brown.

Thrush, Hermit

Length about 7 inches; above, tawny brown, with dull red or rusty tail; below, white, breast heavily spotted brown; nest of moss, coarse grass, and leaves lined with rootlets and pine-needles; eggs, greenish-blue.

Thrush, Olive-backed

Length about 7 inches; above tawny-olive; below, white, breast heavily spotted brown; nest, in bushes or small trees, of coarse grasses, leaves and bark, lined with rootlets and hair; eggs, greenish-blue.

Thrush, Russet-backed

Length 7 inches; ruddy brown above; throat ochre, breast creamy-white, not as strongly spotted as the Olive-backed; nest, of bark strips, moss and grasses, inner mat of dead leaves, in bushes or thickets, occasionally in trees 30 to 60 ft. high; eggs, greenish-blue, marked with brown.

Thrush, Varied

Length 10 inches; male, above slate-gray with eye-stripe, wing-bars and flight feathers, orange; below tawny orange with black breast-bar; female similar but duller; nest of moss, sticks, twigs and rotten wood, in bushes or small trees; eggs, greenish-blue, marked with dark brown.

Thrush, Wilson's, or Veery

Length about 7½ inches; above brown-tawny; below, white, faintly spotted; nest of bark, rootlets and leaves on the ground or near it; eggs, greenish-blue.

Thrush, Wood

Length about 8 inches; above, cinna-mon brown, reddish-brown on head; below, white with large brown spots; nest of leaves, rootlets, etc. with central cup, sometimes of mud, sometimes of leaf-mold, 6 to 10 ft. up on low branch of sapling; eggs usually greenish-blue, smaller than a robin's.

Titmouse

Length 6 inches; above, including wings and tail, gray; head crested, fore-head black; below, whitish; nest, of moss, bark, feathers etc., in deserted woodpecker holes, stumps, or in bird boxes; eggs, white marked with brown.

Towhee, Red-eyed, or Chewink

Length about 8½ inches; male, above black, including neck and chest, wings and tail; sides and flanks, chestnut; breast and belly white; wings marked with white; female, brown replaces black of male; nest of dead leaves and strips of bark, on or near the ground; eggs, white evenly spotted with ashy and brown.

Towhee, Spotted or Spurred

Similar to above but with wings more conspicuously spotted with white.

Veery, *see Thrush, Wilson's*

Vireo, Cassin's

Length about 5½ inches; above, greenish-gray; below, whitish; a white eye ring and two white wing-bars; nest of wood fibers, and bark strips, hanging between forks of a branch; eggs, white or creamy white, marked with dark green spots.

Vireo, Eastern Warbling

Length 5¾ inches; above, dull olive-green, a white line over eye, no wing-bars; below, white, slightly tinged with yellow; nest carefully-woven of plant fibers, grasses, etc. hanging from a branch 8 to 40 ft. up; eggs white specked with black or reddish-brown.

Vireo, Red-eyed

Length 6¼ inches; above, olive-green; crown gray, iris red, eyebrow stripe, white; below, white; nest a hanging cup woven of bark, fiber, and plant down; eggs, white, spotted brown at larger end.

Warbler, Audubon's

Length about 5¾ inches; male, above, grayish-blue; below, white, except yellow throat; breast barred with broad black band; spots on crown, rump, and sides, yellow; female and young, similar but duller; nest of fiber lined with fine roots and grasses, in coniferous trees; eggs, white, marked with browns and purples.

Warbler, Black and White

Length about 5½ inches; above, streaked black and white; below, streaked, except white belly; female similar but duller; nest, of strips of bark, grasses, etc., often placed on the ground, or sometimes in a hollow tree; eggs, white, spotted with brown at larger end.

Warbler, Black-throated Blue

Length 5¼ inches; male, above, deep blue; cheeks, throat, foreneck and flanks black; below, white; female, above, dark olive, below, creamy olive; nest of strips of bark, fine grasses, pine needles, etc., placed low in heavy forest undergrowth; eggs, grayish-white, marked with olive-brown.

Warbler, Black-throated Gray

Length 5 inches; male, striped black and white, solid black cheeks, crown and throat; female and young, similar but duller, lacking black throat; nest, of plant fibers, lined with feathers, in low thickets or high coniferous trees; eggs, creamy-white, marked with blotches of brown, lavender and black.

Warbler, Black-throated Green

Length about 5 inches; male, above, green; sides of head and neck, yellow; below, white, with black throat and breast; female and young similar but duller; nest, of bark, twigs and grasses usually 5 to 15 ft. up in a white pine; eggs, creamy white, marked brown and purple.

Warbler, Cape May

Length 5 inches; male, above, yellow-green, top of head black, chestnut patch on cheek, yellow spot on rump; below, throat, breast and underparts bright yellow, sharply striped with black; white patch on wing; female, above, grayish-olive, below, whitish with faint stripes; nest, of twigs and grasses woven together with spider-webs, partly hanging from a low branch in pasture or woodland; eggs, dull white or buffy, speckled with brown or lilac.

Warbler, Golden-winged

Length about 5 inches; male, above, blue-gray, with yellow cap; below, almost white; throat and cheeks black; wing-patch, yellow; female similar, but with gray instead of black markings; nest, of bark and leaves, wrapped with leaves whose stems point upward, on ground in second growth or bushy fields; eggs, white, speckled brown.

Warbler, Kirtland's

Length 5¾ inches; above, dusky, with head bluish-gray; below, pale yellow, sides streaked and spotted with black; female similar but duller; nest, of fine grasses, fiber, etc., on ground at foot of pine or oak; eggs, white, speckled with umber.

Warbler, Magnolia

Length about 5 inches; male, above, blue-gray; face, cheeks, and saddle, black, and rump yellow; below, yellow, with broken breast-band and stripings of black; white patches on wing and tail; female similar, but coloring subdued; nest, of twigs and leaf stems lined with fine rootlets; eggs, white marked with brown.

Warbler, Myrtle

Length nearly 5¾ inches; male, above, slate-blue; below, throat and breast white; breast-band black; yellow on crown, flank and rump; female and young duller; nest, of vegetable fiber lined with grass, in bush or evergreen tree; eggs, white marked with browns and purples.

Warbler, Northern Parula

Length 4¾ inches; male, back and sides of face and neck, blue, yellow on back; below, throat and breast yellow with dark band crossing the breast; two broad white wing-bars; female duller without the breast-band; nest, in bunches of hanging lichen; eggs, white with reddish-brown markings.

Warbler, Palm

Length 4½ inches; above, olive-brown with chestnut cap and yellow stripe over eye; below, yellow streaked with chestnut; nest of weed stems, grasses, caterpillar webs, etc., on the ground; eggs, buffy or creamy-white, spotted with brown or lilac.

Warbler, Prothonotary

Length 5½ inches; above, yellowish-olive, orange-yellow head and neck; tail ash-gray marked with white; below, orange-yellow, lighter on belly; female similar but duller; nest, quite large, of moss, grass, leaves, etc., in hole or tree, in cavities about buildings and sometimes in gourds or nesting boxes; eggs, creamy-white, marked with brownish.

Water-Thrush, Louisiana

Similar to Northern water-thrush, but larger, darker, and with white line over eye.

Water-Thrush, Northern

Length 5 to about 6 inches; above, dark olive-brown with light buff stripe over eye; below, buffy-yellow, or greenish-yellow, spotted and streaked with olive; nest, principally of moss in hollow in ground or mossy bank; eggs, creamy or pinkish-white, marked with shades of brown.

Waxwing, Bohemian

Length 8 inches; above, grayish-fawn, head crested; below, grayish-fawn, changing to gray on belly; bar through eye and chin spot, black; white wing-bars with red sealing-waxlike append-ages; under tail-coverts chestnut, tail tipped with white; nest, of roots and moss, in trees; eggs, pale bluish-gray or putty-colored, spotted with black or umber.

Waxwing, Cedar

Length about 7 inches; brownish fawn above, head crested, bar through eye and chin spot, black; below brown, yellow on belly; red sealing-waxlike appendages on the wings, no wing-bars; tail broadly tipped with yellow; nest, of bark, leaves, grasses, etc., in bushes, and in fruit or shade trees; eggs, bluish-gray or putty colored, marked with black or umber.

Woodcock

Length 10 to 12 inches; above, cinna-mon-brown and grayish, marked with black, top of head black; below, brighter cinnamon on sides; bill, very long and tapering; nest, a mere hollow with a sprinkling of dead leaves, usu-ally on dry ground near swampland; eggs, creamy or buff marked with brown and gray.

Woodpecker, Downy

Length 6¾ inches; male, above, black

barred and striped with white; below, a dab of red at back of head; female, similar, but without red spot; nest, in hole in stub or limb, excavated by the birds, or in a nesting box; eggs, white.

Woodpecker, Hairy

Length about 9½ inches; male, above, black, barred and striped with white; below, white; red spot on back of head; female, similar, but without red; nest, a hole in a tree, dug by the bird or occasionally a nesting box; eggs, white.

Woodpecker, Lewis's

Length 10½ inches; above, black, face and chin dull crimson; below, gray and rose; gray around neck; nest, excavated in trees and stubs; eggs, white.

Woodpecker, Red-bellied

Length 9½ inches; above, including wings, barred black and white; below, gray; top of head, nape and back of neck, bright scarlet; nest, in tree, stump, post or hole excavated by the birds; eggs dull white.

Woodpecker, Red-headed

Length 9¾ inches; above, black; head, neck and breast, crimson; below, white; white patches on wings; nest, in cavity excavated in dead tree or stub, and occasionally in nesting box; eggs, glossy white.

Woodpecker, Pileated

Length 17 inches; above and below black, with broad masses of white; a conspicuous brilliant scarlet crest; nest, a hole excavated in dead tree or stub; eggs, white, very glossy.

Wren, Bewick's

Length about 5½ inches; above, brown, with white line above eye; below, throat and breast, white, shading to grayish-brown lower down; nest, of dried grasses and leaves, lined with wool, hair or feathers, in holes or crannies in stumps or buildings, or in nesting box; eggs, white, speckled with brown. (The Western form is the Seattle wren.)

Wren, Carolina

Length 5½ inches; above, bright reddish-brown, a whitish or buffy line over eye; underparts creamy-buff, whitish on throat; nest, large, of grasses, feathers, leaves, etc., in holes in trees or crevices about buildings; eggs, creamy, marked with brown.

Wren, House

Length 5 inches; above, ashy-brown; tail and wings barred with dark brown; below, creamy-white; nest, of twigs, lined with grasses, feathers, etc., in hole in tree or in nesting box; eggs, white, speckled reddish-brown.

Wren, Seattle, *see Wren, Bewick's*

Wren, Winter

Length about 4 inches; above rich wood brown, finely cross-barred; below, brown, slightly lighter, heavily barred on belly; nest, in crannies in upturned roots or under logs in deep woods; eggs, white or creamy, marked with reddish-brown.

Yellow-throat, Northern

Length about 5¼ inches; male, above green; below, bright lemon-yellow; black mask across eyes and cheeks; female and young, similar but duller; nest, of dried grasses, near the ground; eggs, white, marked reddish-brown.

Chapter Eighteen

LISTS OF PLANTS TO ATTRACT BIRDS BY SECTIONS OF THE COUNTRY

NORTHEASTERN STATES

From the Atlantic westward to Minnesota, Iowa and Missouri, and from Canada southward to Missouri, Kentucky and Virginia, inclusive

SHRUBS FOR BIRDS (*native*)

Average Conditions

NAME, DESCRIPTION AND FRUITING SEASON	KNOWN TO BE EATEN BY
Arrowwood, *Viburnum dentatum* (and other spp.) To 15 ft.; flowers white, in May and June; fruit blue-black. *June-April*	35 kinds including flicker, bluebird, rose-breasted grosbeak, catbird, robin, phoebe, brown thrasher, red-eyed vireo, ruffed grouse.
Black Alder, *Ilex verticillata* To 10 ft.; deciduous; fruit red, grows best in moist soil. *June-April*	bluebird, cedar waxwing, brown thrasher.
Blackhaw, *Viburnum prunifolium* (and other spp.) To 15 ft.; flowers white in April and May; fruit blue-black with a bloom. *June-May*	35 kinds including yellow-billed cuckoo, robin, bluebird, purple finch, cedar waxwing, bobwhite, olive-backed thrush, pileated woodpecker, brown thrasher.
Buffaloberry, Silver, *Shepherdia argentea* To 18 ft.; thorny with silvery leaves; flow-	16 kinds including pine grosbeak, catbird, hermit thrush, brown thrasher.

NAME, DESCRIPTION AND FRUITING SEASON	KNOWN TO BE EATEN BY
ers small; fruit red; very hardy, good hedge plant. *June-October*	
Burning-Bush, *Euonymus atropurpureus* Tree or shrub to 25 ft.; flowers small, purple; fruit scarlet. *August-November*	hermit thrush, scarlet tanager, robin, bluebird, flicker.
Cranberrybush, American, *Viburnum trilobum* To 12 ft.; flowers white, in May and June; fruit scarlet. *September-October, often persistent until May.*	seldom eaten except by cedar waxwing, ruffed grouse, bluebird.
Dogwood, Alternate-leaved, or Pagoda, *Cornus alternifolia* Shrub or small tree to 25 ft.; flowers white in flat clusters; fruit blue; in open or semi-shade. *June-October*	
Dogwood, Osier, *C. stolonifera* To 8 ft.; twigs red; fruit white; in damp soil. *July-September*	93 kinds including cardinal, brown thrasher, purple finch, flicker, catbird, downy woodpecker, bobwhite, thrushes, cedar waxwing, robin, bluebird, song sparrow.
Dogwood, Round-leaved, *C. rugosa* To 10 ft.; flowers white; fruit light blue. *July-October*	
Dogwood, Silky, *C. amomum* To 10 ft.; flowers white; fruit pale blue; in moist ground and in partial shade. *June-October*	

NAME, DESCRIPTION AND FRUITING SEASON	KNOWN TO BE EATEN BY
Elder, Common, *Sambucus canadensis* (and other spp.) To 12 ft.; flowers white; fruit purple-black; grows best in rich, moist soil. *June-October*	118 kinds including bluebird, mockingbird, rose-breasted grosbeak, flicker, red-headed woodpecker, catbird.
Fringe-tree, *Chionanthus virginica* Shrub or small tree to 30 ft.; flowers white, fringe-like; fruit a dark blue drupe. *September-October*	pileated woodpecker.
Hercules Club or Devil's Walking-Stick, *Aralia spinosa* Shrub to 25 ft.; very spiny; flowers small, in clusters; fruit berrylike. *August-October*	bobwhite, white-throated sparrow, pine grosbeak, olive-backed thrush, ruffed grouse, blue jay, bluebird.
Holly, American, *Ilex opaca* (and other spp.) Shrub or tree, evergreen; flowers inconspicuous; fruit red; plant both pistillate and staminate forms. *All year*	45 kinds including hermit thrush, bluebird, cedar waxwing, mockingbird, flicker, robin.
Nannyberry, *Viburnum lentago* Shrub or tree to 30 ft.; flowers white; fruit blue-black with a bloom. *All year*	cedar waxwing, robin, flicker, bluebird, rose-breasted grosbeak, ruffed grouse, catbird, hermit thrush, bobwhite.
Rose, Pasture, *Rosa carolina* To 3 ft.; flowers pink, usually solitary; fruit a red hip; naturalize in meadows. *All year*	
Rose, Prairie, *R. setigera* To 15 ft.; climbing; flowers pink fading to white, clustered; fruit a red hip. *All year*	38 kinds including bobwhite, ruffed grouse.

LIST OF PLANTS TO ATTRACT BIRDS

NAME, DESCRIPTION AND FRUITING SEASON	KNOWN TO BE EATEN BY
Snowberry, *Symphoricarpos albus* (and other spp.) To 3 ft.; flowers small, pinkish; fruit snow-white. *All year*	33 species including waxwing, pine grosbeak.
Strawberry-bush, *Euonymus americanus* To 8 ft.; flowers inconspicuous; fruit salmon-pink. *August-November*	scarlet tanager, bluebird, robin, hermit thrush, yellow-bellied sapsucker.
Withe-Rod, or Blackhaw, *Viburnum cassinoides* (and other spp.) To 12 ft.; flowers white, in flat clusters; fruit blue-black; in moist soil. *September-October*	35 kinds including brown thrasher, ruffed grouse, bluebird, rose-breasted grosbeak, purple finch.

Enduring Shade

Blueberry, Highbush, *Vaccinium corymbosum* (and other spp.) To 12 ft.; flowers white or pinkish; fruit blue-black with a bloom, acid soil. *June-September*	93 kinds including chickadee, kingbird, bluebird, pine grosbeak, towhee, robin, hermit thrush.
Chokeberry, Black, *Aronia melanocarpa* To 4 ft.; flowers white; fruit black; grows best in low, moist, acid soil. *July-May*	21 kinds including meadowlark, brown thrasher, catbird, ruffed grouse, bobwhite.
Chokeberry, Red, *A. arbutifolia* To 10 ft.; flowers white; fruit red. *July-May*	

231

NAME, DESCRIPTION AND FRUITING SEASON	KNOWN TO BE EATEN BY
Coralberry, or Indian currant, *Symphoricarpos orbiculatus* (and other spp.) To 6 ft.; flowers small, white; fruit dark red; holds leaves late into the fall. *All year*	33 kinds including evening and pine grosbeaks, ruffed grouse, robin, brown thrasher, ring-necked pheasant.
Dangleberry, *Gaylussacia frondosa* To 6 ft.; flowers greenish purple; fruit blue with a bloom; acid soil. *July-August*	flicker, blue jay, catbird, towhee, pine grosbeak, ruffed grouse, bobwhite, cedar waxwing.
Elder, Common, or American, *Sambucus canadensis* To 12 ft.; flowers white; fruit purple-black; prefers moist soil. *July-October*	118 kinds including rose-breasted grosbeak, catbird, bluebird, kingbird, robin, red-headed woodpecker, flicker, brown thrasher.
Elder, Red or Scarlet, *S. pubens* To 15 ft.; flowers creamy-white; fruit scarlet; grows best in moist soil. *June-August*	
Hobblebush, *Viburnum alnifolium* To 10 ft.; flowers white, showy in May and June; fruit purple-black; grows best in moist, acid soil. *July-September*	ruffed grouse, pine grosbeak, brown thrasher, red-eyed vireo, cedar waxwing, olive-backed thrush.
Raspberry, Flowering, *Rubus odoratus* (and other spp.) To 6 ft.; flowers rose-purple; fruit red.	146 kinds including song sparrow, cedar waxwing, rose-breasted grosbeak, orchard and Baltimore orioles, bluebird, wood and olive-backed thrushes.
Snowberry, *Symphoricarpos albus* To 3 ft.; flowers small, pinkish; fruit snow-white. *All year*	33 kinds including evening and pine grosbeaks.

LIST OF PLANTS TO ATTRACT BIRDS

Spicebush,
Benzoin æstivale
To 12 ft.; flower small, yellow, very early
in spring; fruit red.
July-November

KNOWN TO BE EATEN BY

17 kinds including kingbird, red-
eyed vireo, wood thrush, veery,
catbird, flicker, bobwhite.

Viburnum, Mapleleaf,
Viburnum acerifolium
(and other spp.)
To 6 ft.; flowers white; fruit purple-black;
will endure dry shade.
All year

35 kinds including bluebird,
purple finch, cedar waxwing,
ruffed grouse, hermit-, olive-
backed-, gray-cheeked thrush,
robin.

Winterberry,
Ilex lævigata
(and other spp.)
To 6 ft.; fruit red.
August, through winter.

48 kinds including hermit
thrush, catbird, brown thrasher,
bobwhite.

Dry, Sandy Soil in Sun

Bayberry,
Myrica caroliniensis
(and other spp.)
To 9 ft.; fruit gray, waxy.
July-June

85 kinds including flicker, Carolina wren, tree swallow, myrtle
warbler, meadowlark, bluebird,
phoebe, hermit thrush, catbird,
brown thrasher, downy woodpecker.

Blackberry, Highbush,
Rubus canadensis
To 8 ft.; fruit black; in hedgerow or field.
June-September

Blackberry,
R. frondosus
To 6 ft.; at length over-arching; fruit black;
in hedgerows or field.
July-August

146 kinds including robin, cardinal, oriole, bluebird, rose-
breasted grosbeak, catbird, cedar
waxwing, song sparrow, kingbird, tufted titmouse, wood
thrush, bobwhite, flicker.

Blackberry, Highbush,
R. allegheniensis
(and other spp.)
To 10 ft.; fruit black; in hedgerow or field.

NAME, DESCRIPTION AND FRUITING SEASON	KNOWN TO BE EATEN BY
Blueberry, Lowbush, *Vaccinium pennsylvanicum* (and other spp.) To 2 ft.; fruit bluish-black; in acid soil. *June-September*	93 kinds including towhee, kingbird, robin, tufted titmouse, catbird, brown thrasher.
Cherry, Sand, *Prunus pumila* 3 to 5 ft.; flowers white; fruit black. *June-August*	cedar waxwing, catbird, olivebacked thrush, bobwhite, redheaded woodpecker.
Dogwood, Panicled, *Cornus racemosa* To 10 ft.; flowers white; fruit white. *July-November*	ruffed grouse, bobwhite, flicker, cardinal, pine grosbeak, cedar waxwing, bluebird, robin, thrush.
Huckleberry, Black, *Gaylussacia baccata* To 3 ft.; fruit black, shining; in acid soil. *July-November*	towhee, flicker, blue jay, catbird, pine grosbeak.
Plum, Beach, *Prunus maritima* 3 to 20 ft.; flowers white; fruit red. Particularly good for seaside planting. *August-March*	
Raspberry, Blackcap, *Rubus occidentalis,* (and other spp.) From 3 to 5 ft.; fruit black. Plant in hedgerow, field or edge of woods. *June-September*	146 kinds including cedar waxwing, blue jay, catbird, olivebacked thrush, song sparrow, pine grosbeak, bluebird, brown thrasher, towhee.
Red Cedar, *Juniperus virginiana* (and other spp.) To 30 ft. and more, often shrubby dense evergreen; fruit blue, persistent. *All year*	54 kinds including flicker, mockingbird, ruffed grouse, robin, evening and pine grosbeaks, purple finch, bluebird, myrtle warbler, cedar waxwing, tree swallow, phoebe, cardinal, kingbird.

NAME, DESCRIPTION AND FRUITING SEASON	KNOWN TO BE EATEN BY
Rose, Pasture, *Rosa carolina* (and other spp.) To 3 ft.; flowers rose-pink; fruit a hip, bright red. *All year*	38 kinds including bobwhite, ruffed grouse, wood thrush, ring-necked pheasant.
Sweet-fern, *Comptonia asplenifolia* To 2 ft.; forming dense colonies; fruit a nutlet. *September-October*	flicker, mourning dove, ruffed grouse.

Trees for Birds (*native*)

Alder, Speckled, *Alnus incana* Small tree or shrub; forms thickets and protects stream-banks. *August-September* Alder, Smooth, *A. rugosa* Small tree or shrub; in moist soil, in the sun.	23 kinds including redpoll, bobwhite, ring-necked pheasant, ruffed grouse, woodcock, pine siskin, tree sparrow, mallard, great blue heron, buffle-head, green-winged teal, sharp-tailed grouse, mourning dove, ballpate.
Arbor-vitæ, *Thuya occidentalis* An evergreen to 60 ft.; fruit a small cone. *Autumn-Winter*	3 kinds including thrushes, redpolls and pine siskins.
Ash, White, *Fraxinus americana* Tree to 120 ft.; fruit a winged seed. *October-November*	7 kinds including bobwhite, purple finch and pine grosbeak.
Basswood or Linden, *Tilia americana* A large tree; fruit nutlike. *August-October*	4 kinds including redpoll, bobwhite, ruffed grouse.

NAME, DESCRIPTION AND FRUITING SEASON	KNOWN TO BE EATEN BY
Beech, American, *Fagus grandifolia* A large tree; fruit a 3-angled nut; grows best in acid soil except sand. *September-October*	red-winged blackbird, bobwhite, red-bellied woodpecker, flicker, blue jay, downy and hairy woodpecker, wood duck.
Birch, Black or Sweet, *Betula lenta* A large tree to 75 ft.; fruit a small nutlet. *September-October*	junco, wood duck, great blue heron, buffle-head, blue jay, wild turkey, green-winged teal, sharp-tailed grouse, pine siskin, goldfinch, ring-necked pheasant, woodcock, titmouse.
Birch, Gray, *B. populifolia* A small, short-lived tree to 30 ft.; fruit a small nutlet. *September*	
Birch, White or Paper, *B. papyrifera* Tree to 100 ft.; with white bark; fruit a small nutlet. *August-September*	
Birch, Yellow, *B. lutea* Tree to 90 ft.; yellowish bark; fruit a small nutlet. *September-October*	
Blue-Beech, *Carpinus caroliniana* A small bushy tree, occasionally to 40 ft.; fruit a nutlet. *August-October, persistent*	9 kinds including bobwhite, ruffed grouse, mallard, woodcock, wood duck.
Box-elder, *Acer negundo* Tree to 70 ft.; fruit a winged key; only pistillate form bears fruit. (A short-lived, brittle tree.) *September-October, persistent through winter.*	4 kinds including evening grosbeak, ring-necked pheasant.

236

LIST OF PLANTS TO ATTRACT BIRDS

Cherry, Choke,
Prunus virginiana
Shrub or small tree, flowers white; fruit red.
July-September

Cherry, Wild Black,
P. serotina
Large tree; flowers white; fruit purple-black.
June-November

Cherry, Wild Red,
P. pennsylvanica
Small tree to 35 ft.; flowers white; fruit red.
August-October

Dogwood, Flowering,
Cornus florida and other spp.
Tree to 40 ft.; flowers small, surrounded by white bracts; fruit red.
September-February

Elm, American,
Ulmus americana
Tree to 120 ft.; fruit a winged nutlet.
March-May

Fir, Balsam,
Abies balsamea
Evergreen with erect cones breaking up on tree.
September

Hackberry, Eastern,
Celtis occidentalis
A large tree to 120 ft.; fruit orange to purple.
September-October, often persistent

84 kinds including downy and hairy woodpecker, blue jay, cedar waxwing, pileated woodpecker, catbird, wood, hermit, gray-cheeked thrush, song sparrow, mockingbird, chewink, pine grosbeak, bluebird, goldfinch, robin, kingbird, vireo, white-throated and white-crowned sparrow, ring-necked pheasant, mallard, ruffed grouse, sharp-tailed grouse, catbird, flicker, bobwhite.

93 kinds including ruffed grouse, flicker, bobwhite, hermit thrush, robin, bluebird, olive-backed thrush, brown thrasher, red-eyed vireo, purple finch, song sparrow.

9 kinds including bobwhite, purple finch, pine siskin, wood duck, great blue heron.

13 kinds including white-winged crossbill, blue jay, Hudsonian chickadee, long-eared owl, ruffed grouse.

48 kinds including cedar waxwing, cardinal, hermit thrush, bobwhite, flicker, robin, chewink, brown thrasher, ring-necked pheasant, bluebird, mockingbird.

237

NAME, DESCRIPTION AND FRUITING SEASON	KNOWN TO BE EATEN BY
Hawthorn, Arnold's, *Cratægus arnoldiana* To 20 ft.; fruit bright red. *August-September*	
Hawthorn, Cockspur, *C. crus-galli* To 25 ft.; exceedingly long spines; fruit dull red. *October, through winter*	
Hawthorn, Round-leaved, *C. rotundifolia* Bushy to 15 ft.; fruit red with yellow flesh. *September-November*	39 kinds including ruffed grouse, pine grosbeak, robin, bobwhite, fox sparrow, hermit thrush, purple finch.
Hawthorn, Thicket, *C. intricata* Bushy to 10 ft.; spines few; fruit reddish-brown. *September-October*	
Hawthorn, Washington, *C. phænopyrum* To 30 ft.; long spines; fruit scarlet. *September-March*	
Hemlock, *Tsuga canadensis* Tall evergreen; fruit a small cone. *October, seeds falling in winter.*	15 kinds including flicker, sharp-tailed grouse, chickadee, pine siskin, ruffed grouse, red and white-winged crossbill.
Hickory, Shagbark, *Carya ovata and other spp.* A large, long-lived tree; fruit a nut. *September-October*	wood duck, mallard, cardinal, bobwhite, ring-necked pheasant.
Hornbeam, Hop, or Ironwood, *Ostrya virginiana* To 60 ft.; fruit a nutlet. *August-October*	downy woodpecker, American merganser, ruffed grouse, bobwhite, ring-necked pheasant.

238

NAME, DESCRIPTION AND FRUITING SEASON	KNOWN TO BE EATEN BY
Juniper, *see* Red Cedar	
Larch, or Tamarack, *Larix laracina* A large, needle-leaved tree, shedding its needles in the fall; cones oblong. *Autumn, seeds falling through winter*	4 kinds including ruffed grouse, crossbill, pine siskin, ring-necked pheasant.
Locust, Black, *Robinia pseudoacacia* A large tree; flowers white; fruit a pod. *September-April*	5 kinds including bobwhite and mourning dove.
Maple, Red, *Acer rubrum* Tree to 120 ft.; fruit a winged seed. *March-April*	
Maple, Silver *A. saccharinum* A large brittle tree with deeply cut leaves; fruit a winged seed. *April-June*	bobwhite, evening grosbeak, pine grosbeak, cardinal, sharp-tailed grouse, great blue heron.
Maple, Sugar, *A. saccharum* A large, slow-growing, long-lived tree; fruit a winged weed. *July-December*	
Mountain-Ash, American, *Sorbus americana* To 30 ft.; fruit clustered, bright red. Grows readily even in dry soil. *August-March*	14 kinds including Bohemian and cedar waxwings, brown thrasher, robin, Baltimore oriole, evening and pine grosbeaks, catbird, red-headed woodpecker.
Mountain-Ash, Showy, *S. decora* To 30 ft.; fruit red, large. Plant in the open in well-drained soil. *August-March*	

239

NAME, DESCRIPTION AND FRUITING SEASON	KNOWN TO BE EATEN BY
Mulberry, Red, *Morus rubra* To 60 ft.; fruit dark purple. Plant both pistillate and staminate forms. *May-August*	59 kinds including cardinal, scarlet tanager, catbird, robin, kingbird, Baltimore oriole, yellow-billed cuckoo, wood thrush, downy woodpecker, yellow warbler, red-headed woodpecker, red-eyed vireo, bobwhite, cedar waxwing.
Oak, Red, *Quercus borealis* Tree to 80 ft.; fruit an acorn. Makes coppices, is of rapid growth when young. *September-October. Acorn ripening second year.* **Oak, White,** *Q. alba* A large, wide-spreading, long-lived tree; fruit an acorn. *October-November. Acorn ripening first year.*	62 kinds including cardinal, bobwhite, flicker, ruffed grouse, blue jay, downy and hairy woodpeckers, hermit thrush, chewink, white-breasted nuthatch, meadowlark, brown thrasher, mourning dove, red-headed woodpecker, wood duck, mallard, ring-necked pheasant. (Staminate flowers eaten by rose-breasted grosbeak)
Persimmon, Common, *Diospyros virginiana* To 50 ft.; fruit yellow or orange. *August-October*	robin, bobwhite, bluebird, phoebe, pileated woodpecker, mallard.
Pine, Pitch, *Pinus rigida* Evergreen varying in height according to soil and situation; needles in 3s; fruit a cone 4 in. long. *Cone maturing second season, persistent.* **Pine, White,** *P. strobus* A large evergreen; needles in 5s; fruit a cone 4 to 6 in. long. *Cone maturing July of second season, September.*	63 kinds including cedar waxwing, pileated and hairy woodpeckers, bobwhite, crossbill, chickadee, ring-necked pheasant, pine siskin, meadowlark, brown thrasher, wood duck, horned grebe, red-breasted nuthatch. Preferred as nesting-site by purple finch, crossbill, pine siskin, myrtle, magnolia, yellow-throated, pine and Blackburnian warblers.

LIST OF PLANTS TO ATTRACT BIRDS

Poplar, Quaking, or Aspen,
Populus tremuloides
To 90 ft.; leaves ovate; fruit a capsule.
May-June

12 kinds including great blue heron, sharp-tailed grouse, ring-necked pheasant, pine and rose-breasted grosbeaks, northern shrike.

Plum, Canada,
Prunus nigra
To 30 ft.; flowers white turning pink; fruit yellow or red.
August-October

ruffed grouse, ring-necked pheasant.

Red Cedar,
Juniperus virginiana
An evergreen to 60 ft. or more; fruit blue with a bloom.
All year

54 kinds including myrtle warbler, bobwhite, ruffed grouse, bluebird, cedar waxwing, evening and pine grosbeaks, flicker, mockingbird, hermit thrush, tree swallow, cardinal, phoebe, kingbird, blue jay, catbird, chickadee.

Red-bud,
Cercis canadensis
Shrub or small tree to 35 ft.; flowers sweet pea-like, rose-purple; fruit pods to 3½ in.
July-August, often persistent through winter.

ring-necked pheasant, yellow-billed cuckoo, rose-breasted grosbeak, bobwhite.

Sassafras,
Sassafras variifolium
To 60 ft.; fruit dark blue on red stems. Often shrubby, forming coppices.
August-October

18 kinds including bobwhite, catbird, kingbird, red-eyed vireo, pileated woodpecker, great crested flycatcher.

Shadbush, Juneberry or Serviceberry,
Amelanchier canadensis
A small tree or shrub; white flowers before the leaves, fruit a dark red to purple pome.
June-August

42 kinds including cedar waxwing, cardinal, ruffed grouse, flicker, blue jay, downy, hairy, and red-headed woodpeckers, hermit, olive-backed, and wood

NAME, DESCRIPTION AND FRUITING SEASON	KNOWN TO BE EATEN BY
Shadbush, Smooth, *A. lævis* Shrub or usually a small tree; fruit a purple pome. *June-July*	thrushes, Baltimore oriole, phoebe, bluebird, brown thrasher, kingbird, rose-breasted grosbeak, red-winged blackbird, mourning dove, red-eyed vireo, junco, song sparrow, ruffed grouse, redstart, scarlet tanager, robin.
Sour Gum or Pepperidge, *Nyssa sylvatica* Large tree; fruit conspicuous, blue-black. *September-October sometimes falling, sometimes persistent until May.*	cedar waxwing, pileated and downy woodpecker, bluebird, brown thrasher, robin, blue jay, flicker, catbird, hermit, wood, olive-backed thrushes, veery, mockingbird, ring-necked pheasant, wood duck and mallard.
Spruce, Red, *Picea rubra* Evergreen; fruit a cone to 2 in. long. *September, seeds falling by late fall.* **Spruce, White,** *P. glauca* Large evergreen; fruit a cone to 2 in. long. (Sometimes listed as *P. canadensis*.) *September, cones falling*	31 kinds including white-winged crossbill, red crossbill, downy, hairy, pileated woodpeckers, chickadee, olive-backed and wood thrushes, mallard, great blue heron.
Sweet Gum, *Liquidambar styraciflua* Large tree to 140 ft.; fruit a spiny cluster. *September-November, seeds falling in winter.*	12 kinds including bobwhite.
Sycamore or Plane-tree, *Platanus occidentalis* To 100 ft.; bark shedding; fruit in heads. *October, persistent through winter.*	4 kinds including purple finch, and mallard duck.
Tulip tree, *Liriodendron tulipifera* Large tree; fruit a winged seed or samara. *September-November*	4 kinds of birds including bobwhite.

242

LIST OF PLANTS TO ATTRACT BIRDS

Willow, Shining,
Salix lucida
Shrub or tree to 18 ft.; catkins with the
leaves.

20 kinds including redpoll, pine grosbeak, wood duck, mallard duck.

GROUND COVERS AND VINES (*native*)

Bearberry,
Arctostaphylos uva-ursi
Prostrate and creeping evergreen shrub;
flowers white or pinkish; fruit red; in acid
soil in the open or semishade.
All year.

34 kinds including ruffed grouse and fox sparrow.

Bittersweet or Waxwork,
Celastrus scandens
A shrubby vine; flowers small; fruit orange
and red; in sun or shade.
September-June

bobwhite, hermit thrush, bluebird, robin, red-eyed vireo.

Bunchberry,
Cornus canadensis
Dwarf shrub to 4 inches; flowers small, surrounded by white bracts; fruit red, in clusters; in very acid peaty soil in the shade.

ruffed grouse.

Catbrier,
Smilax glauca
A partially evergreen, thorny vine; fruit
bluish-black; excellent cover.

43 kinds including mockingbird, catbird, brown thrasher, robin, hermit thrush, cardinal.

Clintonia,
Clintonia borealis
Perennial plant; flowers yellow; fruit bril-
liant blue; acid soil in the shade.
August

Cloudberry,
Rubus chamæmorus
Herb with creeping rootstock; flowers
white; fruit reddish or yellow; in acid soil.
June-August

ruffed grouse, bobwhite, flicker, white-throated, fox and song sparrows.

BIRDS IN THE GARDEN

Cowberry,
Vaccinium vitis-idæa
var. *minus*
Creeping evergreen shrub; fruit dark red;
in the open or semishade, in acid, peaty soil.
Fall and winter

ruffed grouse, brown thrasher,
catbird towhee.

Cranberry,
V. oxycoccus
Evergreen creeping shrub; fruit red; in
moist acid peaty soil in the open.
All year

Dewberry, Northern,
Rubus flagellaris
Trailing vine, rooting at the tips; fruit
black; in open or near hedgerow for ground
cover in poor soil.
July

white-throated, fox and song
sparrows, ruffed grouse, bobwhite, flicker, kingbird, brown
thrasher, thrushes, robin.

Dewberry, Swamp,
R. hispidus
Slender vine without prickles; leaves glossy,
almost evergreen; in moist ground.
June-July

Crowberry, Black
Empetrum nigrum
Small evergreen shrub to 10 inches; fruit,
berrylike, black; in acid sandy soil in the
open.
All year

40 kinds including pine grosbeak
and snow bunting.

Crowberry, Broom,
Corema conradi
Small evergreen shrub; fruit a dry drupe; in
acid sandy soil in the open.

244

LIST OF PLANTS TO ATTRACT BIRDS

Grape, Fox,
Vitis labrusca
Strong climber; fruit purple-black, with
musky flavor.
July-October

Grape, Frost,
V. cordifolia
High climber; fruit small, dull-black.
July-October

87 kinds including kingbird,
mockingbird, catbird, cedar waxwing, bluebird, thrushes, brown
thrasher, flicker, pileated woodpecker, cardinal.

Grape, River-bank,
V. vulpina
Strong climber; fruit black with a bloom.
July-April

Greenbrier. Bristly,
Smilax hispida
Vine with leaves edged with prickles; fruit
black.
All year

cardinal, bluebird, catbird, brown
thrasher, robin, mockingbird,
hermit thrush.

Honeysuckle, Trumpet,
Lonicera sempervirens
A climber; flowers orange-scarlet; fruit red.

18 kinds including bobwhite,
catbird, brown thrasher, robin,
hermit thrush.

Horsebrier,
Smilax rotundifolia
A thorny vine; fruit bluish-black; as a tangle
or in shrubby hedgerow.
All year

39 kinds including cardinal,
mockingbird, brown thrasher,
catbird, hermit thrush, robin.

Juniper, Ground,
Juniperus communis var. compressa
Dwarf evergreen shrub with crowded
branchlets; fruit berrylike, bluish; in acid
sandy soil in the open.
All year

robin, flicker, bluebird, evening
and pine grosbeaks, purple finch.

BIRDS IN THE GARDEN

Lily-of-the-valley
Convallaria majalis
Flowers white, bell-like, fragrant; leaves glossy; fruit red; in damp soil in shade or semi-shade.
June-July

Mayflower, Canadian,
Maianthemum canadense
Perennial to 6 or 7 inches; leaves glossy; flowers small, white; fruit dull-red, spotted; in moist soil in the shade.
August-September

ring-necked pheasant, ruffed grouse, russet- and olive-backed thrush.

Moonseed,
Menispermum canadense
A woody, twining vine with good foliage; flowers white or yellowish; fruit black; in rich soil, to drape arbors or fences.
September, through winter

robin, brown thrasher, towhee.

Partridgeberry,
Mitchella repens
An evergreen trailer; flowers white, fragrant; fruit red; in acid or semi-acid soil in partial or full shade.
All year

10 kinds including ruffed grouse.

Pokeberry,
Phytolacca americana
An herb to 12 ft.; fruit purple in long clusters.
August-September

52 kinds including mourning dove, flicker, kingbird, mockingbird, catbird, robin, hermit, olive-backed and gray-cheeked thrushes, bluebird, cardinal.

Raspberry, Dwarf, *see* Dewberry, Swamp.

Rose, Wild,
Rosa nitida
Bush to 2 ft.; flowers pink; fruit a red hip. Excellent shrub to plant in ordinary soil.
August, through winter

38 kinds including ruffed grouse, bobwhite, robin, ring-necked pheasant.

LIST OF PLANTS TO ATTRACT BIRDS

Sarsaparilla, Wild,
Aralia nudicaulis
Herb with attractive foliage to 1 ft.; flowers greenish; fruit black. Plant in shade in acid soil.
June-October

14 kinds including bobwhite, robin.

Serviceberry, Dwarf,
Amelanchier stolonifera
Shrub to 4 ft.; flowers white; fruit purple with a bloom; thicket forming.
June-July

flicker, catbird, robin, hermit thrush, veery, cedar waxwing, Baltimore oriole.

Snowberry, Creeping,
Chiogenes hispidula
An evergreen trailing plant; flowers white, bell-shaped; fruit white; in the shade in cool acid soil.
August-September

ruffed grouse, olive-backed thrush, spruce grouse.

Solomon's-seal,
Polygonatum biflorum
A perennial to 2 ft.; fruit blue with a bloom.
August-November

pheasant.

Solomon's-seal, False,
Smilacina racemosa
A perennial to 3 ft.; fruit red.
August-November

gray-cheeked, hermit, wood thrushes, bluebird.

Strawberry, Wild,
Fragaria virginiana
A perennial herb to 5 in.; flowers white; fruit red; semishade or in open.
June

58 kinds including catbird, brown thrasher, robin, wood thrush, towhee.

Strawberrybush, Running,
Euonymus obovatus
Prostrate shrub with branches rooting; fruit pink.
August-October

hermit thrush, bluebird, robin, scarlet tanager, flicker.

NAME, DESCRIPTION AND FRUITING SEASON	KNOWN TO BE EATEN BY
Wintergreen, *Gaultheria procumbens* Small evergreen shrub; leaves glossy; flowers white, fruit bright red, aromatic; in partial or complete shade in very acid soil. *All year*	10 kinds including ruffed grouse.
Yew, Canada, *Taxus canadensis* Evergreen, needle-leaved shrub; fruit red; in shade in acid soil. *August-September, available second season*	ruffed grouse, thrushes.
Virginia Creeper, *Parthenocissus quinquefolia* Hardy vine; fruit blue-black. *Fall through winter*	39 kinds including flicker, robin, mockingbird, bluebird, scarlet tanager, purple finch, thrushes.

SOUTHEASTERN STATES

From the Atlantic westward to Arkansas and Louisiana, and from Arkansas, Tennessee, and North Carolina southward to the Gulf of Mexico, not including Florida

(*native*)

Adelia,
Forestiera ligustrina
A large widely branched shrub; fruit a black
or purple drupe.

American olive,
Osmanthus americanus
Large evergreen shrub or small tree; grows
near coast; fruit a drupe.
September

NAME, DESCRIPTION AND FRUITING SEASON	KNOWN TO BE EATEN BY
Bayberry, *Myrica caroliniensis* A small to large almost evergreen shrub; fruit waxy, nutlike. *June-April*	
Bayberry, Dwarf Wax-Myrtle, *M. pumila* A small evergreen shrub; fruit waxy, nutlike. *All year*	flicker, catbird, tree swallow, mockingbird, towhee, brown thrasher, white-eyed vireo, bobwhite, downy woodpecker, myrtle warbler.
Bayberry, Southern Wax-Myrtle, *M. cerifera* A small to large evergreen shrub; fruit grayish white. *All year*	
Beautyberry, *Callicarpa americana* Shrub to 6 ft.; flowers bluish; fruit violet. *July-January*	cardinal, bobwhite, catbird, mockingbird, brown thrasher, towhee.
Black Haw, Southern, *Viburnum rufidulum* To 30 ft.; flowers white; berries dark blue with a bloom. *June-April*	cedar waxwing, pileated woodpecker, robin, bobwhite, brown thrasher.
Blueberry, Evergreen, *Vaccinium myrsinites* A small evergreen shrub; fruit purple-black.	
Blueberry, or Farkleberry, *V. arboreum* Evergreen shrub or tree to 30 ft.; fruit black. *October-March*	tufted titmouse, blue jay, catbird, orchard oriole, towhee, robin, bluebird, brown thrasher, kingbird.
Blueberry, Highbush, *V. corymbosum* Shrub to 15 ft.; flowers white or pinkish; berries blue with bloom. *April-June*	

249

BIRDS IN THE GARDEN

NAME, DESCRIPTION AND FRUITING SEASON	KNOWN TO BE EATEN BY
Bumelia, or Chittamwood, *Bumelia lanuginosa* Thorny shrub to 25 ft.; fruit purple-black. *September-February*	bobwhite.
Catbrier, *Smilax glauca* Prickly vine; fruit black. *Long persistent*	ruffed grouse, robin, red-bellied woodpecker, flicker.
Chinaberry, (naturalized) *Melia azedarach* Spreading tree to 50 ft.; flowers purple, fragrant; fruit round, yellow. *August-May*	robin.
Chokeberry, Purple, *Aronia atropurpurea* A shrub to 12 ft.; flowers white; fruit purple-black. *August-October, persistent*	catbird, meadowlark, brown thrasher, cedar waxwing.
Chokeberry, Red, *A. arbutifolia* A shrub to 10 ft.; flowers white; fruit red. *July-March*	
Coral bead, or Carolina Moonseed *Cocculus carolinus* A twining shrub; fruit red. *July-April*	mockingbird, phoebe, brown thrasher.
Dangleberry, *Gaylussacia frondosa* Shrub to 6 ft.; flowers greenish-purple; fruit blue with a bloom. *June-July*	flicker, bobwhite, blue jay, mockingbird, catbird, towhee, orchard oriole, scarlet tanager.
Dewberry, Southern, *Rubus trivialis* A prickly partially evergreen vine; flowers white or pinkish; fruit black. *April-July*	tufted titmouse, cedar waxwing, cardinal, brown thrasher, bobwhite, catbird, orchard oriole, song sparrow, mockingbird, towhee, kingbird, flicker.

250

LIST OF PLANTS TO ATTRACT BIRDS

Dogwood, Flowering,
Cornus florida
Tree to 40 ft.; flowers small, surrounded by four white bracts; fruit scarlet.
July-December

cardinal, warbling vireo, bob-white, brown thrasher, kingbird, red-eyed vireo, ruffed grouse, flicker, robin, bluebird, hermit thrush.

Dogwood, Stiff,
C. femina
A shrub to 15 ft., with purplish branches; flowers white; fruit pale blue.
August-October

Elderberry, American,
Sambucus canadensis
Shrub to 12 ft.; flowers white; fruit purple-black.
July-October

red-bellied woodpecker, flicker, catbird, mockingbird, bluebird, brown thrasher.

Fringe-tree,
Chionanthus virginica
A large shrub or small tree; flowers fringe-like, white; fruit purple, olivelike.
September-October

pileated woodpecker.

Grape, Frost,
Vitis cordifolia
Strong high climbing vine; fruit dull black.
August-October

Grape, Summer,
V. æstivalis
Tall, strong climber; fruit black with a bloom.
August-September

cedar waxwing, red-bellied wood-pecker, flicker, blue jay, robin, cardinal, ruffed grouse, bobwhite, boat-tailed grackle, kingbird.

Grape, Winter, or Sweet,
V. cinerea
High climbing vine; fruit black or purple with a bloom.
August-November

251

NAME, DESCRIPTION AND FRUITING SEASON	KNOWN TO BE EATEN BY
Greenbrier, Coral, *Smilax walteri* A smooth-leaved vine; stem prickly below; fruit coral red. *July-April* Greenbrier, Laurel, *S. laurifolia* Vine with leathery, evergreen leaves; stem with straight prickles; fruit black. *All year*	flicker, hermit thrush, pileated woodpecker, ruffed grouse, catbird, mockingbird, robin, brown thrasher, red-bellied woodpecker.
Hackberry, or Sugarberry, *Celtis lævigata* Tree to 100 ft.; fruit orange to purple. *May-November*	cardinal, mockingbird, robin, brown thrasher, bluebird, red-bellied woodpecker, hermit thrush, flicker, robin, bobwhite, phoebe.
Hawthorn, Parsley, *Cratægus apiifolia* A spiny shrub to 20 ft.; fruit scarlet. *September-November*	ruffed grouse, robin, cardinal, bobwhite, blue jay.
Holly, American, *Ilex opaca* Evergreen shrub or tree to 30 ft.; fruit red. *All year*	bobwhite, hermit thrush, robin, brown thrasher, mockingbird, red-bellied woodpecker.
Honeysuckle, Trumpet, *Lonicera sempervirens* Nearly evergreen vine; orange-red flowers; fruit red. *June-September*	catbird, red-eyed vireo, robin, mockingbird, bobwhite.
Inkberry, *Ilex glabra* Evergreen shrub to 8 ft.; fruit black. *All year*	mockingbird, bluebird, flicker, hermit thrush, catbird, towhee, bobwhite.

LIST OF PLANTS TO ATTRACT BIRDS

Mulberry, Red,
Morus rubra
Tree to 60 ft.; fruit purple; plant staminate
and pistillate forms.
May-July

cardinal, catbird, robin, kingbird,
crested flycatcher, bobwhite.

Partridgeberry,
Mitchella repens
Small evergreen trailer; flowers white; fruit
red.
All year

ruffed grouse, catbird, robin,
bluebird, brown thrasher, bobwhite.

Passionflower,
Passiflora incarnata
Vine; flowers white, with lavender or rose-
pink center; fruit yellow.
June-August

bobwhite, mourning dove.

Peppervine,
Ampelopsis arborea
Bushy vine with divided leaves; fruit dark
purple.
July-November

flicker, catbird, bluebird, bobwhite.

Persimmon,
Diospyros virginiana
Tree to 50 ft.; fruit yellow or orange.
August-November

robin, mockingbird.

Pokeberry,
Phytolacca americana
Herb to 12 ft.; fruit fleshy berries in long
clusters.
May-October

catbird, mockingbird, towhee,
robin, bluebird, hermit thrush.
mourning dove.

Possumhaw,
Ilex decidua
Shrub or tree to 30 ft.; berries red or orange.
All year

robin, brown thrasher, red-bellied
woodpecker, flicker, bluebird,
bobwhite.

253

NAME, DESCRIPTION AND FRUITING SEASON	KNOWN TO BE EATEN BY
Red Cedar, *Iuniperus virginiana* Tree to 80 ft.; fruit a bright blue berry. *All year* **Red Cedar, Southern,** *J. lucayana* Tree to 50 ft.; fruit a dark blue berry with a bloom. *All year*	cedar waxwing, robin, bluebird, flicker, mockingbird, bobwhite.
Rose, Cherokee, (naturalized) *Rosa lævigata* Evergreen climber to 15 ft.; flowers white; fruit a solitary red hip. *August-March* **Rose, Pasture,** *R. carolina* Bush to 3 ft.; flowers rose; fruit a solitary hip. *June-October*	ruffed grouse, bobwhite, cardinal, wood thrush, robin.
Sassafras, *Sassafras variifolium* Tree to 60 ft.; fruit dark blue on red stalks. *July-October*	bobwhite, catbird, kingbird, red-eyed vireo, pileated woodpecker, white-eyed vireo.
Shadbush, or Serviceberry, *Amelanchier canadensis* Shrub or tree to 30 ft.; flowers white, before the leaves; fruit dark red to purple. *April-May*	robin, catbird, red-headed woodpecker, flicker, cardinal, scarlet tanager, bluebird.
Sour Gum, *Nyssa sylvatica* Tree often of low, crooked growth; fruit dark blue. *July-December*	robin, flicker, red-bellied woodpecker, mockingbird, bluebird, brown thrasher, pileated woodpecker.

LIST OF PLANTS TO ATTRACT BIRDS

NAME, DESCRIPTION AND FRUITING SEASON	KNOWN TO BE EATEN BY
Spicebush, *Bensoin æstivale* Shrub to 10 ft.; flowers very early, yellow; fruit red. *June-March*	kingbird, wood thrush, catbird, red-eyed vireo, cardinal, robin.
Sumac, Dwarf, *Rhus copallina* Shrub or small tree to 20 ft.; flowers greenish; fruit red and hairy. *June-March*	bobwhite, robin, bluebird, ruffed grouse, red-headed woodpecker, mockingbird.
Sugarberry, *see* Hackberry	
Supplejack, *Berchemia scandens* A climbing shrub to 15 ft.; flowers greenish; fruit bluish-black. *July-October*	mallard, hermit thrush, brown thrasher, robin, mockingbird, bobwhite, wild turkey.
Virginia creeper, *Parthenosissus quinquefolia* Hardy vine; fruit a black berry. *Through winter*	flicker, bluebird, catbird, bobwhite.
Winterberry, *Ilex verticillata* Shrub to 10 ft.; fruit red. *July-December*	catbird, ruffed grouse, flicker, bobwhite, hermit thrush, robin.
Withe-Rod, Smooth, *Viburnum nudum* (and other spp.) Shrub to 15 ft.; flowers white or yellow; fruit blue-black. *All year*	red-eyed vireo, brown thrasher, robin, cardinal, blue jay.
Yaupon, *Ilex vomitoria* Evergreen shrub or small tree to 25 ft.; berries scarlet. *July-April*	catbird, mockingbird, brown thrasher, bobwhite.

BIRDS IN THE GARDEN

PLANTS FOR BIRDS IN TEXAS AND OKLAHOMA

TREES AND SHRUBS (*native*)

NAME, DESCRIPTION AND FRUITING SEASON	KNOWN TO BE EATEN BY
Adelia, Spring Heralds or Spring Golden Glow, *Forestiera pubescens* Small or large shrub; flowers petalless, consisting of clusters of stamens or pistils on separate bushes, the staminate yellow and conspicuous; fruit blue in clusters. Shady, rocky ground; thicket-forming. *May-October* *F. acuminata* Tree to 30 ft.; small yellow flowers; fruit a dark purple drupe. *May-October*	scaled quail.
Anaqua, *Ehretia elliptica* Tree to 50 ft.; small white flowers; fruit a small yellow drupe. *Mid-June-April*	cardinal, Bullock's oriole, mockingbird, scissor-tailed flycatcher.
Beautyberry, or French Mulberry, *Callicarpa americana* Shrub to 6 ft.; flowers bluish; fruit violet. *August-November*	cardinal, catbird, bobwhite, hermit thrush, wood thrush, mockingbird, red-eyed towhee, brown thrasher.
Black Haw, Southern, *Viburnum rufidulum* Tall shrub or small tree; flowers creamy-white, in flat-topped clusters; fruit black with a bloom; in woods and thickets. *July-November, persistent through winter.*	cedar waxwing, pileated woodpecker, robin, brown thrasher.
Blueberry, or Huckleberry, *Vaccinium hirsutum* To 3 ft.; flowers white; berries purplish black. *August*	tufted titmouse, cardinal, blue jay, catbird, hermit thrush, orchard oriole, red-eyed towhee, bluebird, brown thrasher, kingbird.

256

LIST OF PLANTS TO ATTRACT BIRDS

Buckthorn, Woolly, or
Chittamwood or Gum Elastic,
Bumelia lanuginosa
Thorny shrub or small tree; flowers small,
white, greenish, fragrant; fruit like a small
black cherry; river bottoms and rocky hill-
sides.
September-November

Sennett's thrasher.

Chittamwood, *see* Buckthorn, Woolly.

Coral bead, or Carolina Moonseed,
Cocculus carolinus
A twining shrub; flowers inconspicuous;
fruit red.
*September-October, often persistent through
winter in South.*

brown thrasher, mockingbird,
phoebe.

Coralberry, or Indian Currant,
Symphoricarpos orbiculatus
Shrub to 7 ft.; flowers white, bell-shaped;
fruit purple-red.
September-June

bobwhite, prairie chicken, hermit
thrush.

Dogwood, Flowering,
Cornus florida
Tree to 40 ft.; flowers small, surrounded by
large, white bracts, fruit red.
July-December

Dogwood, Roughleaf,
C. asperifolia
Shrub with reddish-brown twigs; flowers
small, white, in clusters; fruit white.
August-October

Dogwood, Silky,
C. amomum
Shrub to 10 ft.; flowers white, in flat-topped
clusters; fruit pale blue.
August-November

yellow-shafted flicker, bobwhite,
hermit thrush, robin, bluebird,
wood thrush, brown thrasher, catbird, cedar waxwing, cardinal,
red-bellied woodpecker, kingbird,
red-eyed vireo.

NAME, DESCRIPTION AND FRUITING SEASON	KNOWN TO BE EATEN BY
Dogwood, Stiff, *C. femina* Shrub to 15 ft.; flowers white in flat-topped clusters; fruit pale blue. *August-November*	yellow-shafted flicker, bobwhite, hermit thrush, robin, bluebird, wood thrush, brown thrasher, catbird, cedar waxwing, cardinal, red-bellied woodpecker, kingbird, red-eyed vireo.
Elderberry, American, *Sambucus canadensis* Shrub to 12 ft.; flowers white, in clusters; fruit purple-black; grows best in moist soil. *July-September*	yellow shafted flicker, catbird, bobwhite, mockingbird, bluebird, brown thrasher, red-eyed vireo.
Farkleberry, *Vaccinium arboreum* Evergreen shrub to 30 ft.; flowers white; fruit black; in acid soil. *June-December*	bobwhite, mockingbird.
Gum Elastic, *see* Bumelia.	
Hackberry, or Sugarberry, *Celtis lævigata* Tree to 100 ft.; fruit orange-red to dark purple. *All year*	cardinal, mockingbird, robin, bluebird, brown thrasher.
Hawthorn, *Cratægus spathulata* Spiny shrub or small tree to 25 ft.; flowers white; fruit bright red. *June-October*	bobwhite, robin, lesser prairie chicken, blue jay.
Hercules'-club or Devil's Walking-Stick, *Aralia spinosa* Shrubby tree, very spiny; flowers in panicles; fruit berrylike. *August-November*	bobwhite, wood thrush, catbird, blue jay.

LIST OF PLANTS TO ATTRACT BIRDS

NAME, DESCRIPTION AND FRUITING SEASON

KNOWN TO BE EATEN BY

Holly, American,
Ilex opaca
Evergreen tree to 30 ft.; flowers inconspicuous, male and female on separate trees; fruit bright red.
August-June

bobwhite, hermit thrush, robin, mockingbird, brown thrasher, red-bellied woodpecker, catbird, yellow-shafted flicker, bluebird.

Honeysuckle, Wild,
Lonicera albiflora
Climbing shrub; flowers white and fragrant; fruit a blue berry; thickets and banks of streams.
October-November

bobwhite, catbird, hermit thrush, robin.

Ironwood, Black,
Condalia obovata
A large spiny shrub; fruit blue or black.
Through summer

Bullock's oriole, mockingbird, scissor-tailed flycatcher, kingbird, bluebird.

Mulberry, Red,
Morus rubra
Tree to 60 ft.; fruit dark purple.
April-August

tufted titmouse, cardinal, catbird, cedar waxwing, bobwhite, wood thrush, orchard oriole, red-headed woodpecker, mockingbird, robin, brown thrasher.

Mulberry, White (naturalized),
M. alba
Tree to 50 ft.; fruit white to purplish.
April-August

bobwhite, red-bellied woodpecker, downy woodpecker, yellow-shafted flicker.

Palmetto, Bluestem or Dwarf,
Sabal minor
Stemless palm; leaves with many short branches; fruit round.
All year

wood thrush.

Persimmon, Common,
Diospyros virginiana
Tree to 30 ft.; fruit yellow or orange.
July-November

bluebird, robin, phoebe, bobwhite, mockingbird.

NAME, DESCRIPTION AND FRUITING SEASON	KNOWN TO BE EATEN BY
Plum, Creek, *Prunus rivularis* A large shrub growing in moist soil; fruit red with a bloom. *June*	
Plum, Texas Sloe, *P. tarda* A small spiny tree; fruit a bright red, yellow or purple drupe. *October-November*	bobwhite.
Plum, Wild or Oklahoma, *P. gracilis* Bush to 15 ft.; straggling thickets; fruit reddish. *June-August*	
Pokeberry, *Phytolacca americana* Herb to 12 ft.; flowers white; fruit a fleshy berry. *June-September*	cedar waxwing, cardinal, yellow-shafted flicker, catbird, hermit thrush, robin, bluebird, mourning dove.
Possumhaw, Redberry, Winterberry, or Hollyberry, *Ilex decidua* Shrub or tree to 30 ft.; berries red or orange; in moist soil. *September-March*	bobwhite, hermit thrush, robin, mockingbird, brown thrasher, red-bellied woodpecker, catbird, yellow-shafted flicker, bluebird.
Redbay, or Sweetbay, Swamp, *Persea pubescens* A small to large evergreen tree; fruit a berry, nearly black. *September, long persistent.*	
Redbay, *P. borbonia* Aromatic evergreen tree; small green flowers; fruit a dark blue berry. Swamps and along streams. *June-November*	robin, bobwhite, bluebird.

NAME, DESCRIPTION AND FRUITING SEASON | KNOWN TO BE EATEN BY

Red Cedar,
Juniperus virginiana
Evergreen shrub or tree to 100 ft.; fruit bluish with a bloom.
All year

cedar waxwing, yellow-shafted flicker, bobwhite, mockingbird, robin, bluebird, cardinal, mourning dove.

Rose,
Rosa macouni
Much branched bush to 6 ft.; flowers rose-pink, solitary; fruit a red hip.
All year

bobwhite, prairie chicken, wood thrush, bluebird.

Rouge plant,
Rivina humilis
An herb to 3 ft.; flowers white; fruit berry-like.
June-November

mockingbird, brown thrasher.

Sassafras,
Sassafras variifolium
Tree to 60 ft.; flowers yellow; fruit dark blue on bright red stalks.
August-October

bobwhite, catbird, kingbird, red-eyed vireo, pileated woodpecker, phoebe, bluebird.

Sour Gum, or Pepperidge,
Nyssa sylvatica
Tree to 100 ft.; fruit dark blue; in moist soil.
September-October, sometimes persistent.

red-bellied woodpecker, yellow-shafted flicker, robin, cedar waxwing, catbird, mockingbird, pileated woodpecker, brown thrasher.

Spicebush,
Benzoin æstivale
Shrub to 15 ft.; flowers yellow, before leaves; fruit scarlet.
August-September, or earlier

cardinal, yellow-shafted flicker, catbird, wood thrush, kingbird, red-eyed vireo.

Spring Heralds, or Spring Golden Glow,
see Adelia.

Sugarberry, *see* Hackberry.

BIRDS IN THE GARDEN

Sumac, Shining Dwarf,
Rhus copallina
Shrub or tree to 20 ft.; fruit red and hairy.
August-April

Sumac, Fragrant,
R. canadensis
Shrub to 8 ft.; leaves aromatic; fruit red and hairy.
April-June

Sumac, Staghorn,
R. typhina
Shrub or tree to 30 ft.; fruit crimson and hairy.
All year

yellow-shafted flicker, bobwhite, hermit thrush, red-headed woodpecker, robin, bluebird, mockingbird, thrasher.

Supplejack,
Berchemia scandens
Twining shrub to 15 ft.; fruit bluish-black; in damp soil.
July-October

robin, brown thrasher, hermit thrush, mockingbird, bobwhite.

Sweetbay, *see* Redbay.

Withe-Rod, Smooth,
Viburnum nudum
Shrub to 15 ft.; flowers white or yellowish in June or July; fruit bluish-black.
September-December

cardinal, blue jay, red-eyed vireo, brown thrasher, robin.

Yaupon,
Ilex vomitoria
Evergreen shrub or small tree; flowers small, greenish-white; berries bright red.
September-October, often persistent.

bobwhite, hermit thrush, robin, mockingbird, brown thrasher, red-bellied woodpecker, catbird, yellow-shafted flicker, bluebird.

LIST OF PLANTS TO ATTRACT BIRDS

VINES (*native*)

NAME, DESCRIPTION AND FRUITING SEASON

KNOWN TO BE EATEN BY

Dewberry, Southern or Zarzamora,
Rubus trivialis
Prickly trailing vine; large white blooms; fruit black, delicious; banks, gravelly creek beds or over underbrush.
March-May

tufted titmouse, cedar waxwing, cardinal, bobwhite, catbird, red-eyed towhee, robin, brown thrasher.

Grape, Frost,
Vitis cordifolia
High climber; fruit dull black.
June-November

Grape, Muscadine,
V. rotundifolia
Strong climber; fruit dull purple.
August-September

Grape, Mustang or Wild,
V. candicans
Vigorous woody vine; to 70 or 100 ft.; flowers greenish, fragrant; large acid grapes; river bottoms.
April-July

cedar waxwing, pileated woodpecker, yellow-shafted flicker, robin, blue jay, cardinal, gray-cheeked thrush, bobwhite, red-headed woodpecker, mourning dove, catbird.

Grape, Riverbank,
V. vulpina
Vigorous climber; flowers fragrant; fruit black with a bloom.
June-November, persistent.

Grape, Sand, Sugar or Mountain,
V. rupestris
A bushy plant, 2 to 7 ft.; sometimes climbing; grapes purple-black, ripening June and July; dry gravelly creek banks.
July-August

Grape, Winter,
V. cinerea
High climber, fruit black or purple with a bloom.
August-November, long persistent.

BIRDS IN THE GARDEN

Greenbrier, Bristly,
Smilax hispida
Vine with leaves edged with prickles; fruit
black.
October-November, persistent until spring.

yellow-shafted flicker, hermit
thrush, pileated woodpecker.

Greenbrier, Laurel,
S. laurifolia
Evergreen woody vine, fruit black.
August-September

Honeysuckle, Trumpet,
Lonicera sempervirens
A climber; flowers orange-scarlet; fruit red.
September-October

robin, hermit thrush, catbird,
bobwhite, Eastern purple finch.

Horsebrier,
Smilax rotundifolia
Woody vine; fruit bluish-black.
October, persistent throughout winter.

robin, bluebird, brown thrasher,
pileated woodpecker, yellow-
shafted flicker.

Ivy, Marine or Yerba del buey,
Cissus incisa
Tiny greenish flowers; fruit grape-like clus-
ters of small black berries; climbs over fences
and brush.
October

Arkansas kingbird.

Maypop, *see* Passionflower.

Partridgeberry,
Mitchella repens
Trailing evergreen vine; flowers white; fruit
scarlet; in shade.
July-April

bobwhite, catbird, robin, bluebird, brown thrasher.

Passionflower,
Passiflora incarnata
Vinelike plants; flowers large handsome,
purplish; fruit large as a lemon, yellow;
makes excellent thick cover.
June-August

bobwhite, mourning dove.

LIST OF PLANTS TO ATTRACT BIRDS

Peppervine,
Ampelopsis arborea
Leaves divided; fruit dark purple.
July-October

yellow-shafted flicker, robin, bluebird, bobwhite.

Virginia Creeper,
Parthenocissus quinquefolia
Hardy and adaptable climber; fruit a black berry.
August-February

red-bellied woodpecker, hermit thrush, mockingbird, robin, bluebird, brown thrasher.

Virginia Creeper, Texas,
P. heptaphylla
Woody-stemmed; vines, clinging to walls, fences and trees; flowers small, greenish; fruit black or dark blue berries.
August-February

Zarzamora, *see* Dewberry.

FLORIDA, NORTH AND CENTRAL ZONES

(*native*)

Adelia,
Forestiera acuminata
Small or large widely-branched, spiny shrub; fruit black or purple; forms thickets.
June-October

wood duck, mallard.

Arrowwood,
Viburnum dentatum
Shrub to 15 ft.; flowers white in small clusters; fruit black.
October-December

robin, phoebe, brown thrasher, white-eyed vireo, catbird.

Bayberry, or Wax-Myrtle,
Myrica cerifera
Evergreen tree to 36 ft.; fruit grayish-white; in moist peaty soil.
July-March

flicker, bobwhite, red-bellied and downy woodpeckers, tree swallow, mockingbird, white-eyed vireo.

BIRDS IN THE GARDEN

NAME, DESCRIPTION AND FRUITING SEASON	KNOWN TO BE EATEN BY
Beautyberry, or French Mulberry, *Callicarpa americana* Shrub to 6 ft.; flowers lavender; fruit violet. *August-November*	cardinal, bobwhite, mockingbird, brown thrasher, red-eyed towhee.
Blackberry, Sand, *Rubus cuneifolius* Spiny and erect; 1 to 3 ft.; flowers white or pinkish; fruit black; excellent cover in sandy soil. *May-July*	tufted titmouse, cardinal, bobwhite, blue jay, catbird, red-headed woodpecker, mockingbird, chewink, brown thrasher.
Black Haw, or Withe-Rod, *Viburnum cassinoides* Shrub to 12 ft.; flowers white in broad, flat clusters. *September-October, falling at once.* Black Haw, Southern, *V. rufidulum* Shrub to 30 ft.; flowers white; fruit dark blue with a bloom. *October-November, often persistent until March.*	bobwhite, pileated woodpecker, robin, brown thrasher.
Blueberry, Highbush, *Vaccinium corymbosum* Shrub to 15 ft.; flowers white or pinkish; berries blue with a bloom. *April-June* Blueberry, Evergreen, *V. myrsinites* Small evergreen shrub, fruit a berry. *April-June*	tufted titmouse, cardinal, orchard oriole, chewink, brown thrasher, kingbird.
Bumelia, or Chittamwood, *Bumelia lanuginosa* Thorny shrub to 25 ft.; flowers small, white; fruit small, black. *August-November*	bobwhite.

266

LIST OF PLANTS TO ATTRACT BIRDS

Chinaberry, (naturalized)
Melia azedarach
A spreading tree to 50 ft.; flowers purple, fragrant; fruit round, yellow.
August-May

robin.

Chokeberry, Black,
Aronia melanocarpa
A shrub to 4 ft.; flowers white; fruit black.
August-September, often persistent.

Chokeberry, Purple,
A. atropurpurea
A shrub to 12 ft.; flowers white; fruit purple-black.
August-October, persistent.

bobwhite, brown thrasher, chewink, catbird.

Chokeberry, Red,
A. arbutifolia
A shrub to 10 ft.; flowers white, fruit red.
July-March

Coral bead, or Carolina Moonseed,
Cocculus carolinus
A twining shrub; fruit red.
September-October, persistent.

mockingbird, thrasher.

Crabapple, Southern,
Pyrus angustifolia
Shrubby, partially evergreen tree to 30 ft.; flowers pink, fragrant; fruit yellow-green, fragrant.
September-October

bobwhite.

Dewberry, Southern,
Rubus trivialis
A prickly, partially evergreen vine; flower white or pinkish; fruit black.
April-July

tufted titmouse, cardinal, bob white, blue jay, catbird, red-headed woodpecker, mockingbird, chewink, brown thrasher.

267

BIRDS IN THE GARDEN

Dogwood, Flowering,
Cornus florida
Tree to 40 ft.; flowers small, surrounded by
four showy petal-like bracts; fruit scarlet.
July-December

Dogwood, Silky,
C. amomum
Shrub to 10 ft.; flowers small; white, in
clusters; fruit white or bluish.
August-September

red-bellied woodpecker, flicker,
bobwhite, bluebird, brown
thrasher, catbird, kingbird, red-
eyed vireo, hairy and downy
woodpeckers.

Dogwood, Stiff,
C. femina
Shrub to 15 ft.; flowers white, in clusters;
fruit pale blue.
September-October

Elderberry, American,
Sambucus canadensis
A shrub to 12 ft.; flowers white in large flat
clusters; fruit black.
July-October

red-bellied woodpecker, flicker,
catbird, bobwhite, bluebird,
brown thrasher, mockingbird,
red-eyed vireo.

Farkleberry,
Vaccinium arboreum
An evergreen shrub to 25 ft.; flowers white;
fruit black.
July-November

bobwhite.

Fringe-tree,
Chionanthus virginica
A large shrub or small tree; flowers white;
fruit purple, olivelike.
September-October

pileated woodpecker.

Gallberry, *see* Inkberry

268

LIST OF PLANTS TO ATTRACT BIRDS

NAME, DESCRIPTION AND FRUITING SEASON   KNOWN TO BE EATEN BY

Grape, Frost,
Vitis cordifolia
Strong, high-climbing vine; fruit dull black.
August-October

Grape, Little Muscadine, or Bird
V. munsoniana
A slender, trailing vine, usually not climbing; fruit purple.
All year

Grape, Riverbank,
V. vulpina
Strong climber; fragrant bloom; fruit black with a bloom.
June-November, persistent.

Grape, Summer,
V. æstivalis
Tall, strong climber; fruit black; with a bloom.
August-September

Grape, Sweet Winter,
V. cinerea
High-climbing vine; fruit black or purple with bloom.
August-November

82 kinds including red-bellied, pileated, and red-headed woodpeckers, blue jay, kingbird, bobwhite, cardinal, boat-tailed grackle.

Greenbrier, Coral,
Smilax walteri
A smooth-leaved vine, stem prickly below; fruit coral-red; in damp soil.
Mid-July-April

Greenbrier, Laurel,
S. laurifolia
Vine with leathery, evergreen leaves; stems with straight prickles; fruit black.
All year

red-bellied woodpecker, flicker, catbird, mockingbird, brown thrasher, cardinal, robin, meadowlark, bluebird, thrushes, phoebe, pileated woodpecker.

Hackberry, *see* Sugarberry.

269

BIRDS IN THE GARDEN

NAME, DESCRIPTION AND FRUITING SEASON	KNOWN TO BE EATEN BY
Hawthorn, Parsley, *Cratægus apiifolia* A spiny shrub to 20 ft.; fruit scarlet. *September-November*	bobwhite, blue jay, cardinal.
Hercules'-Club, *Aralia spinosa* A very spiny shrub; fruit in long clusters. *August-November*	red-bellied woodpecker, catbird, bobwhite.
Holly, American, *Ilex opaca* Evergreen tree or shrub to 40 ft.; leaves toothed, spiny; fruit a red berry. *All year* **Holly, Dahoon,** *I. cassine* Evergreen or shrub; fruit a dull red berry. *Nearly all year*	red-bellied woodpecker, bobwhite, mockingbird, flicker, catbird, brown thrasher.
Honeysuckle, Trumpet, *Lonicera sempervirens* Nearly evergreen vine; orange-red flowers; fruit red. *September-October*	catbird, bobwhite, mockingbird.
Huckleberry, Dwarf, *Gaylussacia dumosa* A low shrub to 1½ ft.; fruit a black berry. *May-July*	cardinal, mockingbird, blue jay, catbird, red-eyed towhee, bobwhite.
Inkberry, or Gallberry, *Ilex glabra* Evergreen shrub to 8 ft.; fruit a black berry. *Nearly all year*	red-bellied woodpecker, flicker, catbird, bluebird, red-eyed towhee, bobwhite, mockingbird.
Ivy, Wild or Marine, *Cissus incisa* Strong vines; three leaflets; fruit a berry. *October*	many birds.

270

LIST OF PLANTS TO ATTRACT BIRDS

Juneberry or Shadbush,
Amelanchier canadensis
Shrub or tree to 30 ft.; white flowers before the leaves; fruit dark red to purple.
April-May

tufted titmouse, blue jay, catbird, brown thrasher, kingbird.

Juneberry, or Shadbush,
A. oblongifolia
Shrub or tree to 25 ft.; flowers white, in erect clusters; fruit purple.
April-May

Maypop, *see* Passionflower.

Mulberry, Red,
Morus rubra
Tree to 60 ft.; fruit purple; plant staminate and pistillate forms.
May-July

tufted titmouse, cardinal, bob-white, catbird, kingbird, Florida grackle.

Palm, Needle,
Rhapidophyllum hystrix
Stemless palm; fruit round, nearly black.

Palm, Saw-Cabbage,
Acœlorraphe wrighti
Tree often over 50 ft.; rather small head of leaves; fruit nearly round, black.
June-November

bobwhite, cardinal, phoebe, red-bellied woodpecker.

Palmetto, Scrub,
Serenoa repens
Shrub or tree, evergreen; fruit an almost round, black drupe.
June-November

Partridgeberry,
Mitchella repens
Evergreen trailer; flowers white; fruit scarlet.
July-October, often persistent throughout year.

bobwhite, catbird, brown thrasher, bluebird, ruffed grouse.

BIRDS IN THE GARDEN

NAME, DESCRIPTION AND FRUITING SEASON	KNOWN TO BE EATEN BY
Passionflower, Maypop, *Passiflora incarnata* A vine; flowers white with lavender or rose-pink center; fruit yellow. *June-August*	bobwhite, mourning dove.
Peppervine, *Ampelopsis arborea* A bushy vine with divided leaves; fruit dark purple. *July-November*	bobwhite, catbird, bluebird.
Persimmon, *Diospyros virginiana* Tree to 50 ft.; fruit yellow or orange. *August-November*	mockingbird, bobwhite, phoebe, bluebird, robin, pileated woodpecker.
Plum, Hog, *Prunus umbellata* Bush or small tree; thicket forming; flowers white; fruit yellow or purple. *June-August*	no data.
Pokeberry, *Phytolacca americana* Herb to 12 ft.; fruit fleshy berries in long clusters. *July-August*	cardinal, flicker, catbird, mockingbird, red-eyed towhee, bluebird, kingbird, mourning dove.
Possumhaw, or Withe-Rod, Smooth *Viburnum nudum* Shrub to 15 ft.; flowers creamy; fruit black. *September-March*	bobwhite.
Redbay, *Persea borbonia* Evergreen tree to 35 ft.; fruit nearly black. *All year* Redbay, Swamp, *P. pubescens* Evergreen tree or shrub; fruit dark blue with a bloom. *Nearly all year.*	bobwhite, bluebird, robin.

LIST OF PLANTS TO ATTRACT BIRDS

Red Cedar, or Juniper,
Juniperus virginiana
Evergreen tree to 100 ft.; fruit blue with a
bloom.
All year

cardinal, flicker, bobwhite, mockingbird, bluebird, kingbird.

Red Cedar, Southern,
J. lucayana
Evergreen tree to 50 ft.; fruit dark blue with
a bloom.
All year

Redhaw,
Cratægus viridis
A tree to 35 ft.; leaves dark green, shining;
fruit red or orange; plant in moist ground.
October through winter

bobwhite, blue jay, cardinal, bluebird.

Rose, Cherokee, (naturalized)
Rosa lævigata
Evergreen climber to 15 ft.; flowers white;
fruit a solitary red hip.
August-March

bobwhite, cardinal, bluebird.

Rose, Swamp,
R. palustris
Bush to 6 ft.; flowers in clusters; fruit a hip.
Almost all year.

Rouge plant, Bloodberry,
Rivina humilis
A slender plant to 3 ft.; flowers white or
pink; fruit a red berry.
All year

mockingbird, brown thrasher.

Sageretia,
Sageretia minutiflora
A spiny straggling shrub; fruit a purple
berrylike drupe.
June

BIRDS IN THE GARDEN

NAME, DESCRIPTION AND FRUITING SEASON	KNOWN TO BE EATEN BY
Sassafras, *Sassafras variifolium* A tree to 60 ft.; fruit dark blue on red stalks. *August-October*	pileated woodpecker, bobwhite, catbird, bluebird, kingbird, red-eyed vireo.
Shadbush, *see* Juneberry.	
Sour Gum, *Nyssa sylvatica* Tree often of low crooked growth; fruit dark blue. *July-December*	pileated and red-bellied woodpeckers, blue jay, catbird, mockingbird, brown thrasher, bluebird, thrushes, cedar waxwing, wood duck.
Spicebush, Hairy, or Southern *Benzoin melissæfolium* A shrub to 20 ft.; flowers small, yellow; fruit a red drupe. *September-October*	cardinal, flicker, bobwhite, catbird, kingbird, red-eyed vireo.
Stinking-Cedar, *Torreya taxifolia* Evergreen to 40 ft.; fruit a purple drupe. *August-October*	
Sugarberry, or Hackberry, *Celtis lævigata* Tree to 100 ft.; fruit orange to purple. *May-November*	cardinal, bobwhite, mockingbird, red-eyed towhee, brown thrasher, bluebird.
Sumac, Dwarf or Shining, *Rhus copallina* Shrub or small tree to 20 ft.; flowers greenish; fruit red and hairy. *June-March* **Sumac, Smooth,** *R. glabra,* Shrub or tree to 20 ft.; flowers green; fruit scarlet and hairy. *September-October, persistent all year.*	flicker, bobwhite, red-headed woodpecker, mockingbird, bluebird, blue jay, catbird, brown thrasher, red-eyed vireo, cardinal,

274

LIST OF PLANTS TO ATTRACT BIRDS

NAME, DESCRIPTION AND FRUITING SEASON   KNOWN TO BE EATEN BY

Sumac, Staghorn,
R. typhina
Shrub or tree to 30 ft.; flowers greenish;
fruit crimson and hairy.
September, persistent all year.

flicker, bobwhite, red-headed
woodpecker, mockingbird, bluebird, blue jay, catbird, brown
thrasher, red-eyed vireo, cardinal.

Supplejack,
Berchemia scandens
A climbing shrub to 15 ft.; flowers green-
ish; fruit bluish-black.
July-October

mockingbird, brown thrasher,
catbird, bobwhite.

Virginia Creeper,
Parthenocissus quinquefolia
A hardy climber; fruit a black berry.
August-February

red-bellied woodpecker, flicker,
mockingbird, bluebird, brown
thrasher, red-eyed vireo.

Wax-Myrtle, *see* Bayberry.

Wild olive,
Osmanthus americanus
An evergreen tree or shrub to 45 ft.; flow-
ers very fragrant; fruit a drupe.
August-March

Withe-Rod, Smooth, *see* Possumhaw

Yaupon,
Ilex vomitoria
Evergreen shrub or tree to 20 ft.; fruit a
bright red berry.
July-March

catbird, mockingbird, brown
thrasher, bobwhite.

ARIZONA AND NEW MEXICO
(*native*)

Adelia, Spring Heralds or Spring Golden
Glow,
Forestiera pubescens
A small or large shrub; flowers yellow and
conspicuous, fruit in clusters; thicket form-
ing.
June-October

scaled quail.

275

NAME, DESCRIPTION AND FRUITING SEASON	KNOWN TO BE EATEN BY
Allthorn, *Kœberlinia spinosa* Shrub or tree, very spiny; thicket-forming; fruit a black berry. *September*	scaled quail.
Bearberry, *Arctostaphylos uva-ursi* Trailing evergreen shrub; fruit red. *All year*	no data.
Blueberry, *Vaccinium oreophilum* Small shrub; fruit blue-black. *July-October*	cardinal, hermit thrush, red-shafted flicker, Cassin's kingbird, long-tailed chat.
Buffaloberry, Russet, *Shepherdia canadensis* Shrub to 4 ft.; fruit red. *July-September*	} hermit thrush, hairy woodpecker.
Buffaloberry, Silver, *S. argentea* Shrub to 15 ft.; thorny; fruit red. *July-September*	
Chittamwood, or False Buckthorn, *Bumelia lanuginosa* Shrub or small tree, spiny; fruit black. *September-November, sometimes persistent.*	curve-billed thrasher, Sennett's thrasher.
Creeper, Thicket, *Parthenocissus quinquefolia* Hardy vine; fruit black. *August-February*	hairy woodpecker, mockingbird, Arkansas kingbird, red-shafted flicker, hermit thrush.
Dogwood, *Cornus stolonifera* Shrub to 6 ft.; twigs red; fruit white; moist soil. *July-September, sometimes persistent.*	cardinal, hermit thrush, Bullock's oriole, mockingbird, phainopepla.

276

LIST OF PLANTS TO ATTRACT BIRDS

Elderberry, Black,
Sambucus melanocarpa
Shrub to 10 ft.; fruit black.
July-September

Elderberry, Blue,
S. cærulea, var. *neomexicana*
Large shrub or tree; fruit blue with a bloom.
August-October

cardinal, red-shafted flicker, band-tailed pigeon, Steller's jay, Western flycatcher, cactus wren, Gambel's quail, phainopepla, Arkansas flycatcher, black-headed grosbeak.

Grape, Canyon,
Vitis arizonica
A weak vine or small shrub; fruit black.
July-September, often persistent until October.

cardinal, red-shafted flicker, mockingbird, Western bluebird, Western kingbird.

Hawthorn,
Cratægus cerronis
Spiny shrub to 15 ft.; fruit black or brown.
July-November

Hawthorn,
C. rivularis
Shrub or small tree to 20 ft.; fruit dark red becoming black.
July-November

cardinal, Mearns' quail, black-headed grosbeak.

Honeysuckle,
Lonicera albiflora
Bushy shrub, sometimes climbing; fruit orange.
October-November

hermit thrush, Gambel's quail, mockingbird.

Ironwood, Black, or Squawbush,
Condalia spathulata
Evergreen, stiff shrub densely branched; fruit a drupe.
July-August

Bullock's oriole, mockingbird, scissor-tailed flycatcher, curve-billed thrasher, bluebird.

BIRDS IN THE GARDEN

NAME, DESCRIPTION AND FRUITING SEASON	KNOWN TO BE EATEN BY
Juniper, Alligator, *Juniperus pachyphlæa* Tree to 60 ft.; fruit reddish-brown with a bloom. *All year*	
Juniper, Cherrystone, *J. monosperma* Tree to 50 ft.; fruit bright blue with a bloom. *All year*	evening grosbeak, mockingbird, pine grosbeak.
Juniper, Colorado, or Red Cedar, *J. scopulorum* Tree to 30 ft.; fruit bright blue with a bloom. *All year.*	
Lotebush, Texas Buckthorn or Chaparral, *Condalia obtusifolia* Thorny, intricately branched shrub; flowers inconspicuous; fruit mealy, bluish-black. *June*	golden-fronted woodpeckers feed it to their young, phainopepla, masked bobwhite, Mearns' quail.
Madrona, *Arbutus arizonica* Large evergreen tree; flowers white; fruit red. *July-December*	no data.
Manzanita, *Arctostaphylos pungens* Evergreen shrub; branches rooting; fruit red. *July-April*	Gambel's quail.
Mountain-Ash, *Sorbus dumosa* Large shrub or small tree; fruit red. *July-December*	evening grosbeak, pine grosbeak, robin, dusky grouse.

278

LIST OF PLANTS TO ATTRACT BIRDS

Mulberry, Mexican,
Morus microphylla
Large shrub or small tree; fruit purple or black; thicket-forming.
May-June

cardinal, robin, mockingbird, phainopepla, black-headed grosbeak, Gambel's quail.

Paloblanco,
Celtis lævigata
Large shrub or tree; fruit orange to purple.
September

mockingbird, scissor-tailed flycatcher, Gambel's quail, band-tailed pigeon, Bullock's oriole.

Raspberry, Arizona Red,
Rubus arizonicus
Small bush; fruit red
June

cardinal, house finch, Steller's jay, Bullock's oriole, mockingbird, pine grosbeak, spurred towhee, bluebird.

Rose,
Rosa suffulta
To 1 ½ ft.; flowers pink, in clusters; fruit a red hip.
All year

Rose,
R. woodsi, var. fendleri
Bush to 4 ft.; flowers pink, occasionally white, solitary; fruit a red hip.
All year

cardinal, hermit thrush, bluebird.

Serviceberry, or Shadbush, Western,
Amelanchier alnifolia
To 7 ft.; flowers white in erect clusters; fruit purple.
July-September

Serviceberry, Cluster,
A. polycarpa
Large shrub or small tree; flowers white; fruit purple, very abundant.
August

Western tanager, Western bluebird, cardinal, Bullock's oriole, evening grosbeak, black-headed grosbeak.

Shadbush, *see* Serviceberry.

NAME, DESCRIPTION AND FRUITING SEASON	KNOWN TO BE EATEN BY
Snowberry, Mountain *Symphoricarpos oreophilus* Shrub to 5 ft.; often trailing; fruit white or pinkish. *August-September*	russet-backed thrush, pine grosbeak, spurred towhee, evening grosbeak, hermit thrush.

Spring Heralds, or Golden Glow, *see* Adelia.

NORTHERN PLAINS STATES
The Dakotas, Kansas and Nebraska
(native)

American Spikenard, *Aralia racemosa* A perennial herb to 6 ft.; fruit a brown-purple berry.	ruffed grouse, catbird, olive-backed thrush.
Bearberry, *Arctostaphylos uva-ursi* A prostrate creeping evergreen shrub; flowers white; fruit red; in acid soil in open or semi-shade. *All year*	ruffed grouse, Canada jay, Harris' sparrow.
Blackberry, Highbush, *Rubus allegheniensis* Erect to 10 ft.; fruit sweet and aromatic, on edge of woods or in a field.	cedar waxwing, ruffed grouse, flicker, blue jay, catbird, olive-backed thrush, wood thrush, red-headed woodpecker, pine grosbeak, chewink.
Blackcap, or Raspberry, *Rubus occidentalis* Erect prickly bush with recurving canes; fruit black. *June-September*	kingbird, cedar waxwing, flicker, bobwhite, catbird, olive-backed thrush, red-headed woodpecker, pine grosbeak, towhee.
Blackhaw, *Viburnum prunifolium* Shrub to 15 ft.; flowers white; fruit blue-black with a bloom. *June-May*	cedar waxwing, robin, olive-backed thrush.

280

LIST OF PLANTS TO ATTRACT BIRDS

NAME, DESCRIPTION AND FRUITING SEASON   KNOWN TO BE EATEN BY

Buffaloberry, Russet,
Shepherdia canadensis
Shrub to 4 ft.; fruit red or yellow.
July-September

olive-backed thrush, pine grosbeak, flicker, catbird, ruffed grouse, brown thrasher, hermit thrush, pine grosbeak, red-headed woodpecker, towhee.

Buffaloberry, Silver,
S. argentea
Thorny shrub; leaves silvery; fruit red or yellow.
July-September

Bunchberry,
Cornus canadensis
A small woody plant to 4 in.; fruit red, clustered.
July-October

ruffed grouse, pine grosbeak, ring-necked pheasant, bobwhite, Lapland longspur, prairie chicken.

Carrionflower,
Smilax herbacea
Strong vine; fruit clustered, blue-black.
July-September

cedar waxwing, ruffed grouse, robin, brown thrasher.

Crab, Prairie,
Pyrus ioensis
A large shrub or small tree to 30 ft.; fruit a pome.
September-October

Cranberry, American,
Viburnum trilobum
Shrub to 12 ft.; flowers white; fruit scarlet.
July, persistent

ruffed grouse, bluebird.

Creeper, Virginia,
Parthenocissus quinquefolia
Hardy vine for walls and tangles; fruit a black berry.
August-February

bobwhite, flicker, catbird, robin, bluebird.

281

NAME, DESCRIPTION AND FRUITING SEASON	KNOWN TO BE EATEN BY
Dogwood, Gray, *Cornus racemosa* To 10 ft.; flowers white; fruit white. *July-November*	
Dogwood, Prairie, *C. bayleyi* Shrub to 10 ft.; with reddish branches; fruit white.	
Dogwood, Red-osier, *C. stolonifera* Shrub to 10 ft.; with dark crimson branches; flowers white; fruit white or bluish. *June-December*	ruffed grouse, flicker, downy woodpecker, olive-backed thrush, red-headed woodpecker, robin, bluebird, catbird, sharp-tailed grouse, bobwhite, grosbeak, cedar waxwing, kingbird.
Dogwood, Roughleaf, *C. asperifolia* Shrub to 15 ft.; with reddish-brown branches; fruit pale blue. *June-September*	
Dogwood, Silky, *C. amomum* Shrub to 10 ft.; branches purplish; fruit pale blue. *June-September*	
Elderberry, *Sambucus canadensis* Shrub to 12 ft.; flowers white; fruit purple-black. *June-August*	flicker, catbird, hermit thrush, ruffed grouse, bobwhite, olive-backed thrush, robin, bluebird, brown thrasher.
Grape, Riverbank, *Vitis vulpina* Strong vine, fragrant in bloom; fruit black with a bloom. *July-October*	red-headed woodpecker, ruffed grouse, bobwhite, kingbird, flicker, catbird, robin, ring-necked pheasant, brown thrasher.
Grape, Winter, *V. cinerea* High climber; fruit black or purple.	

LIST OF PLANTS TO ATTRACT BIRDS

Greenbrier, Bristly,
Smilax hispida
Woody vine with rough-edged leaves; fruit black.
July-March

ruffed grouse, flicker, catbird, hermit thrush, robin, sharp-tailed grouse, ring-necked pheasant.

Hackberry,
Celtis occidentalis
Tree to 120 ft.; fruit orange to purple.
July-April

flicker, robin, hermit thrush, bob-white, bluebird.

Hawthorn, Downy,
Cratægus mollis
Spiny shrub or small tree to 25 ft.; fruit scarlet.
August-October

Hawthorn,
C. intricata
Dense, almost spineless shrub to 10 ft.; fruit reddish-brown.
September-October

ruffed grouse, robin, bobwhite, pine grosbeak, ring-necked pheasant.

Honeysuckle,
Lonicera dioica
Shrub with vine-like branches; flowers yellowish-green; fruit red.
May-October

Honeysuckle,
L. hirsuta
A climber; flowers orange; fruit red.

Honeysuckle, Trumpet,
L. sempervirens
A climber; flowers orange-scarlet; fruit red.

hermit and olive-backed thrushes, pine grosbeak, robin, catbird, ring-necked pheasant.

Huckleberry, Big,
Vaccinium membranaceum
Small shrub; fruit black or blue.
July-September

flicker, blue jay, catbird, hermit thrush, black-capped chickadee, towhee, robin, brown thrasher, kingbird.

BIRDS IN THE GARDEN

NAME, DESCRIPTION AND FRUITING SEASON	KNOWN TO BE EATEN BY
Juniper, Colorado, *Juniperus scopulorum* Shrub or tree to 30 ft.; fruit bright blue. *All year*	
Juniper, Common, *J. communis* Evergreen shrub or tree; fruit blue. *All year*	olive-backed thrush, robin, ruffed grouse, bobwhite, Hungarian partridge, ring-necked pheasant.
Juniper, Creeping, *J. horizontalis* Evergreen with trailing branches; fruit blue. *All year*	
Moonseed, *Menispermum canadense* A woody twining vine; fruit black. (Berries poisonous to humans) *September-October*	robin, brown thrasher, towhee.
Mountain-Ash, *Sorbus decora* Large shrub or small tree; fruit red. *July-December*	ruffed grouse, sharp-tailed grouse, olive-backed thrush, robin, catbird.
Mulberry, Red, *Morus rubra* Tree to 60 ft.; fruit dark purple. *April-August*	cedar waxwing, bobwhite, catbird, robin, kingbird, hairy woodpecker.
Nannyberry, *Viburnum lentago* To 30 ft.; fruit blue-black with a bloom. *July, long persistent*	ruffed grouse, catbird, hermit thrush, robin.
Plum, Canada *Prunus nigra* A tree to 30 ft.; fruit red; on borders of woods. *August*	

284

LIST OF PLANTS TO ATTRACT BIRDS

Plum, Wild,
Prunus americana
Tree to 20 ft.; fruit yellow or red.
July-October

pine grosbeak.

Pokeberry,
Phytolacca americana
Herb to 12 ft.; fruit purple.
July-November

cedar waxwing, flicker, catbird, hermit thrush, olive-backed thrush, towhee, robin, bluebird.

Red Cedar
Juniperus virginiana
Evergreen tree; fruit blue with a bloom.
All year

olive-backed thrush, robin, ruffed grouse, bobwhite, Hungarian partridge, ring-necked pheasant, cedar waxwing, bluebird.

Rose, Wild,
Rosa acicularis
Bush to 3 ft.; flowers deep rose; fruit a red hip.
All year

Rose, Prairie,
R. setigera
Bush to 15 ft.; branches climbing; flowers in clusters; fruit a red hip.
All year

bobwhite, ruffed grouse, ring-necked pheasant, sharp-tailed grouse, prairie chicken.

Rose, Arkansas,
R. arkansana
Bush to 1½ ft.; flowers in clusters; fruit a red hip.
All year

Sarsaparilla, Wild,
Aralia nudicaulis
A perennial herb to 1 ft.; fruit berrylike, purplish-black.
June-August

ruffed grouse, catbird, olive-backed thrush.

NAME, DESCRIPTION AND FRUITING SEASON	KNOWN TO BE EATEN BY
Serviceberry, *Amelanchier alnifolia* Shrub to 7 ft.; flowers white in upright clusters; fruit purple. *June-August* Serviceberry, *A. canadensis* Shrub or tree to 30 ft.; flowers white, drooping; fruit purple. *June-August*	catbird, robin, cedar waxwing, ruffed grouse, flicker, red-headed woodpecker, downy woodpecker, blue jay.
Silverberry, *Elæagnus argentea* A bushy shrub or tree; fruit silvery. *July-October*	catbird, hermit thrush, towhee, brown thrasher.
Skunkbush, *Rhus trilobata* Shrub to 6 ft.; fruit red in clustered spikes. *All year*	ruffed grouse, evening grosbeak, robin, bobwhite, prairie chicken.
Snowberry, *Symphoricarpos albus* Shrub to 3 ft.; flowers pinkish; fruit white. *July-December*	ruffed grouse, hermit thrush, olive-backed thrush, ring-necked pheasant.
Strawberry, Wild, *Fragaria americana* Small perennial, usually with silky leaves; fruit red. *July-August*	cedar waxwing, catbird, towhee, brown thrasher, blue jay, white-throated sparrow.
Sumac, Shiny, *Rhus copallina* Shrub or tree to 20 ft.; flowers greenish; fruit red. *All year* Sumac, Smooth, *R. glabra* Shrub to 6 ft.; fruit red. *All year.*	ruffed grouse, flicker, bobwhite, hermit thrush, red-headed woodpecker, robin, bluebird, prairie chicken.

286

LIST OF PLANTS TO ATTRACT BIRDS

NAME, DESCRIPTION AND FRUITING SEASON	KNOWN TO BE EATEN BY
Thimbleberry, *Rubus parviflorus* Upright bush to 6 ft.; flowers white; fruit red. *June-August*	kingbird, cedar waxwing, flicker, bobwhite, catbird, olive-backed thrush, red-headed woodpecker, pine grosbeak, towhee.
Virginia Creeper, *Parthenocissus quinquefolia* Hardy vine; fruit black. *July-March*	flicker, robin, bluebird, hermit thrush, olive-backed thrush, brown thrasher, red-eyed vireo.

ROCKY MOUNTAIN STATES
Montana, Wyoming, Colorado
(*native*)

Adelia, *Forestiera neomexicana* A shrub to 10 ft.; fruit a small black or purple drupe. *June-September*	ruffed grouse, pine grosbeak.
Arrowwood, Western, *Viburnum pauciflorum* A small or large shrub; fruit red. *July-September*	ruffed grouse, pine grosbeak.
Bearberry, or Kinnikinnick, (*see also* Buffaloberry) *Arctostaphylos uva-ursi* An evergreen trailing shrub; fruit red. *August-March*	ruffed grouse, solitaire, Rocky Mountain jay.
Blackcap, or Raspberry *Rubus leucodermis* Erect shrub with trailing branches; fruit purple-black. *June-August*	cedar waxwing, ruffed grouse, Steller's jay, dusky grouse, catbird, olive-backed thrush, red-headed woodpecker, pine grosbeak, Arctic towhee.
Blackhaw, *Viburnum lentago* Shrub or small tree to 30 ft.; fruit blue-black with a bloom. *August-September*	hermit thrush, robin, ruffed grouse.

NAME, DESCRIPTION AND FRUITING SEASON	KNOWN TO BE EATEN BY
Blueberry, Dwarf, *Vaccinium cæspitosum* A small shrub; fruit a berry. *July-September*	cedar waxwing, ruffed grouse, hermit thrush, olive-backed thrush, sharp-tailed grouse, red-shafted flicker, ring-necked pheasant, pine grosbeak.
Blueberry, and other spp. *V. occidentale* *July-August*	
V. oreophilum *July-October*	
Buffaloberry, Russet, *Shepherdia canadensis* Shrub to 4 ft.; fruit a bitter acid berry. *July-September*	robin, olive-backed thrush, sharp-tailed grouse.
Buffaloberry, Silver, *S. argentea* A thorny bush to 18 ft.; excellent for hedges; fruit red. *July-October*	
Bunchberry, *Cornus canadensis* A small woody plant to 4 in.; fruit red, clustered. *July-October*	ruffed grouse, pine grosbeak, ring-necked pheasant.
Cranberrybush, American, *Viburnum trilobum* Shrub to 12 ft.; fruit scarlet. *September-October, often persistent until May.*	bluebird, ruffed grouse.
Dogwood, Red-osier, *Cornus stolonifera* Shrub to 10 ft.; branches red; fruit white or bluish. *June-October, often persistent until May.*	olive-backed thrush, sharp-tailed and ruffed grouse, pine grosbeak.

LIST OF PLANTS TO ATTRACT BIRDS

Elderberry, Blue,
Sambucus cærulea
Shrub or small tree; flowers white; fruit blue
with a bloom.
August-October

Elderberry, American,
S. canadensis
Shrub to 12 ft.; fruit purple-black.
August-October

Elderberry, Black,
S. melanocarpa
Shrub to 12 ft.; fruit shiny, black.
July-September

> 43 kinds including cedar waxwing, hermit thrush, olive-backed thrush, ruffed grouse, robin, song sparrow, ring-necked pheasant, black-headed grosbeak.

Grape, Riverbank,
Vitis vulpina
Strong climber; fruit black with a bloom.
June-November, persistent.

> red-headed woodpecker, kingbird, ruffed grouse.

Hackberry,
Celtis douglasi
Small shrub-like tree to 20 ft.; fruit brown.
July-January

> solitaire, hermit thrush, robin, evening grosbeak.

Hawthorn,
Cratægus cerronis
A spiny shrub to 15 ft.; fruit black or
brown.
July-November

Hawthorn, Black,
C. douglasi
Thorny shrub or tree to 25 ft.; flowers
white; fruit black.
August-October

Hawthorn, River,
C. rivularis
Spiny shrub to 20 ft.; fruit dark red or black.
August-October

> solitaire, robin, ruffed grouse, cedar waxwing, pine grosbeak, hermit thrush, black-headed grosbeak.

BIRDS IN THE GARDEN

Honeysuckle, Fly, *Lonicera canadensis* A shrub to 5 ft.; flowers yellowish; fruit red. *June-July* Honeysuckle, Utah, *L. utahensis* Low shrub; flowers pale yellow; fruit red. *June-September*	hermit thrush, solitaire, robin, pine grosbeak, sharp-tailed grouse, ring-necked pheasant.
Huckleberry, Grouse, *Vaccinium scoparium* Low bush with green stems; fruit light red. *July-September*	ring-necked pheasant, pine grosbeak, hermit and olive-backed thrushes.
Juniper, Colorado, *Juniperus scopulorum* Small tree to 30 ft.; fruit bright blue with a bloom. *All year* Juniper, Cherrystone, *J. monosperma* A tree to 50 ft.; fruit dark blue with a bloom. *All year* Juniper, Common, *J. communis* Spreading shrub or tree to 35 ft.; fruit dark blue with a bloom. *All year* Juniper, Creeping, *J. horizontalis* Shrub with trailing branches; fruit blue. *All year* Juniper, Utah, *J. utahensis* A tree to 20 ft.; fruit reddish-brown with a bloom. *September, all year*	solitaire, olive-backed thrush, robin, ruffed grouse, Hungarian partridge, ring-necked pheasant, pine grosbeak, evening grosbeak.

LIST OF PLANTS TO ATTRACT BIRDS

NAME, DESCRIPTION AND FRUITING SEASON	KNOWN TO BE EATEN BY

Kinnikinnick, *see* Bearberry.

Mountain-Ash,
Sorbus dumosa
Large shrub or small tree; fruit red.
June-December

robin, ruffed grouse, dusky grouse, sharp-tailed grouse, olive-backed thrush, evening grosbeak, pine grosbeak.

Nannyberry,
Viburnum lentago
Usually a large shrub; fruit a blue-black drupe.
August-September

hermit thrush, robin, ruffed grouse.

Plum, Wild,
Prunus americana
Small tree to 30 ft.; fruit yellow or red.
June-September

pine grosbeak.

Raspberry, Boulder,
Rubus deliciosus
Upright shrub to 6 feet.; flowers white; fruit reddish-purple.
July-September

cedar waxwing, ruffed grouse, Steller's jay, dusky grouse, catbird, olive-backed thrush, red-headed woodpecker, pine grosbeak, Arctic towhee.

Rose, Wild,
Rosa arkansana
To 1¼ ft.; flowers pink in clusters; fruit a red hip.
All year

Rose,
R. woodsi, var. *fendleri*
To 4 ft.; flowers pink or white; fruit a red hip.
All year

ruffed grouse, hermit and olive-backed thrushes, solitaire, sharp-tailed grouse, ring-necked pheasant, dusky grouse.

Rose,
R. macouni
To 6 ft.; flowers rose; fruit a red hip.
All year

291

BIRDS IN THE GARDEN

NAME, DESCRIPTION AND FRUITING SEASON	KNOWN TO BE EATEN BY
Rose, *R. nutkana* To 5 ft.; flowers pink, large, solitary; fruit a red hip. *All year*	ruffed grouse, hermit and olive-backed thrushes, solitaire, sharp-tailed grouse, ring-necked pheasant, dusky grouse.
Sarsaparilla, Wild, *Aralia nudicaulis* A perennial herb to 1 ft.; fruit berrylike, purplish-black. *June-August*	hermit thrush, pine grosbeak, ruffed grouse.
Serviceberry, or Shadbush *Amelanchier alnifolia* Shrub to 7 ft.; flowers white; fruit purple. *June-September*	catbird, robin, evening grosbeak, cedar waxwing, ruffed and dusky grouse, hairy woodpecker, solitaire, black-headed grosbeak.
Silverberry, *Elæagnus argentea* Silvery-leaved shrub to 12 ft.; flowers fragrant; fruit silvery. *All year*	catbird, hermit thrush, red-headed woodpecker, pine grosbeak, hairy woodpecker.
Skunkbush, *Rhus trilobata* Shrub to 6 ft.; fruit red in clustered spikes. *All year*	ruffed grouse, red-shafted flicker, evening grosbeak, mountain bluebird, robin.
Snowberry, or Wolfberry, *Symphoricarpos occidentalis* Shrub to 5 ft.; flowers pinkish; fruit white. *June-October*	
Snowberry, Mountain, *S. oreophilus* Shrub to 5 ft.; flowers pinkish; fruit white or pink. *August-September*	ruffed grouse, evening grosbeak, ring-necked pheasant, dusky grouse, pine grosbeak, robin.
Snowberry, *S. albus* Shrub to 3 ft.; flowers pinkish; fruit snow-white. *July-October*	

NAME, DESCRIPTION AND FRUITING SEASON	KNOWN TO BE EATEN BY
Strawberry, Wild, *Fragaria americana* Small perennial, usually with silky leaves; fruit red. *July-August*	cedar waxwing, dusky grouse, ruffed grouse, catbird, robin, kingbird, black-headed grosbeak.
Sumac, Smooth, *Rhus glabra* Shrub or tree to 20 ft.; fruit scarlet and hairy. *September-October, persistent.*	ruffed grouse, robin, catbird, hermit thrush, red-headed woodpecker, pine grosbeak.
Thimbleberry, *Rubus parviflorus* Unarmed, erect shrub to 6 ft.; flowers white; fruit red. *July-October*	cedar waxwing, ruffed grouse, Steller's jay, dusky grouse, catbird, olive-backed thrush, red-headed woodpecker, pine grosbeak, Arctic towhee.
Twinberry, *Lonicera involucrata* Shrub to 8 ft.; fruit black, shiny, surrounded by purple bracts. *August-September*	cedar waxwing, olive-backed thrush, pine grosbeak, Arctic towhee.
Wintergreen, *Gaultheria humifusa* Small evergreen creeping shrub; fruit red. *August-September*	ruffed grouse, hermit thrush, sharp-tailed grouse, ring-necked pheasant.

Wolfberry, *see* Snowberry.

GREAT BASIN STATES
Utah and Nevada
(*native*)

Bearberry, *see* Kinnikinnick.

Blackcap, or Raspberry *Rubus leucodermis* Erect shrub with trailing branches; fruit hemispheric, blue-black. *June-August*	house finch, hairy woodpecker, olive-backed thrush, mockingbird, Bullock's oriole, pine grosbeak, spurred towhee, black-headed grosbeak.

BIRDS IN THE GARDEN

NAME, DESCRIPTION AND FRUITING SEASON	KNOWN TO BE EATEN BY
Blueberry, *Vaccinium occidentale* Small shrub; fruit black or blue. *July-August*	hermit thrush, long-tailed chat, red-shafted flicker, Rocky Mountain jay.
Buffaloberry, or Bearberry, Russet, *Shepherdia canadensis* Shrub to 4 ft.; fruit red. *July-September* Buffaloberry, Silver, *S. argentea* Shrub to 15 ft.; thorny; fruit red. *July-August*	olive-backed thrush, pine grosbeak, hermit thrush, hairy woodpecker.
Creeper, Thicket, *Parthenocissus quinquefolia* Hardy vine; fruit black. *August-February*	hairy woodpecker, robin, red-shafted flicker, mockingbird, olive-backed thrush.
Dogwood, *Cornus occidentalis* Shrub to 15 ft.; fruit white. *July-October*	Steller's jay, evening grosbeak, hermit, and olive-backed thrushes, mockingbird, pine grosbeak, red-shafted flicker.
Elderberry, Blue, *Sambucus cærulea* Shrub or small tree to 30 ft.; fruit blue with a bloom. *July-October* Elderberry, Red, *S. microbotrys* Small shrub; fruit clustered. *July-September*	house finch, red-shafted flicker, band-tailed pigeon, Steller's jay, olive-backed thrush, pine grosbeak, Western bluebird, Arkansas kingbird, black-headed grosbeak.
Grape, Canyon, *Vitis arizonica* A weak vine or small shrub; fruit black. *July-August, often persistent until October.*	red-shafted flicker, russet-backed thrush, hermit thrush, mockingbird, Western bluebird, Cassin's kingbird.

294

LIST OF PLANTS TO ATTRACT BIRDS

NAME, DESCRIPTION AND FRUITING SEASON | KNOWN TO BE EATEN BY

Hackberry,
Celtis douglasi
Shrub or small tree; fruit brown.
July-January

band-tailed pigeon, hermit bird, evening grosbeak, road-runner.

Hawthorn, Black,
Cratægus douglasi
Small tree; fruit black, shiny.
July-November

Hawthorn, River,
C. rivularis
Shrub or small tree to 20 ft.; fruit dark red becoming black.
July-November

solitaire, pine grosbeak, black-headed grosbeak, hermit thrush.

Honeysuckle,
Lonicera ciliosa
High-climbing vine; flowers orange and scarlet; fruit red.
July-September

Honeysuckle,
L. conjugialis
Small much-branched shrub; flowers dark red; fruit red.
August-September

olive-backed thrush, pine grosbeak, spurred towhee, hermit thrush, solitaire.

Honeysuckle, Utah,
L. utahensis
Small shrub; flowers yellow; fruit red.
June-August

Huckleberry, *see* Whortleberry.

Juniper, Cherrystone,
Juniperus monosperma
Large evergreen shrub or tree; fruit dark blue.
September, persistent all year.

solitaire, evening grosbeak, mockingbird, pine grosbeak.

NAME, DESCRIPTION AND FRUITING SEASON	KNOWN TO BE EATEN BY
Juniper, Western, *J. occidentalis* Small or large evergreen tree; fruit bluish-black with a bloom. *September of second year. Persistent all year.* Juniper, Rocky Mountain, or Red Cedar, *J. scopulorum* Large shrub or small tree; fruit bright blue with a bloom. *All year*	solitaire, evening grosbeak, mock-ingbird, pine grosbeak.
Kinnikinnick, or Bearberry, *Arctostaphylos uva-ursi* Evergreen, trailing shrub; flowers white; fruit red. *All year*	solitaire, Rocky Mountain jay, band-tailed pigeon.
Manzanita, Pine nut, *Arctostaphylos nevadensis* Small evergreen shrub; flowers white; fruit red. *July-September, persistent.*	solitaire, Rocky Mountain jay, band-tailed pigeon.
Mountain-Ash, *Sorbus dumosa* Large shrub or small tree; fruit red. *July-December*	olive-backed thrush, evening and pine grosbeaks, sharp-tailed grouse.
Plum, Wild or Bitter Cherry, *Prunus emarginata* Large shrub or tree; flowers white; fruit becoming black. *May-September*	grouse.
Raspberry, Western Red, *Rubus melanolasius* Bristly bush; fruit red or purplish, sour. *July*	house finch, hairy woodpecker, olive-backed thrush, mocking-bird, Bullock's oriole, pine gros-beak, spurred towhee, black-headed grosbeak.

296

LIST OF PLANTS TO ATTRACT BIRDS

NAME, DESCRIPTION AND FRUITING SEASON	KNOWN TO BE EATEN BY
Rose, Wild, *Rosa woodsi*, var. *fendleri* Low bush; flowers solitary, pink; fruit a red hip. *All year*	olive-backed thrush, solitaire, ring-necked pheasant, hermit thrush, sharp-tailed grouse.
Serviceberry, or Shadbush, *Amelanchier alnifolia* To 7 ft.; flowers white in erect clusters; fruit purple. *July-September* Serviceberry, Cluster, *A. polycarpa* Large shrub or small tree; flowers white; fruit purple, very abundant. *August*	evening grosbeak, cedar waxwing, hairy woodpecker, russet-backed thrush, solitaire, pine and black-headed grosbeaks.
Silverberry, *Elæagnus argentea* A bushy shrub or tree; fruit silvery; thicket-forming. *July-October*	hermit thrush, pine grosbeak, hairy woodpecker.
Skunkberry, *see* Sumac.	
Snowberry, *Symphoricarpos albus* Erect shrub; flowers pinkish; fruit white; thicket-forming. *All year*	evening grosbeak, ring-necked pheasant, pine grosbeak.
Squaw-apple, *Peraphyllum ramosissimum* An intricately branched shrub; fruit a pome, yellow tinged with purple; good cover. *July-September*	
Strawberry, Wild, *Fragaria glauca* Small perennials; fruit red. *July.* Strawberry, other spp. *F. platypetala* *F. truncata*	cedar waxwing, house finch, mockingbird, sharp-tailed grouse, pine and black-headed grosbeaks.

NAME, DESCRIPTION AND FRUITING SEASON	KNOWN TO BE EATEN BY
Sumac, Skunkbush, *Rhus trilobata* Shrub to 6 ft.; flowers greenish; fruit red. *All year*	red-shafted flicker, piñon jay, evening grosbeak, mountain bluebird.
Thimbleberry, *Rubus parviflorus* Unarmed, erect shrub to 6 ft.; flower white; fruit red.	house finch, hairy woodpecker, olive-backed thrush, mockingbird, Bullock's oriole, pine grosbeak, spurred towhee, black-headed grosbeak.
Twinberry, *Lonicera involucrata* Shrub to 8 ft.; flowers yellowish; fruit shiny black, surrounded by purple bracts. *August-September*	olive-backed thrush, pine grosbeak, spurred towhee, hermit thrush, solitaire.
Whortleberry, or Thinleaf Huckleberry, *Vaccinium membranaceum* A small shrub; fruit black or blue. *July-September* Whortleberry, or Grouse Huckleberry, *V. scoparium* Low bush with green stems; berries small, light red. *July-September*	cedar waxwing, olive-backed thrush, sharp-tailed grouse, red-shafted flicker, long-tailed chat, pine grosbeak, Rocky Mountain jay.
Wintergreen, *Gaultheria humifusa* Small-trailing evergreen; fruit spicy; excellent ground cover. *August-September*	hermit thrush, sharp-tailed grouse.

CALIFORNIA GENERAL
(*native*)

Adelia,
Forestiera neo-mexicana
Shrub or tree to 10 ft.; flowers small, yellowish; fruit dark purple to black; in moist situation.

NAME, DESCRIPTION AND FRUITING SEASON	KNOWN TO BE EATEN BY

Aralia,
Aralia californica
Perennial herb to 10 ft.; flowers whitish; fruit berrylike, blue-black.
October

by many birds.

Ash, Oregon,
Fraxinus oregona
Tree to 40 ft. or more; inconspicuous flowers before the leaves; fruit winged seeds in clusters; in rich moist soil.

Bay, *see* Myrtle, California Wax-

Bearberry, *see* Kinnikinnick.

Blackberry, California, or Dewberry,
Rubus macropetalus
Climbing or on the ground; flowers white; male and female on different vines; fruit black, delicious.
June-August

California jay, house finch, wren-tit, Steller's jay, Brewer's blackbird, russet-backed thrush, California quail, Bullock's oriole, fox sparrow, brown towhee, spotted towhee, black-headed grosbeak.

Cascara,
Rhamnus purshiana
Tree from 10 to 40 ft.; flowers inconspicuous; fruit black; in rich soil in partial shade.
July-September

California jay, mockingbird, russet-backed thrush, California thrasher.

Cherry, Bitter,
Prunus emarginata
Tree to 30 ft.; often in thickets; flowers white, in loose round clusters; fruit in scattered clusters, coral red.
May-September

Cherry, Western Choke,
P. virginiana, var. *demissa*
A shrub; flowers white; fruit bright red.
July-September

California jay, cedar waxwing, house finch, Brewer's blackbird, russet-backed thrush, Bullock's oriole, Western tanager, black-headed grosbeak, band-tailed pigeon.

299

NAME, DESCRIPTION AND FRUITING SEASON	KNOWN TO BE EATEN BY
Condalia, or Lotebush, *Condalia lycioides* A small or large, spiny, straggling shrub; fruit a drupe; forms thickets.	quail, band-tailed pigeon.
Crabapple, Oregon, *Pyrus fusca* Shrub or small tree; flowers white, fragrant; fruit greenish yellow or red. *July-October*	grouse, robin, cedar waxwing, woodpecker, ring-necked pheasant, mockingbird, purple finch.
Dogwood, California, *Cornus californica* Shrub resembling red osier; fruit white. *July-November* Dogwood, Pacific, *C. nuttalli* Tree to 60 ft.; flowers small surrounded by large white bracts; fruit scarlet. *August-November* Dogwood, Miners', *C. sessilis* A large shrub or small tree; fruit a small drupe. *August-September*	grouse, quail, flicker, woodpecker, kingbird, thrasher, bluebird, purple finch, russet-backed and other thrushes.
Elderberry, Blue, *Sambucus cærulea* (and other spp.) Shrub or small tree to 50 ft.; flowers yellowish white; fruit blue-black with a bloom; in rich, moist soil. *August-October, rarely to December.* Elderberry, Red, *S. callicarpa* Shrub to 20 ft.; flowers white; fruit bright scarlet. *June-September*	quail, flicker, woodpecker, kingbird, black phoebe, mockingbird, robin, thrasher, bluebird, black-headed grosbeak, California towhee, russet-backed thrush, phainopepla, band-tailed pigeon.

LIST OF PLANTS TO ATTRACT BIRDS

NAME, DESCRIPTION AND FRUITING SEASON   KNOWN TO BE EATEN BY

Grape, California,
Vitis californica
Tall climber; flowers very fragrant; fruit
purple with a bloom.
August-October

red-shafted flicker, grouse, quail,
woodpecker, mockingbird, wren
tit, thrasher, thrushes, Western
bluebird, cedar waxwing.

Greenbrier, California,
Smilax californica
Smooth or prickly vine; fruit a berry.
July-November

mockingbird, thrasher, robin,
russet-backed thrush.

Hackberry, *see* Paloblanco.

Hawthorn, or Western Blackhaw,
Cratægus douglasi
Spiny shrub or small tree to 25 ft.; flowers
white; fruit black.
July-November

grouse, robin, purple finch, solitaire, black-headed grosbeak, hermit thrush.

Honeysuckle, Bristly,
Lonicera hispidula
Erect shrub to 12 ft.; flowers white or pur-
ple; fruit red; on banks.
June-January

solitaire, quail, thrasher, robin,
russet-backed thrush, spotted
towhee, wren-tit.

Honeysuckle, Chapparal,
L. interrupta
Bushy vine or small evergreen shrub; fruit
a berry.
June-December

Huckleberry, or Box Blueberry,
Vaccinium ovatum
Evergreen shrub to 12 ft.; flowers white or
pink; fruit blue or black.
July-September

grouse, quail, robin, chickadee,
thrasher, wren-tit, russet-backed
thrush, red-shafted flicker.

Huckleberry, Red,
V. parvifolium
Shrub to 6 ft.; flowers pinkish; fruit clear
translucent red.
June-September

Indian plum, *see* Osoberry.

NAME, DESCRIPTION AND FRUITING SEASON	KNOWN TO BE EATEN BY
Juniper, California, *Juniperus californica* Shrub to 12 ft., rarely a tree; fruit berry-like, blue. *All year*	flicker, mockingbird, robin, cedar waxwing, evening grosbeak, purple finch, russet-backed thrush, solitaire, varied thrush, plumed quail.
Juniper, Sierra, *J. occidentalis* Shrub to tree of 40 ft.; fruit blue-black, with a bloom. *All year*	
Kinnikinnick, or Bearberry, *Arctostaphylos uva-ursi* A small evergreen trailing shrub; berries red. *All year*	grouse.
Laurel, California, *Umbellularia californica* Evergreen tree to 80 ft.; flowers yellowish-green in many-flowered clusters; fruit a drupe, pale yellow when ripe; in moist soil. *October, somewhat persistent.*	Steller's jay, Townsend's solitaire.
Madrona, *Arbutus menziesi* Evergreen tree to 75 ft.; flowers creamy white; fruit red. *July-January*	yellow-breasted chat, solitaire.
Maple, Bigleaf, *Acer macrophyllum* Tree to 50 ft.; flowers greenish-yellow; fruit hard, winged seeds, hanging in dense clusters. *July-September, persistent until winter.*	evening grosbeak.
Maple, Vine, *A. circinatum* Small tree, 8 to 35 ft.; flowers reddish; fruit a hard winged seed. *September*	

302

LIST OF PLANTS TO ATTRACT BIRDS

Manzanita,
Arctostaphylos diversifolia
Shrub or small tree to 15 ft.; flowers light
pink; fruit red or brownish.
All year

Manzanita,
A. manzanita
Evergreen shrub to 12 ft.; flowers white or
pinkish; fruit red or brownish.
All year

California jay, band-tailed
pigeon, fox sparrow, California
quail, California thrasher, wren-
tit, dusky grouse, mockingbird.

Mountain-Ash, Western,
Sorbus americana, var. sitchensis
Tree to 30 ft.; flowers white; fruit bright
red.
August-March

woodpecker, thrasher, robin,
cedar waxwing, evening grosbeak, dusky grouse, russet-backed
thrush.

Myrtle, California Wax-
Myrica californica
Shrub or tree to 35 ft.; fruit purple; in dry
sandy soil.
All year

flicker, quail, woodpecker, tree
swallow, chestnut-backed chickadee, towhee, wren-tit, Audubon's
warbler.

Osoberry, or Indian Plum,
Osmaronia cerasiformis
Shrub to 6 ft.; flowers greenish-white; fruit
a purple-black drupe.
July-August

many birds.

Palm, Fan,
Washingtonia filifera,
Tree to 80 ft.; fruit thin-fleshed drupe;
about streams and springs on borders of
Colorado Desert.
December-February

Paloblanco, or Hackberry,
Celtis reticulata
Large shrub or tree; fruit orange-red.
September

Bullock's oriole, road-runner, red-
shafted flicker, robin.

BIRDS IN THE GARDEN

Plum, Wild,
Prunus subcordata
Small crooked tree from 5 to 15 ft.; flowers
white, like apple blossoms; fruit a small
purplish-red or yellowish plum.
August-September

Raspberry, Whitebark, or Blackcap,
Rubus leucodermis
Erect canes 3 to 5 ft.; fruit purple or black.
June-August

California jay, house finch, wren-
tit, Steller's jay, russet-backed
thrush, California quail, mockingbird, brown and spotted tow-
hees, robin, Bullock's oriole, California thrasher.

Rose, Baldhip,
Rosa gymnocarpa
Bush to 10 ft.; flowers pink, solitary; fruit
a red hip.
June-October

Rose, California Wild,
R. californica
Shrubby bush to 10 ft.; flowers pink, in
clusters; fruit a red hip.
All year

dusky grouse, russet-backed
thrush, solitaire, ring-necked
pheasant.

Rose, Ground,
R. spithamea
Bush to 1 ft.; flowers rose, in clusters; fruit
a red hip.
All year

Rose, Nutka,
R. nutkana
A bush to 5 ft.; flowers rose-pink, solitary;
fruit a red hip; in damp soil.
All year

Salal,
Gaultheria shallon
Shrub to 8 ft.; flowers pinkish white; fruit
purple-black.
June-September

wren-tit, ring-necked pheasant.

304

LIST OF PLANTS TO ATTRACT BIRDS

Salmonberry,
Rubus spectabilis
Upright bush to 6 ft.; flowers rosy-purple; fruit yellow or orange-red, juicy.
May-August

California jay, house finch, wren-tit, Steller's jay, Brewer's black-bird, russet-backed thrush, California quail, Bullock's oriole, fox sparrow, brown towhee, spotted towhee, black-headed grosbeak.

Serviceberry, or Saskatoon,
Amelanchier alnifolia
Shrub to 7 ft.; flowers white; fruit purple.
May-October

Serviceberry, or Western Shadbush,
A. florida
Clumps of bushes or tree to 30 ft.; flowers white; fruit blue.
July-September

flicker, cedar waxwing, hermit thrush, robin, Western tanager, Western bluebird, evening grosbeak, dusky grouse, russet-backed thrush, black-headed grosbeak.

Skunkbush, *see* Sumac.

Snowberry,
Symphoricarpos occidentalis
Shrub to 5 ft.; flowers pinkish; fruit pure white.
June-May

varied thrush, California quail, wren-tit, russet-backed thrush, ring-necked pheasant, spotted towhee, robin.

Squawbush, *see* Sumac.

Squawthorn,
Lycium torreyi
Small or large, thorny shrub; fruit a berry.
June-September

road-runner, Gambel's quail.

Strawberry, California,
Fragaria californica
Perennial plant to 5 in.; fruit red, acid-sweet.
April-July

Strawberry, Sand,
F. chiloensis
Perennial to 8 in.; flowers white; fruit red.
April-July

dusky grouse, Brewer's black-bird, California quail, mocking-bird, brown towhee, robin, black-headed grosbeak.

305

NAME, DESCRIPTION AND FRUITING SEASON	KNOWN TO BE EATEN BY
Sumac, Laurel, *Rhus laurina* Evergreen shrub; flowers greenish-white; fruit whitish. *September, persistent.*	golden-crowned sparrow, Audubon's warbler, goldfinch, thrasher, mockingbird, bluebird, robin, chickadee, wren-tit, red-shafted flicker, hermit thrush, California quail, road-runner, mockingbird, evening grosbeak.
Sumac, or Lemonadeberry, *R. integrifolia* Shrub or tree to 30 ft.; flowers white or pinkish; fruit dark red, hairy. *February-October*	
Sumac, Squawbush or Skunkbush, *R. trilobata* Shrub to 6 ft.; flowers greenish-white; fruit red, in clustered spikes. *All year*	
Sumac, or Sugarbush, *R. ovata* Evergreen shrub to 10 ft.; flowers light yellow; fruit dark red, hairy; thicket forming. *August-September*	
Thimbleberry, *Rubus parviflorus* Unarmed, erect shrub to 6 ft.; flowers white; fruit bright red, rather dry. *May-October*	California jay, house finch, wren-tit, Steller's jay, Brewer's blackbird, russet-backed thrush, California quail, Bullock's oriole, fox sparrow, brown towhee, spotted towhee, black-headed grosbeak.
Toyon, or Christmasberry, *Heteromeles arbutifolia* Evergreen shrub to 15 ft.; flowers in white clusters; fruit bright red or yellow. *October-February*	wren-tit, band-tailed pigeon, California quail.
Twinberry, *Lonicera involucrata* Shrub to 8 ft.; fruit black, shiny; surrounded by purple bracts. *August-September*	solitaire, quail, thrasher, robin, russet-backed thrush, spotted towhee, wren-tit.

LIST OF PLANTS TO ATTRACT BIRDS

Water Jacket,
Lycium andersoni
Small spiny shrub; fruit a berry; in sandy,
alkaline soil.
April-May

road-runner, Gambel's quail,
black-chinned hummingbird.

NORTHWESTERN STATES

Washington, Oregon and Idaho

SHRUBS AND PERENNIALS (*native*)

Bearberry, *see* Kinnikinnick.

Blackberry, or Dewberry,
Rubus macropetalus
A biennial trailing vine; flowers white,
male and female on separate vines; fruit,
black, delicious.
June-August

robin, bluebird, russet-backed
thrush, cedar waxwing, pine and
black-headed grosbeaks.

Blackcap or Black Raspberry,
R. leucodermis
Erect shrub with trailing branches; flowers
white; fruit hemispherical, purple-black.
June-August

Buffaloberry,
Shepherdia canadensis
Shrub to 4 ft.; flowers small, white; fruit
a bitterly acid berry; undershrub with pines.
July-September

Bohemian and cedar waxwings,
russet-backed thrush, ruffed
grouse, pine grosbeak.

Bunchberry,
Cornus canadensis
Small woody plant to 4 in.; flowers small,
surrounded by white bracts; fruit red, clus-
tered.
August-October.

grouse, pine grosbeak, ring-
necked pheasant.

307

BIRDS IN THE GARDEN

Cranberrybush, Western,
Viburnum pauciflorum
Shrub to 5 ft.; flowers white; fruit, round, red; near water.
June-January

ruffed grouse, bluebird, pine grosbeak, ring-necked pheasant.

Currant, Red-flowering,
Ribes sanguineum
Shrub to 9 ft.; flowers light to dark red; fruit a black berry with a heavy bloom; open, or open dry woods.
July-August

red-shafted flicker, russet-backed thrush, solitaire, robin, rufous hummingbird, (flowers).

Devil's-Club,
Echinopanax horridum
Stout, very prickly shrub; flowers greenish-yellow; fruit scarlet; valuable cover.
May-July

no data.

Dogwood, Western Osier,
Cornus pubescens
Shrub to 15 ft.; twigs red; flowers cream-colored; fruit white; wet ground in open.
July-October

red-shafted flicker, evening grosbeak, Lewis's woodpecker.

Elderberry, Blue,
Sambucus cærulea
Shrub or small tree to 50 ft.; flowers yellowish-white; fruit blue-black with a bloom; in rich moist soil.
July-October

California and valley quail, russet-backed thrush, black-headed grosbeak, grouse.

Elderberry, Red,
S. callicarpa
Shrub to 20 ft., flowers creamy-white; fruit bright scarlet; in semi-shade in rich ground.
June-September

band-tailed pigeon, russet-backed thrush, robin, grouse, California quail, buffle-head, robin.

308

LIST OF PLANTS TO ATTRACT BIRDS

Fairybells,
Disporum oreganum
Perennial; fruit orange-red; in rich wood-
land soil.
August

Grouse.

False Lily-of-the-Valley, Western,
Maianthemum unifolium,
Low perennial herb; fruit a reddish berry;
ground cover in shady moist situation.
July

russet-backed thrush.

Honeysuckle, Bristly,
Lonicera hispidula
A slender twining shrub; flowers red and
yellow; berries red; ground cover on banks.
July-February

Honeysuckle, Orange,
L. ciliosa
High-climbing vine; flowers orange and
scarlet; fruit an orange-red berry; edge of
open woods.
July-September

russet-backed thrush, Townsend's
solitaire, pine grosbeak, ring-
necked pheasant.

Huckleberry, Grouse,
Vaccinium scoparium
Low bush with green stems; flowers small,
pink; berries small, light red.
July-September

Huckleberry, Evergreen,
V. ovatum
Evergreen shrub, much-branched, to 12 ft.;
flowers pink or white; berries black, with or
without a bloom; fine cover, in acid soil.
August-December

Huckleberry, Red,
V. parvifolium
Tall shrub with green stems; flowers, small
pink-tinged; berries clear red, acid; in acid
soil in the shade.

cedar waxwing, red-shafted
flicker, russet-backed thrush, California quail, robin, bluebird,
ring-necked pheasant.

BIRDS IN THE GARDEN

NAME, DESCRIPTION AND FRUITING SEASON	KNOWN TO BE EATEN BY
Indian plum, *Osmaronia cerasiformis* Shrub to 12 ft.; flowers greenish-white in drooping clusters; fruit plumlike, purple-black. *July-August*	many birds.
Juniper, Common, *Juniperus communis* Low spreading shrub or tree to 45 ft.; fruit blue with a bloom; on sandy banks. *All year*	ruffed grouse, russet-backed thrush, robin, ring-necked pheasant.
Kinnikinnick or Bearberry, *Arctostaphylos uva-ursi* Trailing shrub; leaves evergreen, leathery; flowers urn-shaped, pink; fruit bright red; groundcover in open; makes dense mats and may be planted to trail over a wall. *All year*	Hungarian partridge, ruffed and dusky grouse, Townsend's solitaire, California quail, band-tailed pigeon, fox sparrow.
Manzanita, *A. columbiana* A branched evergreen shrub to 9 ft.; flowers white; fruit round, red-cheeked. *All year*	dusky grouse, California quail.
Oregon-grape, *Mahonia aquifolium* Evergreen shrub to 6 ft. or more; flowers yellow; berries black with a bloom. *September to October* Oregon-grape, Low-growing, *M. nervosa* Low shrubby plant to 2 ft.; flowers yellow; fruit purple-black with a bloom; excellent ground cover in the shade. *July-October*	ruffed and dusky grouse, cedar waxwing.

310

LIST OF PLANTS TO ATTRACT BIRDS

Rose, Baldhip,
Rosa gymnocarpa
Small shrub to 3 ft.; flowers small, pale pink; fruit an oblong hip; dry woods.
All year

Rose, Nutka,
R. nutkana
A stout bush to 6 ft.; flowers to 2 in.; pink to deep rose-red, solitary; fruit a red hip.
All year

    ruffed and dusky grouse, russet-backed thrush, solitaire, ring-necked pheasant, bluebird.

Rose, Wild,
R. spithamea
Low bush to 1 ft.; flowers rose in few-flowered clusters; fruit a red hip; good ground cover.
All year

Salal,
Gaultheria shallon
Evergreen shrub to 9 ft.; flowers white; fruit a black or dark-purple berry; excellent ground cover.
July-December

    ruffed grouse, ring-necked pheasant, band-tailed pigeon, sooty and blue grouse.

Salmonberry,
Rubus spectabilis
Upright bush to 6 ft.; flowers rosy-purple; fruit yellow or orange-red, juicy.
June-August

    robin, bluebird, russet-backed thrush, cedar waxwing, pine and black-headed grosbeaks, band-tailed pigeon, dusky grouse, Lewis's woodpecker.

Serviceberry or Shadbush,
Amelanchier florida
Clumps of bushes to tree of 30 ft.; flowers white; fruit blue.
May-October

    36 kinds including robin, bluebird, evening, pine and black-headed grosbeak, Lewis's woodpecker, russet-backed thrush, solitaire, sooty grouse.

Skunkbush, or Sumac,
Rhus trilobata
Shrub to 6 ft.; flowers greenish-white; fruit red, in clustered spikes.
All year

    ruffed grouse, red-shafted flicker, ring-necked pheasant, evening grosbeak, mountain bluebird, robin, California quail.

NAME, DESCRIPTION AND FRUITING SEASON	KNOWN TO BE EATEN BY
Snowberry, *Symphoricarpos albus* Erect shrub; flowers pink; berries white. Open woods. *All year*	ruffed grouse, russet-backed thrush, varied thrush, ring-necked pheasant, spurred towhee, California quail.
Solomon's-seal, False, *Smilacina amplexicaulis* Perennial herb to 3 ft.; fruit and berries in a cluster; in a shady spot.	hermit thrush, bluebird, russet-backed thrush.
Strawberry, Prairie, *Fragaria chiloensis* A perennial with thick silky leaves; fruit red, hemispherical; in open places. *May-June*	cedar waxwing, ruffed and dusky grouse, California quail, song sparrow, pine grosbeak, robin, black-headed grosbeak.
Strawberry, Wood, *F. bracteata* A perennial herb; fruit red, oblong, held above the leaves; on edge of prairies and in the woods; excellent ground cover. *May-June*	
Sumac, *see* Skunkbush.	
Thimbleberry, *Rubus parviflorus* Unarmed, erect shrub to 6 ft.; forming colonies; flowers white; fruit bright red, rather dry. *June*	dusky and sooty grouse.
Twinberry, *Lonicera involucrata* Shrub to 3 ft.; flowers yellowish; fruit black, shiny, surrounded by purple bracts; near streams or in rich moist soil. *August-September*	cedar waxwing, russet-backed thrush, pine grosbeak, spurred towhee, hummingbird for flowers.
Viburnum, Oregon, *Viburnum ellipticum* Shrub to 8 ft.; flowers cream-color; fruit black; rich moist soil. *July-September*	magpie.

LIST OF PLANTS TO ATTRACT BIRDS

Wintergreen,
Gaultheria ovatifolia and *G. humifusa*
Small trailing evergreen shrubs; flowers white; fruit red, spicy; excellent ground cover in acid soil.
August-September

grouse and quail.

TREES (*native*)

Alder, Red or Western,
Alnus rubra
To 60 ft.; fruit a nutlet in a small woody cone, hanging in loose clusters.
Autumn through winter

goldfinch, pine siskin, buffle-head, green-winged teal, bald-pate.

Aspen,
Populus tremuloides also var. *vancouveriana.*
To 50 ft.; quick growing; fruit small, hard seed capsules.
May-June

great blue heron, California and valley quail, dusky grouse, siskin, goldfinch, pine grosbeak.

Cascara,
Rhamnus purshiana
From 10 to 40 ft.; flowers inconspicuous; fruit black; rich soil in partial shade.

evening grosbeak, purple finch, pileated woodpecker, ruffed grouse, band-tailed pigeon, Stel-ler's jay, robin, Western tanager.

Cedar, Alaska,
Chamæcyparis nootkatensis
Evergreen to 80 ft.; fruit a small, rough, almost round, erect cone, falling to ground entire.
September-October

buffle-head, Barrow's golden-eye, greater scaup, russet-backed thrush, pine grosbeak, ruffed grouse.

Cedar, Port Orford, or Lawson Cypress,
C. lawsoniana
Evergreen to 200 ft.; fruit a small cone, roughly roundish; shelter planting.
September-October of second season.

Cedar, Western Red, or Arbor-vitæ,
Thuya plicata
Evergreen to 150 ft.; fruit a small cone, scattered over the branches.
August-September, persistent.

NAME, DESCRIPTION AND FRUITING SEASON	KNOWN TO BE EATEN BY
Cherry, Bitter, *Prunus emarginata* To 30 ft.; flowers white, in loose clusters; fruit in scattered clusters, coral red; thicket-forming. *May-September*	Lewis's woodpecker, ruffed grouse, band-tailed pigeon, Townsend's solitaire, cedar waxwing, ring-necked pheasant, robin, bluebird, sharp-tailed grouse.
Cherry, Western Choke, *P. virginiana* var. *demissa* To 20 ft.; flowers apple-blossomlike in dense drooping clusters; fruit blackish, hanging in 6-inch clusters; moist soil; excellent for thickets. *June-October*	
Cottonwood, Black or Balm, *Populus trichocarpa* Large tree to 125 ft.; fruit small hard capsules; plant for quick growth. *May-June*	ruffed grouse.
Dogwood, *Cornus nuttalli,* Tree to 60 ft.; flowers small greenish, surrounded by 4-6 prominent white bracts; fruit orange red, clustered. Occasionally blooms a second time in the fall. *June-December*	flicker, robin, hermit thrush, russet-backed thrush, cedar waxwing, warbling vireo, evening and pine grosbeaks, purple finch, song sparrow, robin, bluebird, pileated woodpecker, band-tailed pigeon.
Douglas Fir, *Pseudotsuga taxifolia* Evergreen tree to 200 ft.; fruit a cone 3 in. long with 3-pointed bracts. *September-October*	dusky grouse.
Fir, Grand, *Abies grandis* Evergreen tree to 125 ft.; needles in flat glossy sprays; fruit a cone to 4 in., erect on topmost branches. *September-October*	crossbill, mountain chickadee, long-eared owl, dusky grouse, horned grebe, Steller's jay.

314

LIST OF PLANTS TO ATTRACT BIRDS

Hackberry,
Celtis douglasi
Small tree, fruit cherrylike, purplish-brown; endures dry soil but thrives in rich moist situation.
All year

solitaire, cedar waxwing, pileated woodpecker, robin, russet-backed thrush, red-shafted flicker.

Hawthorn or Western Thornapple,
Cratægus douglasi
Thorny shrub or tree to 25 ft.; flowers white; fruit berrylike, shining black in bunches.

solitaire, Lewis's woodpecker, ruffed grouse, fox sparrow, pine grosbeak, robin, bluebird, black-headed grosbeak, hermit thrush, ring-necked pheasant, Gairdner's woodpecker, Louisiana tanager.

Hemlock, Lowland,
Tsuga heterophylla
Evergreen tree to 200 ft.; fruit a small cone, hanging from ends of twigs.
September-October

white-winged crossbill, flicker, California quail.

Juniper, Colorado,
Juniperus scopulorum
Shrub to 30 ft.; fruit bright blue with a bloom.
All year

Juniper, Common,
J. communis
Low spreading shrub or tree to 45 ft.; fruit blue with a bloom; on shady banks.
All year

Juniper, Western,
J. occidentalis
Shrub or tree to 40 ft.; foliage gray-green; fruit blue-black with a bloom.
All year

evening and pine grosbeaks, purple finch, ruffed grouse, russet-backed thrush, robin, ring-necked pheasant.

Laurel, Oregon or California,
Umbellularia californica
Evergreen tree to 80 feet.; flowers yellowish-green in many-flowered clusters; fruit green or purple; in moist soil.
October

Steller's jay.

NAME, DESCRIPTION AND FRUITING SEASON	KNOWN TO BE EATEN BY

Madrona,
Arbutus menziesi
Evergreen tree to 100 ft.; bark dark red; flowers in clusters, fragrant, white; fruit round, orange-red.
July-January

Bohemian waxwing, band-tailed pigeon, mourning dove, solitaire, cedar waxwing, robin, flicker.

Maple, Bigleaf,
Acer macrophyllum
Tree to 50 ft.; flowers greenish yellow; fruit hard, winged seeds, hanging in dense clusters.
July-September and through winter.

Maple, Dwarf,
A. glabrum
Small slender tree, 10 to 25 ft.; flowers in clusters; fruit a hard winged seed.
Late autumn

evening and pine grosbeaks, great blue heron.

Maple, Vine,
A. circinatum
Small tree 8 to 35 ft.; flowers reddish; fruit a hard winged seed; damp rich soil, very tolerant of shade.
September

Mountain-Ash, Dwarf,
Sorbus dumosa
Tall shrub to 15 ft.; flowers white, in dense clusters; fruit bright red.
August-December

evening and pine grosbeaks, robin, ruffed grouse, dusky grouse, russet-backed thrush, bluebird.

Mountain-Ash, Western,
S. americana, var. *sitchensis*
Tree to 30 ft.; flowers white; fruit berrylike, orange-yellow in flat clusters.
August-November

316

LIST OF PLANTS TO ATTRACT BIRDS

NAME, DESCRIPTION AND FRUITING SEASON	KNOWN TO BE EATEN BY
Plum, Pacific, *Prunus subcordata,* Small shrubby tree to 20 ft.; flowers white in loose clusters; fruit a purplish-red or yellowish; valuable cover. *August-September*	no data.
Yew, Western, *Taxus brevifolia* Low evergreen tree to 40 ft.; fruit berrylike, coral red. *September-October*	ruffed grouse.

II. PLANTING TO ATTRACT WATER FOWL

List of trees, shrubs and moisture-loving plants providing cover and food

TREES

Ash, American
Fraxinus americana

Ash, Black
F. nigra

Maple, Red
Acer rubrum

Maple, Silver
A. saccharinum

Oak, Pin
Quercus palustris

Oak, Swamp White
Q. bicolor

Poplar, Balsam
Populus balsamifera

Poplar, Large-toothed or Aspen
P. grandidentata

Poplar, Quaking or Aspen
P. tremuloides

Tupelo or Sour Gum
Nyssa sylvatica

Sycamore
Platanus occidentalis

Willow, Black
Salix nigra

BIRDS IN THE GARDEN

SHRUBS

Alder, Speckled
Alnus incana

Azalea, Clammy
Rhododendron viscosum

Bayberry (high, sandy ground)
Myrica caroliniensis

Black Alder
Ilex verticillata

Blueberry, Highbush
Vaccinium corymbosum

Buttonbush
Cephalanthus occidentalis

Dogwood, Osier
Cornus stolonifera

Elder, American
Sambucus canadensis

Elder, Scarlet
S. pubens

Hardhack or Shrubby Cinquefoil
Potentilla fruticosa

Meadowsweet
Spiræa latifolia

Pinxter flower or Pink azalea
Rhododendron nudiflorum

Rose, Swamp
Rosa carolina

Rose, Wild
R. virginiana

Spicebush
Benzoin æstivale

Steeplebush
Spiræa tomentosa

Sweet Pepperbush
Clethra alnifolia

Withe-Rod
Viburnum cassinoides

Water Willow or Swamp Loosestrife
Decodon verticillatus

Willow, Pussy
Salix discolor

Willow, Shining
S. lucida

FERNS

Cinnamon,
Osmunda cinnamomea

Marsh
Dryopteris thelypteris

Royal
Osmunda regalis

Sensitive
Onoclea sensibilis

318

LIST OF PLANTS TO ATTRACT BIRDS

Emergent Vegetation of value for food or cover or both

DESCRIPTION	HOW PLANTED	KNOWN TO BE EATEN BY
Arrow Arum or Wampee, *Peltandra virginica* To about 1 ft.; leaves arrow-shaped, dark green; fruit fleshy, green.	Seeds or root-stocks in spring or fall.	wood ducks.
Blue flag, *Iris versicolor* To 2 ft.; attractive lavender flowers; foliage making excellent cover.	Roots, in spring, summer or fall.	
Bulrush, *Scirpus spp.* From 3 to 6 ft.; seeds are eaten; foliage makes cover.	Transplant root-stocks in spring or fall or sow seeds.	31 species of ducks including mallard and blue-winged teal.
Bur-reed, *Sparganium spp.* Slender leaves and fruiting heads on main branches.	Roots, spring, summer or fall.	mallard, black duck, green- and blue-winged teals, and wood duck.
Cat-tail, *Typha spp.* From 8 to 10 ft.; long slender leaves; excellent cover.	Rootstocks, in spring or fall, and will grow much more slowly from the minute seed.	wild geese.
Duck Potato or Wapato, *Sagittaria latifolia* To 4 ft.; large leaves furnish cover; the tubers are eaten.	Tubers or roots, in spring or fall.	16 species including mallard, pintail, canvas-back, and geese.
Pickerelweed, *Pontederia cordata* To 2 ft.; attractive blue flowers; profuse foliage; valuable for cover.	Roots, in spring or fall.	10 species including mallard and Northern and Southern black ducks.

319

BIRDS IN THE GARDEN

DESCRIPTION	HOW PLANTED	KNOWN TO BE EATEN BY
Reed Grass, *Phragmites phragmites* To 8 ft.; principally valuable for cover and to prevent soil erosion.	Roots, in spring or fall.	
Smartweed, Water, *Polygonum amphibium* Pink flowers on surface of water; dark seeds which are valuable duck food. This plant often springs up spontaneously after flooding or cultivation.	Seeds or roots.	21 species including mallard, pintail, green- and blue-winged teals, and others.
Water Cress, *Nasturtium officinale* A smooth, fleshy plant; small white flowers; much divided leaves. Very valuable because it grows so fast ducks cannot eat it out. Grows only where water is clear and cold, in ponds, brooks or streams.	Seeds or cuttings.	by many species; valuable on duck farms.
Wild Rice, *Zizania aquatica* To 10 ft.; profuse grassy foliage; seeds eaten; makes good cover for molting and young ducks.	Seeds, in the spring.	14 species including lesser scaup, mallard, black and canvas-back ducks.

Surface Vegetation, floating or with floating leaves

Duckweeds, or Duck's meat, *Lemna minor* and *Spirodela polyryza* Very small disklike leaves floating at or near the surface. An important duck food and also valuable because they harbor snails and insects eaten by many ducks. Duckweeds will grow only on still water.		many species.

LIST OF PLANTS TO ATTRACT BIRDS

DESCRIPTION	HOW PLANTED	KNOWN TO BE EATEN BY
Pondweed, Celery-leaved, *Potamogeton epihydrus* An upright stem with long ribbon-like leaves resembling wild celery; seeds, leaves, and rootstocks eaten.	Roots, in summer or fall.	34 species including mallard, canvasback, red-head, black ducks and pintail.
Pondweed, Floating, also called Brownleaf, *Potamogeton natans* Oval, pointed leaves, floating on the water; will grow in protected water or where there is some motion; holds seeds until October and November.	Roots, in summer or fall.	mallard, and other surface feeding ducks.
Waterlily, White, *Nymphæa odorata* Leaves 3 to 10 in. across; flowers white, fragrant. Ducks eat insects or algae below waterlily leaves and also the seeds. The white waterlily is less likely to take possession of the pond than the spatterdock.	Seeds or roots, spring, summer or fall.	17 species including blue-winged teal.
Waterlily, Yellow, or Spatterdock, *Nymphozanthus advena* Leaves sometimes extending a foot or more above water; flowers yellow; furnishes cover and food.	Seeds or roots, spring, summer and fall.	mallard and wood duck.
Water Shield, *Brasenia schreberi* Oval leaves 3 to 4 in. wide; flowers small, purple; plant in same situation as yellow waterlily; seeds eaten.	Seeds or roots in spring, summer or fall.	22 species including ring-necked, lesser scaup, and wood duck.

BIRDS IN THE GARDEN

Submerged foliage

DESCRIPTION	HOW PLANTED	KNOWN TO BE EATEN BY
Coontail, *Ceratophyllum demersum* Dense masses of foliage which harbor many water animals such as snails, shrimps and sow bugs on which ducks feed; seeds eaten, also foliage.	Pieces of stem in quiet water; watch that colonies do not crowd out more valuable species.	23 species including wood duck, mallard, and ring-necked.
Mud Plantain, *Heteranthera dubia* Grassy leaves, round stems; will grow in warm, still water where wild celery or rice will not grow.	Seed in summer or fall.	9 species including pintail.
Musk grass, *Chara spp.* The musk grasses are one of the highly organized algae. They form fluffy masses at the bottom of fresh water ponds. The plants are fragile, pale green in color and often encrusted with lime. They grow very luxuriantly, often beneath other water plants.	Transplant in masses.	22 species including blue-winged teal, ruddy duck, greater scaup. Golden-eye eats tubers.
Pondweed, Bushy, *Naias flexilis* Masses of foliage in various depths; foliage and seeds eaten.	Plant seed as soon as mature in summer.	20 species including mallard, lesser scaup, and black duck.
Pondweed, Clasping-leaved, (Sometimes called Red-head grass), *Potamogeton perfoliatus* A leafy plant which supplies not only foliage for food, but seeds and rootstocks.	Roots, summer and fall.	wood duck, black duck, mallard.

322

LIST OF PLANTS TO ATTRACT BIRDS

DESCRIPTION	HOW PLANTED	KNOWN TO BE EATEN BY
Pondweed, Sago, *P. pectinatus* Horsetail-like foliage; tubers, and rootstocks eaten by diving ducks; surface-feeding ducks eat seeds.	Tubers or roots, in spring, summer or fall.	all ducks.
Pondweed, White-stemmed, *Potamogeton prælongus* Lance-shaped leaves on white stems; foliage, seeds, and rootstocks are all eaten; growing in water from 12 to 15 ft. deep.	Roots, in summer or fall.	by both diving and surface feeding ducks.
Water Weed, *Elodea canadensis* Rapidly-growing plant of translucent green; long branching stems; foliage and rootstocks eaten; grows only in water no deeper than 3 ft.	Leaf, buds or seeds, in spring, summer or fall.	mallard, and other dabbling ducks.
Wild celery, *Vallisneria americana* The grasslike leaves and thickened winter buds are eaten.	Winter buds.	Many ducks including the canvasback, which is supposed to gain its delicious flavor from this food.

III. PLANTS TO ATTRACT BIRDS IN THE CITY GARDEN

TREES (*native and exotic*)

Honey Locust
Gleditsia triacanthos var. *inermis*
Slender tree, with finely-cut delicate foliage and fragrant white flowers.

Cork tree
Phellodendron amurense
Slow-growing tree with corky bark, the pistillate forms bearing small black berry-like fruit, remaining long on the tree.

Mountain-Ash
Sorbus americana
Attractive tree with feather-form leaves, white flowers and brilliant scarlet fruit greatly relished by migrating birds.

Crabapple, Showy
Pyrus floribunda
Large bush or tree to 25 ft. with rose-red flowers changing to nearly white and small red fruit.

Crabapple, Siberian
P. baccata
Tree to 40 ft. with fragrant white flowers, fruit, waxy, yellow or red.

Black Cherry
Prunus serotina
Becoming a large tree with fragrant white flowers in long clusters, fruit purple-black.

Mulberry, Siberian
Morus alba var. *tatarica*
Small, hardy tree, the pistillate form carrying blackberrylike fruits exceedingly attractive to birds.

SHRUBS (*native and exotic*)

Blackhaw
Viburnum prunifolium
Shrub to 15 ft., flowers white, fruit blue-black.

Black alder
Ilex verticillata
Shrub shedding its leaves but bearing conspicuous red fruit greatly loved by thrushes.

Cornelian Cherry
Cornus mas
Shrub blooming very early in the spring, small yellow flowers, fruit, bright red.

Hawthorn, Washington Thorn
Cratægus crus-galli
Thorny shrub with white flowers followed by red fruits.

Hawthorn, English
C. oxycantha
Shrub wreathed in white flowers followed by bright red fruit.

Inkberry
Ilex glabra
Shrub very tolerant of city conditions, evergreen foliage and shining black fruit.

Privet, Common
Ligustrum vulgare
Shrub to 15 ft. having black berries.

Privet, Regel's
L. obtusifolium var. *regelianum*
Shrub to 10 ft., low branching and having black fruit.

Privet, California
L. ovalifolium
Shrub to 15 ft., nearly evergreen, making good cover and having black fruit.

Honeysuckle, Bush
Lonicera tatarica
Shrub to 10 ft.; flowers white; fruit red.

Elder, American
Sambucus canadensis
Shrub to 12 ft.; flowers white; fruit purple black in clusters.

VINES (*native and exotic*)

Bittersweet, American
Celastrus scandens
Vine with red and orange fruits; plant pistillate and staminate forms.

Bittersweet, Chinese
C. articulatus
Vine with fruits similar to above, but more tolerant of city conditions.

Boston Ivy
Parthenocissus tricuspidata
Clinging vine; black berries.

BIRDS IN THE GARDEN

Grape, Wild
Vitis æstivalis or *V. vulpina*
Makes good cover, but seldom fruits in the city.

Honeysuckle, Japanese
Lonicera japonica, var. *halliana*
Profusely growing, nearly evergreen vine; fruit red.

Virginia Creeper
Parthenocissus quinquefolia
Hardy and adaptable vine; fruit black berries.

REFERENCES

Allen, A. A., *The Book of Bird Life*. D. Van Nostrand. New York, 1935.

——, *American Bird Biographies*. Comstock. Ithaca, N. Y., 1934.

Bailey, Florence Merriam, *Handbook of the Birds of the Western United States*. Houghton Mifflin. Boston, 1920.

Baynes, Harold E., *Wild Bird Guests*. E. P. Dutton and Co. New York, 1915.

Chapman, Frank M., *Handbook of Birds of Eastern North America*. Appleton-Century Co. New York, 1932.

——, *The Warblers of North America*. Appleton-Century Co. New York.

Dawson, William Leon, and Bowles, John Hooper, *The Birds of Washington*. The Occidental Publishing Co. Seattle, 1909.

Forbush, Edward H., *Birds of Massachusetts and other New England States*. Massachusetts Commonwealth. Boston, 1925-1929.

——, Useful Birds and their Protection. Massachusetts State Board of Agriculture, 1907.

Henderson, Junius, *The Practical Value of Birds*. Macmillan. New York, 1927.

Henshaw, H. W., Editor, *The Book of Birds*. National Geographic Association, Washington, D. C., 1927.

McAtee, W. L., *Wildfowl Food Plants*. Collegiate Press Inc. Ames, Iowa, 1939.

May, John Bichard, *The Hawks of North America*. The National Association of Audubon Societies. New York, 1935.

Merriam, Florence A., *Birds of Village and Field*. Houghton Mifflin. Boston, 1898.

Lincoln, Frederick C., *The Migration of American Birds*. Doubleday Doran. New York, 1939.

Mathews, F. Schuyler, *Fieldbook of Wild Birds and Their Music*. Putnam. New York, 1910.

Pearson, T. Gilbert, Editor, *Birds of America*. Doubleday Doran. Garden City, 1936.

——, *The Bird Study Book*. Doubleday Page. Garden City, 1925.

Peattie, D. C., *Singing in the Wilderness*. Putnam. New York, 1935.

Pellett, F. C., *Birds of the Wild*. Delamare. New York, 1928.

Peterson, Alvin M., *The ABC of Attracting Birds*. The Bruce Publishing Co. Milwaukee.

Peterson, Roger Tory, *A Field Guide to the Birds*. Houghton Mifflin. Boston, 1934.

————, *The Junior Book of Birds*. Houghton Mifflin. Boston, 1939.

Priestley, Mary, *A Book of Birds*. The Macmillan Co. New York, 1938.

Roberts, T. S., *Birds of Minnesota*. University of Minnesota Press, 1934.

Saunders, A. A., *A Guide to Bird Songs*. Appleton-Century Co. New York, 1935.

Shoffner, C. P., *The Bird Book*. Stokes. New York, 1932.

Snedigar, Robert, *Our Small Native Animals*. Random House. New York, 1939.

Sutton, George Miksch, *Birds in the Wilderness*. Macmillan. 1936.

Taverner, P. A., *Birds of Western Canada*. Museum Bulletin No. 41, Canada Department of Mines. Ottawa, 1926.

Trafton, Gilbert H., *Methods of Attracting Birds*. Houghton Mifflin. Boston, 1910.

Weber, W. A., *Traveling with the Birds*. Donahue. 1923.

Wyman, L. E., and Burnell, E. F., *Field Book of Birds of the Southwestern United States*. Houghton Mifflin. Boston, 1925.

GOVERNMENT PUBLICATIONS

(Write to the Superintendent of Documents, Washington, D. C.)

Beal, F. E. L., *Some Common Birds Useful to the Farmer*. Farmers' Bulletin 630.

Beal, F. E. L., and McAtee, W. L., *Food of Some Well-Known Birds of Forest, Farm and Garden*. Farmers' Bulletin 506.

————, *Fifty Common Birds of Farm and Orchard*. Farmers' Bulletin 513.

Kalmbach, E. R., and McAtee, W. L., *Homes for Birds*. Farmers' Bulletin 1456.

McAtee, W. L., *Local Bird Refuges*. Farmers' Bulletin 1644.

————, *Usefulness of Birds on the Farm*. Farmers' Bulletin 1682.

————, *Propagation of Aquatic Game Birds*. Farmers' Bulletin 1612.

————, *Propagation of Upland Game Birds*. Farmers' Bulletin 1613.

————, *Groups of Plants Valuable for Wildlife Utilization and Erosion Control*. U. S. Department of Agriculture. Circular 412.

————, *Fruits Attractive to Birds—Northeastern States*. Wildlife Research and Management Leaflet BS-44.

————, *Fruits Attractive to Birds—Southern Plain States*. Wildlife Research and Management Leaflet BS-48.

————, *Fruits Attractive to Birds—Northwestern States*. Leaflet BS-41.

———, *Fruits Attractive to Birds—California.* Leaflet BS-45.

———, *Fruits Attractive to Birds—Northern Plains States.* Leaflet BS-43.

———, *Fruits Attractive to Birds—Rocky Mountain States.* Leaflet BS-42.

———, *Fruits Attractive to Birds—Great Basin States.* Leaflet BS-46.

———, *Fruits Attractive to Birds—Florida.* Leaflet BS-50.

———, *Fruits Attractive to Birds—Southwestern States.* Leaflet BS-47.

———, *Fruits Attractive to Birds—Southeastern States.* Leaflet BS-49.

———, *Eleven Important Wild-Duck Foods.* Bulletin of the U. S. Department of Agriculture 205.

McAtee, W. L., Beal, F. E. L., and Kalmbach, E. R., *Common Birds of Southeastern States in Relation to Agriculture.* Farmers' Bulletin 755.

McAtee, W. L., and Beattie, J. H., *Gourds for Bird Houses and Other Purposes.*

McAtee, W. L., and Grange, Wallace B., *Improving Farm Environment for Wild Life.* Farmers' Bulletin 1719.

Van Dersal, Wm. R., *Native Woody Plants of the United States.* Miscellaneous Publication 303 U. S. Department of Agriculture.

PUBLICATIONS OF THE NATIONAL ASSOCIATION OF AUDUBON SOCIETIES

1006 Fifth Avenue, New York City

Nature Study for Schools:

Part   1: *Class-room Projects.*
Part   2: *Field Activities.*
Part   3: *Winter Feeding.*
Part   4: *Bird Houses.*
Part   5: *Bird Day.*
Part   6: *Owl Study.*
Part   7: *Electric Nature Games.*
Part   8: *How Should Nature Be Taught?*
Part   9: *Soil—How Wild Life Depends upon It.*
Part 10: *Water—Life-blood of the Earth.*
Part 11: *Swamps and Marshes.*
Part 12: *Forests.*
Part 13: *Grasslands.*
Part 14: *Nature Trails.*
Part 15: *Small Nature Museums.*
Part 16: *Building a Nature Interest.*

BIRDS IN THE GARDEN

Bird Study for Camps.
Winter Birds as Guests.
The Rainey Wildlife Sanctuary.
The Roosevelt Bird Sanctuary.
John James Audubon.
Song-Bird Sanctuaries by Roger Tory Peterson.
Enter Hawk—Exit Mouse (out of print.)
What Hawks Eat.

330

INDEX

Figures given in boldface indicate descriptive material.

INDEX

332

333

INDEX

INDEX

336

INDEX

INDEX

INDEX

INDEX

344

INDEX

INDEX